Multilingual Families in a Digital Age

This book offers new insights into transnational family life in today's digital age, exploring the media resources and language practices parents and children employ toward maintaining social relationships in digital interactions and constructing transnational family bonds and identities.

The book seeks to expand the boundaries of existing research on family multilingualism, in which digital communication has been little studied until now. Drawing on ethnographic studies of four families of Senegalese background in Norway, Lexander and Androutsopoulos develop an integrated approach which weaves together participants' linguistic choices for situated interaction, the affordances of digital technologies, and the families' language and media ideologies. The book explores such key themes as the integration of linguistic and media resources in family repertoires, creative practices of digital translanguaging, engagement in diaspora practices, and opportunities of digital communication for the development of children's heritage language skills.

With an innovative perspective on 'doing family' in the digital age, this book will be of interest to students and scholars in multilingualism, sociolinguistics, digital communication, language and communication, and language and media.

Kristin Vold Lexander, PhD, is a researcher at Inland Norway University of Applied Sciences, and a former postdoctoral fellow at MultiLing Center for Multilingualism in Society Across the Lifespan, University of Oslo. She has worked on digital interaction in Senegalese contexts since 2005 and has published a range of articles and book chapters on the subject.

Jannis Androutsopoulos, Dr. Phil., is Professor of German and Media Linguistics at Universität Hamburg, Germany, and from 2016 to 2023 was a research professor at MultiLing, University of Oslo. His research interests include the sociolinguistics of mediated communication and multilingualism online. He is editor of *Polymedia in Interaction*, Special Issue of *Pragmatics and Society* 12:5 (2021), and *Digital language practices: media, awareness, pedagogy*, Special Issue of *Linguistics and Education* 62 (2021).

Routledge Critical Studies in Multilingualism
Edited by Marilyn Martin-Jones, *MOSAIC Centre for Research on Multilingualism, University of Birmingham, UK* and Joan Pujolar Cos, *Universitat Oberta de Catalunya, Spain*

Titles include:

Spaces of Multilingualism
Edited by Robert Blackwood and Unn Røyneland

Language Education in Multilingual Colombia
Edited by Norbella Miranda, Anne-Marie de Mejía, and Silvia Valencia Giraldo

Multilingualism in the Andes
Policies, Politics, Power
Rosaleen Howard

Global CLIL
Critical, Ethnographic and Language Policy Perspectives
Edited by Eva Codó

Southernizing Sociolinguistics
Colonialism, Racism, and Patriarchy in Language in the Global South
Edited by Bassey E. Antia and Sinfree Makoni

Multilingual Texts and Practices in Early Modern Europe
Edited by Peter Auger and Sheldon Brammall

Multilingual Families in a Digital Age
Mediational Repertoires and Transnational Practices
Kristin Vold Lexander and Jannis Androutsopoulos

For a full list of titles and more information about this series, please visit: www.routledge.com/Routledge-Critical-Studies-in-Multilingualism/book-series/RCSM09

Multilingual Families in a Digital Age

Mediational Repertoires and Transnational Practices

Kristin Vold Lexander and
Jannis Androutsopoulos

First published 2023
by Routledge
605 Third Avenue, New York, NY 10158

and by Routledge
4 Park Square, Milton Park, Abingdon, Oxon, OX14 4RN

Routledge is an imprint of the Taylor & Francis Group, an informa business

© 2023 Kristin Vold Lexander and Jannis Androutsopoulos

The right of Kristin Vold Lexander and Jannis Androutsopoulos to be identified as authors of this work has been asserted in accordance with sections 77 and 78 of the Copyright, Designs and Patents Act 1988.

With the exception of Chapter 6, no part of this book may be reprinted or reproduced or utilised in any form or by any electronic, mechanical, or other means, now known or hereafter invented, including photocopying and recording, or in any information storage or retrieval system, without permission in writing from the publishers.

Chapter 6 of this book is available for free in PDF format as Open Access from the individual product page at www.routledge.com. It has been made available under a Creative Commons Attribution 4.0 license.

Trademark notice: Product or corporate names may be trademarks or registered trademarks, and are used only for identification and explanation without intent to infringe.

ISBN: 9781032130248 (hbk)
ISBN: 9781032130279 (pbk)
ISBN: 9781003227311 (ebk)

DOI: 10.4324/9781003227311

Typeset in Sabon
by Newgen Publishing UK

The Open Access version of chapter 6 was funded by Universitetet i Oslo

Contents

List of tables, images, and figures viii
Preface xi
Acknowledgements xiii

1 **Introduction: Doing family and language in a digital age** 1
  1.1 *A day in the digital life of a young multilingual family member* 1
  1.2 *Theoretical dimensions: Family multilingualism, digital interaction, and polymedia* 3
  1.3 *Fieldwork for this book* 4
  1.4 *Outline of the book* 5

2 **Multilingual families online: Repertoires and practices** 8
  2.1 *Multilingual practices* 8
    2.1.1 Practice approaches to multilingualism 9
    2.1.2 Repertoires and registers 13
  2.2 *Family multilingualism* 16
    2.2.1 Family language policy and beyond 16
    2.2.2 Heritage language practices and heritage language socialisation 19
    2.2.3 The discursive construction of multilingual family space 21
    2.2.4 A 'digital turn' in FLP research 22
  2.3 *Multilingualism online* 23
    2.3.1 Code-switching approaches 24
    2.3.2 Networked multilingualism and digital translanguaging 27
    2.3.3 Affordances for mediated interaction in the digital ecology 31
  2.4 *Transnational families and digitally mediated communication* 34
    2.4.1 'Doing family' transnationally 34
    2.4.2 Digital co-presence in transnational families 36
    2.4.3 Polymedia: An ecology of media choices 38
    2.4.4 Language and media in family-making practices 40
  2.5 *Conclusion: Towards the study of mediational repertoires* 42

vi Contents

3 Media and language use in multilingual families: An ethnographic study in Norway   46
  3.1 Sociolinguistic research with Senegalese migrants in Norway 46
    3.1.1 Language and society in Senegal 46
    3.1.2 Language and immigration in Norway 50
    3.1.3 Senegalese immigrants in Norway 51
  3.2 Presentation of participants 52
    3.2.1 The Diagne family 53
    3.2.2 The Bâ family 54
    3.2.3 The Sagna family 55
    3.2.4 The Coly family 56
  3.3 The families' linguistic repertoires 57
    3.3.1 Wolof 58
    3.3.2 Joola 60
    3.3.3 Peul 62
    3.3.4 French 64
    3.3.5 Arabic 66
    3.3.6 English 67
    3.3.7 Norwegian 67

4 Visualising languages, modalities, and media: From language portraits to mediagrams   70
  4.1 Visualising repertoires 70
    4.1.1 Language portraits and network graphs 71
    4.1.2 Media maps 73
    4.1.3 Mediagrams 76
  4.2 Data collection 77
  4.3 Developing mediagrams 80
  4.4 Data analysis 85
  4.5 Ethical considerations and other challenges 86

5 Analysing mediagrams: Mediational choices in polymedia environments   91
  5.1 Pleasure and pressure: Balancing co-presence 91
  5.2 Multilingualism and multimodality: Managing a network of generations 97
  5.3 Media, language, and connectedness: A comparison of three fathers 99
  5.4 Media choices 103
  5.5 Conclusions 104

6 'Doing family' online: Translocality, connectivity, and affection   106
  6.1 Language, power, morality, and solidarity in the family 107
  6.2 Translocal connectivities 109

    6.2.1 Mediated interaction in the household: Coordinating family issues 110
    6.2.2 Translocal household interaction: Making decisions and sharing 112
    6.2.3 Transnational family-making: Power, solidarity, and teasing 117
 6.3 *Multilingual expressions of affection* 124
    6.3.1 Wife and husband 125
    6.3.2 Parents and children 127
    6.3.3 Extended family and beyond 130
 6.4 *Conclusions* 133

7 **Transnational families, diaspora practices, and digital polycentricity** 135
 7.1 *Diaspora and digital diaspora* 135
 7.2 *Digital diaspora and polycentricity* 139
 7.3 *Polycentric participation: A kaleidoscope of practices* 142
    7.3.1 Digital spaces of diasporic sociality 144
    7.3.2 The Senegalese public sphere 148
    7.3.3 Religious discourse 150
    7.3.4 Beyond diaspora: Traces of Norway and global pop culture 156
 7.4 *Conclusions* 160

8 **Heritage language repertoires** 164
 8.1 *Parents' ideologies of linguistic heritage* 167
 8.2 *Heritage language repertoires in time and space* 172
 8.3 *Children's transnational heritage language practices* 179
    8.3.1 Heritage language repertoires by interlocutors 180
    8.3.2 Heritage language registers 183
    8.3.3 Learning Wolof through online interaction 190
 8.4 *Conclusions: Heritage languages and mediational repertoires* 196

9 **Conclusions** 198
 9.1 *Multi-sited ethnography: Studying mediational repertoires* 199
 9.2 *Transnational connectivity and family multilingualism* 200
 9.3 *A digital perspective on heritage language repertoires* 202

References 205
Index 231

Tables, images, and figures

Tables

3.1	Overview of participating families	53
4.1	Overview of collected data	79
7.1	Data for digital diaspora analysis by participant, platform, and audience	143
7.2	Digital polycentricity: Overview	160

Images

4.1	Media map of Aida Coly	74
4.2	Media map of Cheikh Bâ	74
4.3	Media map of Mamadou Bâ	75
7.1	*Ma carte mon arme*, 'My voting card, my gun' (data by Ousmane Diagne)	149
7.2	Video-stills from 'Bon Vendredi' video (data by Oumou Diagne)	153
7.3	Banner of YouTube channel *Diwaanu Xassaides TV*	155
7.4	'Happy birthday' postings by Ousmane Diagne to his three children	157
7.5	Text area of 'NWE' dance videos (data by Aida Coly)	159
8.1	Sara Bâ, Facebook post (screenshot)	164
8.2	Language portrait of Ousmane Diagne	173
8.3	Language portrait of Momar Diagne	176
8.4	Ibou Coly with 'Uncle', Facebook Messenger	187

Figures

4.1	Visual representation of Nadya's network	72
4.2	Legend mediagrams	81
4.3	Mediagram of Awa Coly, compiled after the first meeting	81
4.4	Mediagram of Awa Coly, compiled after the second meeting	83
4.5	The mediagram research process step by step	84
5.1	Mediagram of Oumou Diagne	95

5.2	Mediagram of Sara Bâ	95
5.3	Mediagram of Rama Sagna	97
5.4	Mediagram of Cheikh Bâ	100
5.5	Mediagram of Ousmane Diagne	101
5.6	Mediagram of Felipe Sagna	102
6.1	World map with locations of transnational interlocutors	117
8.1	Mediagram of Awa Coly (replication of Figure 4.4)	181
8.2	Mediagram of Momar Diagne	182

Preface

This book is about transnational interaction. It is also an outcome of transnational collaboration by the authors, mediated by email, video calls, and physical meetings. There are many people that we are thankful to. First, we are deeply grateful to the Norwegian Center of Excellence 'Multilingualism in Society across the Lifespan' (MultiLing) at the University of Oslo for generously facilitating our research with the Flagship project, Multilingualism and Mediated Communication. MultiLing is funded by the Research Council of Norway through its Centers of Excellence funding scheme, project number 22326. At MultiLing we would especially like to thank the Center directors, Elizabeth Lanza and Unn Røyneland, as well as Jan Svennevig, Haley de Korne, Kellie Gonçalves, Jessica B.P. Hansen, Rafael Lomeu Gomes, Maria Obojska, Judith Purkarthofer, Elisabeth Neuhaus, Toril Opsahl, Hanna G. Andreassen, Ingvild Badhwar Valen-Sendstad, and Anne Golden. We are also grateful to people who helped us with the interpretation and visualisation of data, in particular independent researcher Samba Diop who offered expert advice on various aspects of the data; Natacha Céline Buntinx for her support with graphic design during an internship at MultiLing; and research assistant Marit Johanne Furunes. The final stages of writing this book have been financed partly by the Research Council of Norway Young Research Talents scheme, project number 300820, DigiMulti, at the Faculty of Education, Inland Norway University of Applied Sciences. Kristin is grateful for support from the research group 'Language Didactics in Multilingual Contexts' at Inland Norway University, in particular to her colleagues Lise I. Kulbrandstad, Hilde Thyness, administrator Julie K. Mjelva and research assistant Florian Gorqaj. Jannis acknowledges the permission by Universität Hamburg to take on a professor II position at Multiling from 2016 to 2023. He also thanks his former associate Florian Busch, now at the University of Bern, for methodological feedback, and Sarah Abdelmonem, DAAD scholar at Universität Hamburg, for explanations on Arabic data.

We also thank a number of transnational colleagues who have participated in discussions about this book and given valuable feedback over time. These include LLACAN and Lacito colleagues (CNRS, Paris) Sandra Bornand, Cécile Léguy and Bertrand Masquelier; Åsa Palviainen and the entire WhatsinApp team, including Xiao Lan Curdt-Christiansen. Thanks also to Aïssatou Mbodj-Pouye (Institut des mondes africains, Paris), Rachel Watson (SOAS, London), Ingse Skattum (University of Oslo), Caroline Tagg (Open University), Andreas Stæhr (University of Copenhagen) and Abou Bakry Kébé (Université Gaston Berger, Saint Louis du Sénégal).

Finally, we would like to thank the four families for taking part in the research, for sharing so generously from their interaction with us, for interesting discussions and enjoyable meetings, and for their *teranga*. *Jërëjëf, a jaaraama, emit eramben, takk*!

Acknowledgements

The authors would like to express their thanks for the following permissions to use copyright material:

- Chapter 4 presents reworked text and figures (Figures 4.2, 4.5), and Chapters 5 and 7 present images (Image 8.3) and reworked figures (Figures 5.3, 5.5, 5.6) from the article 'Working with mediagrams: a methodology for collaborative research on mediational repertoires in multilingual families' by Kristin V. Lexander & Jannis Androutsopoulos in *Journal of Multilingual and Multicultural Development*, 42:1 (2021): 1–18. Published by Taylor & Francis https://tandfonline.com. DOI: 10.1080/01434632.2019.1667363
- Chapter 7 is in part based on the article 'Digital polycentricity and diasporic connectivity: a Norwegian-Senegalese case study' by Jannis Androutsopoulos and Kristin V. Lexander in *Journal of Sociolinguistics*, 25:5 (2021): 720–736. Published by John Wiley & Sons Ltd. DOI: 10.1111/josl.12518
- Part of the analysis in Chapter 8 draws on heavily reworked material from the article 'Polymedia and family multilingualism. Linguistic repertoires and relationships in digitally mediated interaction' by Kristin Vold Lexander, *Pragmatics and Society*, 12:5 (2021): 782–804. Figure 4.4, Image 8.4, and Excerpt 8.5 are adapted from this article. Published by John Benjamins Publishing Company. DOI: 10.1075/ps.20052.lex
- Part of Excerpts 6.10 and 7.9 and Image 8.2 are reproduced from the article 'Norsk som digitalt samhandlingsspråk i fire familier med innvandrerbakgrunn – identitet og investering' by Kristin Vold Lexander, *Nordand: nordisk tidsskrift for andrespråksforskning*, 1 (2020), pp. 4–21. Published by Scandinavian University Press (Universitetsforlaget). DOI: 10.18261/issn.2535-3381-2020-01-01
- The mediagrams have been designed using logos from Freepik.com created by rawpixel.com and with permission from Facebook.

1 Introduction
Doing family and language in a digital age

1.1 A day in the digital life of a young multilingual family member

> *Rama hangs up after a phone call with her grandmother in Senegal, who only accepts Joola language in their conversations. She notices that she has received a Snapchat video in Norwegian from her friends from school, and then a Facebook messenger voice message in Wolof from her cousin in France comes in, just as she is reading the usual good night message from her mother, in French and English. In a couple of minutes, Rama uses several parts of her linguistic repertoire to communicate on various media with family and friends in Norway and elsewhere in the world.*

Rama's ways with digital media are emblematic for the subject of this book: the language and media practices by which families maintain local and transnational connections with family members and close friends. These practices are regular, yet fluid, and diverse. They involve a wide range of semiotic resources, including several languages, media channels, and relevant interlocutors. We examine here the language and media practices of four Senegalese families who live in Norway. Transnational migration – a life experience for the parents, a family background for their children – has shaped their linguistic repertoires and social connectivities, and digital media offer indispensable means of maintaining connections to spatially distant relevant others: mothers and brothers, uncles and cousins, former schoolmates or neighbours. The kaleidoscope of these three dimensions – languages, media, and translocal interlocutors – is at the centre of this book, and defines its starting questions: how is family multilingualism being transformed in the digital age? How do people use linguistic resources in digitally mediated interaction to maintain and develop family relationships? How do digital language and literacy practices transform family linguistic repertoires?

To answer these questions, **this book develops an integrated perspective on language and media practices in family contexts.** An important part of this perspective is the notion of a *mediational repertoire*, which

DOI: 10.4324/9781003227311-1

integrates the semiotic and technological choices people make in order to conduct mediated interaction. For example, Rama's everyday practices, sketched out above, draw on her personal mediational repertoire. Rama knows not just whom to address in Joola or French, but also what media channels to select for certain interlocutors. She is in the process of developing more or less conventional, and expected, combinations of linguistic and media choices when communicating with certain (types of) interlocutors. We argue in this book that understanding how such language and media combinations emerge and are maintained or negotiated is an increasingly important dimension of linguistic practice in the early 21st century.

The social environment in which we examine this process is that of the family, in particular the **transnational multilingual family**. These two attributes – transnational and multilingual – are not co-extensive, but overlap considerably: the majority of transnational families, with migration backgrounds, are in some way multilingual, in that several languages are bound up with the family members' linguistic biographies, the everyday language practices of different family members and metapragmatic awareness of the role of language in the construction of social identity (see Chapter 3). And in turn, the multilingualism of different family members is actively maintained through local and transnational family interaction (Chapters 5–7). Moreover, transnational digital interaction presents an opportunity for migrants and their children to engage with language resources that are not necessarily in use in the everyday social arenas where they find themselves, so they can develop their language competences (Chapter 8).

This **nexus of digital media, transnational interaction and family multilingualism** has been rather marginal to research on family multilingualism until very recently (see Chapter 2). With this book, we place it centre stage, taking into account the fact that the discursive construction of relations in a multilingual family is intertwined with the construction of digital family life. As research beyond linguistics makes clear, transnational family-making relies heavily on digital media. Mobility and technology come together as 'More and more, family bonds are being stretched across great distances and, for members of the developing world in particular, this distance and separation is part of what it means to have intimate relationships in the contemporary era.' (Hannaford 2017: 130). This leads to various forms of transnational 'care circulation' (Baldassar & Merla 2014a, 2014b), constructions of co-presence (Baldassar 2008, Nedelcu & Wyss 2016) and 'connected presence' (Christensen 2009, Licoppe 2004). However, it also enhances social control (Hannaford 2017) and facilitates the solicitation of remittances (Tazanu 2012). Our aim is to flesh out these observations with a detailed examination of language use in different aspects of family-making.

The specific social context studied in this book is that of Senegalese families in Norway. Even though there is only a small group of Senegalese in the Norwegian context, Senegalese families provide a particularly good example of sustainable multilingual practices in the diaspora. The 'Culture of mobility' that characterises the Senegalese 'Culture of migration' (Riccio & degli Uberti 2013: 211), is expressed multilingually, and reveals considerable creativity and agency (Smith 2019: 160). Rama was mobile within Senegal before she moved to Norway, and Norwegian was in Rama's words 'just' the seventh language in which she started interacting as she joined the household of her father, who had migrated earlier. There is not *one* heritage or home language used in the Senegalese families studied here, rather a diverse repertoire is accessed. In this book, we examine how Rama and other participants draw on these linguistic resources in digital interactions where family relationships are negotiated, and we show how this affects the family multilingualism.

1.2 Theoretical dimensions: Family multilingualism, digital interaction, and polymedia

In constructing the theoretical backdrop for this study, we integrate a number of fields. These are fully explored in Chapter 2. To outline the main ideas here, we approach the family practices from a family multilingualism perspective. Current work in this field investigates how families are constructed through multilingual language practices, and how language functions as a resource for this process of family-making and meaning-making (King & Lanza 2019: 718). This implies the use of ethnographic methods, often as a combination of interview and interactional data (see for instance Lomeu Gomes 2020). Moreover, the importance of extended family members' multilingualism has been accentuated in recent studies (Coetzee 2018, Curdt-Christiansen 2016, Smith-Christmas 2014), and children's agency has also been foregrounded (Gafaranga 2010, Obojska 2019). Recently, and in line with current sociolinguistic research considering language as social practice, the notion of repertoire has been found useful for the study of family multilingualism (Hiratsuka & Pennycook 2020). Repertoires are often considered in relation to mobility. As Blommaert and Backus (2013: 28) note: 'Repertoires in a superdiverse world are records of mobility: of movement of people, language resources, social arenas, technologies of learning and learning environments.' In a biographical perspective, languages and codes are understood as related to each other, and the meanings attributed to them are linked to how linguistic practices are experienced in discursive constructions of social affiliation (Busch 2012). To investigate Rama's mediational repertoire, we need to know the environments in which she moves, the language resources available in the social arenas where she interacts with others, and the technologies she uses.

Sociolinguistic research on computer-mediated communication has explored a wide range of multilingual practices online (see Lee 2017). Linguistic resources are deployed for playfulness and creativity (Deumert

2014a) and in forms of writing that the users rarely draw on in other contexts (Lee 2017), for instance, as resources that are usually associated with spoken practices appear in digital literacy practices (Lexander 2011). The overwhelming majority of the research on multilingualism in digital interaction, however, is based on data from one specific channel, platform, or communication mode. Linguistic choices of the same user(s) across various communication modes are hardly ever examined. While the early research on multilingualism online focused on digital data only, recent studies combine on- and offline data to investigate digital practices as integrated into people's everyday lives (Androutsopoulos & Stæhr 2018). Moreover, everyday family life unfolds in the alternation between online and offline modes, or in both simultaneously (Stæhr & Nørreby 2021).

Polymedia theory (Madianou & Miller 2012a, 2012b) offers a useful approach to Rama's use of communication technologies, as it treats multiple tools available to users as an environment of affordances. It links the proliferation of new tools for digital interaction with social and emotional aspects, considering relationship-building as affected by the choices that interlocutors make with regard to tools and modality. We therefore incorporate their approach with the sociolinguistic theories referred to above, as we study how families are constructed through language use in digital interaction.

1.3 Fieldwork for this book

This book is the outcome of a three-year research project, combining ethnographic interview data with interactional data related to a diversity of communicational tools. The data was collected 2017–2019 with four families of Senegalese background living in Norway. In all of the families, the parents had stayed in Norway for 10–15 years, which means they had experienced substantial technological development affecting how they kept in touch with their relatives in Senegal and elsewhere. After many years in Norway, all families had also adopted Norwegian as the main means of everyday communication. The use of Senegalese languages differed, due to the families' diverse geographical and ethnic origins, as well as their religious orientation. All used Wolof, Senegal's most widely spoken language, while some families' repertoires also included languages like Peul (Pulaar, Fula) and Joola, and some had learnt to read and write Arabic to varying degrees. All the parents of Senegalese origin had had Senegal's official language, French, as the language of instruction in school, and some of the children had learnt it as a second foreign language in the Norwegian school system. These language labels should not be taken as given, as they cover heteroglossic and varied language practices, and the speakers draw on various linguistic resources in their communication.

Furthermore, the household member composition differed, a dimension that may have an impact on family multilingualism (Vorobeva 2021).

Single-parent families have often been omitted in research on multilingual parenting, but are included here, as two of the research participants were single parents, a mother and a father. In one family both parents were from Senegal, and in another family the mother had been born in Norway and the father had been born in Senegal. Some children had been born in Norway, some had migrated with their parents, and some had joined their parents after the latter had been resident in Norway for some time. The families' communication with relatives outside the household is also included in the analysis through transnational interactional data. Close friends of the family are moreover included in the study. We give a fuller introduction to the families in Chapter 3. Then, in order to analyse the data set, from Chapter 5 onwards, we draw mainly on family multilingualism research, but incorporate conceptual compasses from sociolinguistics and polymedia theory, as well as from family discourse studies and language socialisation theories. Our aim is to present an innovative perspective on language practices in transnational families.

1.4 Outline of the book

The theoretical rationale informing our study is discussed in Chapter 2, where we review research on language as social practice with a focus on family interaction and family multilingualism, multilingualism online, and media-ethnographic research on digital family communication. In Chapter 3 we present the three relevant sociolinguistic settings for this study: language and society in Senegal, language and immigration in Norway, and Senegalese migrants in Norway. We then introduce the four Norwegian-Senegalese families who participated in the study and sketch out the linguistic repertoires of all family members, also describing the mobilisation of linguistic resources across the families.

Chapter 4 provides a methodology to follow in the study of mediational repertoires, based on visuals as fruitful in the study of language as a set of resources (Busch 2012). We outline the conception and realisation of *mediagrams*, the technique developed in the project for collaborative data collection, visualising patterns of language and media choices among participants. In relation to this, we discuss the multi-sited fieldwork and the innovative data-collection methodology applied in the project, including ethical considerations and solutions regarding personal digital data. In Chapter 5, we analyse selected mediagrams to examine how family members' linguistic and media repertoires pattern together in their situated choices for transnational family communication. More specifically, we investigate how participants manage languages and media channels to construct various forms of co-presence (Greschke 2021, Nedelcu & Wyss 2016) to communicate with relatives and friends, in Senegal and elsewhere.

In Chapter 6, we look more closely at what is being communicated and how relationships are co-constructed in these interactions. Through the analysis of digital power and connection manoeuvres (cf. Kendall 2006, Tannen 2006, Tannen et al. 2007) and morality practices (Ochs & Kremer-Sadlik 2007a, 2007b), we show how their interactional practices differ between local and transnational digital connectivity as well as between regular and occasional family contacts. We further examine expressions of affection in these mediated interactions and how they differ according to the various types of local to global connectivity in the data. We draw on Hiratsuka and Pennycook's (2020) notion of translingual family repertoire, and on framing and intertextuality in family communication (Tannen et al. 2007) to demonstrate how the diversity of linguistic repertoires becomes a resource to articulate emotions between adults, parents, and their children.

Chapter 7 extends this scope, moving from family relationships to spaces of cultural participation. We examine how family members and their interlocutors deploy their repertoires of mediation for diasporic communication across various media channels and digital platforms, including social media timelines and group-chats for Senegalese in the diaspora. Drawing on the notion of polycentricity (Blommaert et al. 2005a), we examine how language practices differ by channel, and how family members construct themselves as members of Senegalese diaspora, for example by displaying their affiliation with Senegalese culture and by circulating political and religious messages from and about Senegal.

In Chapter 8, we explore the importance of transnational digital family interaction for the cultivation of heritage language repertoires. We first examine how parents negotiate the indexical meanings of linguistic resources (cf. Bailey 2007) that are emblematic of identity and belonging in the transnational Senegalese family context, i.e. how they define and value their linguistic heritage. Participant reports suggest that family members do not conceive of a single heritage language, but view different linguistic resources as worth maintaining and developing with regard to their Senegalese cultural background. An analysis of two selected language portraits (Busch 2012) delves deeper into the time-space dimension and emotional aspects of the participants' linguistic repertoires. Thirdly, we discuss examples where the children's generation in the families mobilise their heritage language repertoires in interaction. These show that although 'Wolof' appears as a dominant resource, this term covers differentiated and heteroglossic practices, orienting to different registers, related to language mode and interlocutors' age. The analysis portrays transnational family interaction as a space where children can mobilise the heritage language repertoire without necessarily having a full command of particular languages. They experiment with and develop their competences, even by creating frames for language learning.

The final chapter sums up how the linguistic repertoires of these Norwegian-Senegalese families are made and remade in a digital interactional context, affected by local language use in Senegal and Norway as well as by global linguistic resources. It discusses how these factors interact with the affordances of digital communication media, especially regarding the multimodal resources they make available, and how languages and media are coordinated to manage family relationships and identities.

Overall, this book seeks to extend our knowledge of how local and transnational family relationships and identities are constructed in digitally mediated interaction and how digital practices affect family repertoires. It suggests methods for investigating this, and it combines different disciplines to provide a complex and nuanced account of multilingual family-making across national borders in a digital age.

2 Multilingual families online
Repertoires and practices

Multilingualism research is broad and transdisciplinary, and family multilingualism has been studied from many different angles. For example, neurolinguistic and psycholinguistic approaches to multilingualism study the competence of adults and children in two or more languages. Sociolinguistic approaches are more interested in linguistically diverse family interaction and in the language policies and ideologies that shape the preference for certain languages and avoidance of others in family talk. In this book we focus on multilingual practices and mediated communication in transnational families, and the theoretical background to our approach is organised in four areas, outlined in this chapter. Our point of departure is research in sociolinguistics and applied linguistics that conceptualises language as social practice and approaches multilingualism from a repertoire perspective (2.1). We then trace practice-based approaches to multilingualism in research on family language policy (FLP) and on heritage language use, and draw on recent theorising of families as discursively constructed (2.2). Our research is also informed by work on digitally mediated communication and multilingualism online (2.3), and we build on this research to argue that digital literacy practices need to be taken into consideration in the study of family multilingualism. However, since digital literacy practices in a family context have mainly received attention outside of applied linguistics and sociolinguistics, we also draw on relevant research from media studies and media anthropology (2.4). We synthesise these strands of research into a framework for the study of multilingual families and transnational communication in a digital age (2.5).

2.1 Multilingual practices

We start this section with a definition of practice before turning to theoretical concepts associated with practice approaches to multilingualism, and to recent critique of the very concept of multilingualism (2.1.1). We then discuss current understandings of linguistic repertoire and register that are supported by practice-based perspectives to language (2.1.2).

DOI: 10.4324/9781003227311-2

2.1.1 Practice approaches to multilingualism

Sociolinguistics and applied linguistics have not been left untouched by the 'practice turn' across humanities and social sciences (Schatzki et al. 2001). This turn is manifest in a shift of attention from language as innate knowledge and formal structure to speakers' deployment of linguistic resources to produce specific effects in communicative action (Pennycook 2010: 17). Our understanding of practice in this book orients to linguistic anthropology, applied linguistics and literacy studies. For example, Hanks (1996, 2005) theorises practice as a 'moment of synthesis' where different dimensions of language – as form, communicative activity, and ideology – come together. In a practice approach, regularities in language use (i.e. usage patterns) are not explained by formal rules, but by embodied dispositions and generic 'schemas' that are actualised in speech (Hanks 2005: 72). The tension between 'schematic' and 'emergent' aspects of practice is considered constitutive for the reproduction and production of language itself (Hanks 1996).

For Pennycook, practices are repeated 'bundles of activities' (2010: 2) and distinguished from individual, situated action. Practices constitute an organising principle behind communicative action, mediating between social structure and individual activity. Language practices are intertwined with other social practices and always take place locally, drawing here on a sense of locality that encompasses local knowledge, worldviews, and language ideologies (Pennycook 2010: 128). The study of language practices is therefore not reduced to microanalysis of language in action, but also considers the material, political and ideological conditions as well as consequences of practice (Pennycook 2010: 29, 31). In this line of thinking, language in a grammatical/systemic sense emerges from language practices: by practising language, we produce language.

A well-known example of a practice approach in applied linguistics is the notion of literacy practices in New Literacy Studies, which shifts from an understanding of literacy as a 'neutral' skill or technology to an ideological and culturally sensitive conception of reading and writing practices in a community (Street 1984, Barton & Hamilton 1998, Barton 2007). A telling example is Martin-Jones & Jones' (2000) collection of ethnographic accounts of multilingual literacies in a migrant context, which demonstrates how people take on shifting identities in various domains through their literacy practices. Scholarship on literacy practices influenced the later understanding of digital literacy practices (Lee 2007, Lexander 2011, 2012, Jones & Hafner 2012, Jones et al. 2015). In this perspective, digital literacy refers not just to the ability to use digital media for purposes of information-seeking, interpersonal communication, and self-presentation, but also about 'doing something in the social world' and 'being able to adapt the affordances and constraints of the tools to particular circumstances' (Jones & Hafner 2012: 13).

In multilingualism research, practice approaches have been influential in challenging systemic and bounded conceptions of bilingualism and in developing new concepts by which to capture the contextual complexity of language use. In her introduction to *Bilingualism: a social approach*, Heller (2007) argues that to understand language in society, the analysis of linguistic form must be linked to practice, ideology, and political economy. Language practices are viewed from this angle as socially and politically embedded ways in which speakers draw on linguistic resources. The study of multilingualism as social practice consequentially foregrounds speakers as social actors as well as processual and materialist aspects of social action (Heller 2007: 1).

These ideas are reflected in several theoretical concepts whose confluent emergence in the late 2000s and early 2010s has been dubbed a 'trans-super-poly-metro movement' (Pennycook 2016): metrolingualism, poly-languaging, translanguaging, superdiversity (discussed in the next section) and heteroglossia all share an interest in historically new sociolinguistic processes and a critical view of received approaches to multilingualism. As these notions inform our scholarly thinking and research, they are briefly reviewed below.

First, **heteroglossia**: originally developed by Mikhail Bakhtin (Bakhtin & Holquist 1981, Russian *raznorečie*), heteroglossia is part of a conception of language that challenges the structuralist notion of a language as a formal system and instead draws attention to the varying ideological viewpoints and antagonistic social relations that surround language in general, and linguistic features in particular. Recent sociolinguistics and linguistic ethnography have drawn on heteroglossia to emphasise how linguistic signs in multilingual communities are linked to historical, social, political, and cultural tensions (Bailey 2007, Blackledge & Creese 2020). From a practice viewpoint, heteroglossia describes how the simultaneous use of different kinds of signs, which are ideologically framed as belonging to distinct languages or different registers of a language, may be used strategically in order to evoke social or ideological tensions (Androutsopoulos 2011, Mc Laughlin 2014). Second, **polylingual languaging or polylanguaging** is a concept developed by Jørgensen (2008) in research with Danish youth of diverse backgrounds (Jørgensen et al. 2011, Ag & Jørgensen 2013). Key to a polylanguaging analysis is the attempt to avoid the assignment of data to named languages, which are considered language-ideological constructs, and to focus instead on linguistic features as the main unit of analysis, reconstructing their trajectories of usage and tracing their associations from the viewpoint of speakers themselves. On a language-ideological level, polylanguaging is understood as a process in which speakers deploy 'whatever linguistic features are at their disposal' (Jørgensen 2008: 169) in order to achieve their aims, thereby transgressing conventional perceptions of language boundaries and counteracting normative expectations of 'appropriate' language conduct.

Third, **translanguaging** was originally developed as an approach to bilingual education (García 2009) and reached wider currency as a 'practical theory of language' (Li 2018). A key idea in translanguaging is that multilinguals' language skills and practices are not organised in separate, bounded languages, but rather integrated parts of one linguistic repertoire, whose separation into distinct languages is an effect of monolingual ideologies. As García & Li (2014) argue, the strategic selection of features from an integrated repertoire is the normal mode of communication in the world. Through the act of translanguaging, Li (2011) argues, multilingual individuals create a 'translanguaging space' where knowledge and resources that have been ideologically separated from one another can be integrated. The translanguaging analysis developed by García & Li (2014) programmatically embraces the entire range of semiotic means that can be deployed alongside linguistic resources, and the interface of multilingualism and multimodality has been taken up in recent research (De Meulder et al. 2019, Kusters 2021, and see Section 2.1.2). Fourth, and distinct from translanguaging, the concept of **translingual practice** (Canagarajah 2013a, 2013b) refers to a social-interactionist perspective on communication in conditions of diversity and contact. Building on Pratt's (1991) notion of contact zones, Canagarajah argues that language resources always come into contact in actual use and shape each other as 'people engage with each other, tailor their language uses reciprocally, display uptake, resist dominant conventions, and co-construct meanings in relation to existing norms and ideologies in actual interactions' (Canagarajah 2013a: 28). Finally, communicative practices in urban space inspire **metrolingualism**, a notion that embraces both fluidity and fixity. While speakers engage in fluid conversations drawing on a variety of linguistic resources, they may also mobilise ascriptions of fixed identities (Otsuji & Pennycook 2010, Pennycook & Otsuji 2015). In this view, contemporary mixed linguistic repertoires are the outcome of transnational flows of linguistic and cultural resources.

These conceptual innovations in multilingualism theory are joined by a critical perspective towards code-switching and the notion of multilingualism itself. Code-switching (especially, it seems, syntactic approaches to code-switching), is critically understood as imposing ideologically construed boundaries on multilingual practices (e.g. Makoni & Pennycook 2007: 22, Otheguy et al. 2015). However, from the viewpoint of conversational approaches to code-switching, as pioneered by Gumperz (1982) and further developed by Auer (1984, 1995) and others, this critique seems to overshoot its target (cf. Auer 2022). Interactional approaches to code-switching assume that participants hold a joint awareness of distinct 'codes' in their jointly shared repertoires, and negotiate choices of, and alternations between, these resources to index various aspects of conversational and situational context (Auer 1984, 1995). A 'code' in this sense does not only refer to a distinct named language but includes any kind of metalinguistic entity that is perceived and/or treated as interactionally distinct from the participant's viewpoint (Auer 1998). While interactional approaches to code-switching indeed hypothesise distinct 'codes', the aim of the analysis is to show how participants themselves define and negotiate boundaries between these codes, rather than to apply externally predefined boundaries between linguistic (sub)systems to the data. Interactional approaches to code-switching paved the way to Rampton's (1995) notion of crossing, i.e. a conscious use of features from languages that the speaker does not know in full, representing a transgression of social or ethnic boundaries (cf. Quist & Jørgensen 2008). Crossing, in turn, built a bridge from code-switching research to new conceptions of emergent linguistic complexity under conditions of increased ethno-cultural diversity ('superdiversity', see Section 2.1.2).

Code-switching is not alone in this critique. Associated terms like 'mixing', 'hybrid' and 'syncretic', too, have been discredited as implicitly sustaining an ideology of monolingualism, i.e. an understanding of languages as bounded entities, while at the same time disregarding how people actually deploy linguistic resources in communicative practice (cf. Bailey 2007, Makoni & Pennycook 2007: 22, Canagarajah 2013b, Otheguy et al. 2015). In the same spirit, the notion of multilingualism has been heavily criticised for implicating an 'enumerative approach' (Pennycook 2016) or 'a pluralisation of singularity' (Makoni 2011). 'Complexity' has been proposed as a better-suited term with regard to the dynamic borders between socially constructed categories (Blommaert 2013), and Makoni (2015: 217) even prefers a 'humanistic monolingualism' to multilingualism.

While we endorse an understanding of language as social practice in this book, we still retain 'multilingualism' as an overarching term. For one thing, we do so for pragmatic reasons: 'multilingualism' is still an overarching label in several socio and applied linguistics venues, including much recent critical research (not least the series this book is part of). Indeed, much research on multilingualism and code-switching casts a critical view on etic and emic understandings of 'languages' and 'codes' (e.g. Auer 1998, MacSwan 2017). A second reason is that multilingualism aptly captures a sense of 'organised diversity' that matters to speakers themselves, at least so to participants in our research. While we agree that multilingualism does not fully capture the processual dimension of languaging, of 'doing language' by drawing on all available resources, it does cover the fact that participants themselves identify with, and talk about, named languages. This is not to deny that distinctions between named languages are politically and ideologically defined, but to underscore that these distinctions nonetheless seem consequential to the participants' language and media practices and also figure in their metalinguistic discourse.

Against this backdrop, we use code-switching in the interactional perspective outlined above and distinguish it from translanguaging in several ways. On a theory plane, we link translanguaging to other figurative notions that emphasise the boundary-transcending dimension of social and communicative processes, such as transnationalism (cf. Section 2.4) and translocality (Chapter 6).[1] Analytically we use translanguaging to include the interplay of linguistic and semiotic resources in mediated interaction. We also explore translanguaging as practice and ideology among adolescents and young adults, especially with regard to their engagement with heritage languages (Chapter 8). As discussed below, these participants adopt a stance of accepting all linguistic resources in order to engage in language learning practices, and this stance surfaces at times in their metalinguistic comments, where boundaries between named languages are cast as alien to how the participants think about their own language practices.

2.1.2 Repertoires and registers

Practice approaches to multilingualism have led to successive and substantial reconceptions of the linguistic repertoire, a notion as old as modern sociolinguistics itself. John J. Gumperz originally defined a verbal or linguistic repertoire as the totality of 'linguistic forms used in the course of socially significant interaction' (Gumperz 1964: 137), including sets of linguistic varieties that are deployed in a community (Gumperz 1982: 155). Gumperz' starting point is thus the speech community, delimited by the regularity and frequency of interaction (1964: 137).

The rethinking of repertoire in early-21st-century sociolinguistics is closely related to the discourse on superdiversity, a term coined in anthropology to theorise an unprecedented diversification of ethnic and linguistic diversity from a European viewpoint (Vertovec 2007). Superdiversity is conceived as a new order of transnational diversity propelled by an interplay of human mobility (including forced migration) and technological connectivity (Vertovec 2004). A wide range of factors interact in the emergence of superdiverse societies in Europe, including countries of origin, migration channels, migrants' legal status, their human capital and access to the labour market, locality, transnationality, and the reactions of local institutions and the native population (Vertovec 2007: 1049). The reception of superdiversity in sociolinguistics (Blommaert & Rampton 2011) entails a critical rethinking of multilingualism (as already outlined) and a reconsidering of basic assumptions in urban sociolinguistic research. For example, consequences of superdiversity discussed by Blommaert and Rampton (2011) include a loss of predictability in language behaviour, as participants in urban encounters can no longer be presumed to belong to a homogenous speech community, as well as increasingly fuzzy boundaries between a speaker's ethnic origin and the linguistic resources at their disposal. As we shall see below, mobility and connectivity are also closely linked to (digital) diaspora (Chapter 7).

Within the language and superdiversity discussion, a linguistic repertoire is reconceived in a much more individualised and fluid fashion

(Blommaert & Backus 2013). In conditions of late-modern superdiversity, individual repertoires are increasingly detached from the norms of particular communities. Repertoires are formed as speakers engage in various ways of learning – formal and informal, long-lasting and ephemeral, deliberate and accidental – and become more diverse and fluid in this process. A multilingual repertoire is thus understood as a set of mobile resources which index particular contexts of interaction that are relevant to speakers' biographies and trajectories (Otsuji & Pennycook 2010, Androutsopoulos 2014b). Repertoires grow as speakers acquire linguistic knowledge, sometimes limited to single words or even to recognition skills regarding a particular language. Hence, repertoires can be understood as 'records of mobility' that index how people and their language and literacy resources move in space and time (Blommaert & Backus 2013: 15, 28). In addition, Blommaert (2010, Blommaert et al. 2005a) theorises repertoires in close connection to processes of hierarchy-building among linguistic resources (orders of indexicality). For example, transnational (including forced) mobility leads to linguistic repertoires being shaped not by a single sociolinguistic authority, but by several (e.g. learning languages before, during, and post-migration). This leads to patterns of polycentricity, whereby speakers orient to different 'centres of authority', or language-ideological models, in their situated selections of language or language style (Blommaert et al. 2005a, Androutsopoulos & Lexander 2021). As speakers move across encounters and activities, the 'centres' they orient to shift as well, and the indexical value of a given language may also shift in this process (see Chapter 7). For instance, the status of French in Senegal, as official language and language of instruction, is quite different from its status in Norway, where it is an optional second foreign language in school. Expressing oneself in French has quite a different social meaning in Norway and in Senegal. Likewise with Wolof, unknown to most Norwegians, but spoken by the large majority in Senegal (cf. Chapter 3).

Busch (2012) draws on phenomenological and post-structuralist approaches to introduce a biographical approach to the linguistic repertoire. In her view, languages and codes make up 'a heteroglossic whole' and the meanings that speakers attribute to parts of their linguistic repertoire are closely related to their personal experiences and feelings of belonging. Not only the subject's past experiences, but also future ideas, desires, and imaginations are key to people's *Spracherleben*, their 'lived experience of language'. This includes speakers' subjective views of how others perceive them. A telling example of the emotional load Busch describes is found in Monz' (2020) description of homecomers to Mali, whose language practices were affected by negative migration experiences. To enhance our understanding of the embodied experiences of language, Busch (2012) has developed the language portrait as a visualisation method, a method we have applied in our research (cf. Chapter 4).

The notion of spatial repertoires builds on Pennycook's (2010) conception of language as a local practice. With this concept, linguistic repertoires formed through individual life trajectories are linked to the particular places in which these linguistic resources are deployed (Pennycook & Otsuji 2015: 83). Spatial repertoires are assembled *in situ*, in collaboration with others, as language works with 'an assemblage of semiotic resources, artefacts, and environmental affordances' (Canagarajah 2018: 37). Relevant spaces here are sites of social action and interaction, such as restaurants (Pennycook & Otsuji 2015), academia (Canagarajah 2018), and the family (Lanza 2021). Space-making through interaction can also take place online, as exemplified in Mc Laughlin's (2014) study of online communication in the Senegalese diaspora context, where forum members draw on shared linguistic and orthographic resources to reconstruct a distant locality. This conception of space and language is thus highly relevant for our research, involving how linguistic practices are shaped by artefacts and activities.

Through the inclusion of non-linguistic resources, the spatial repertoire approach also points to semiotic repertoires. The theorisation around the semiotic repertoire builds on the understanding that all human interactions and linguistic repertoires are multimodal, and that a holistic focus on repertoires as both multilingual and multimodal allows us to tap into social questions (Kusters et al. 2017). Kusters (2021) furthermore suggests decentralising the individual, to move away from an understanding of semiotic repertoires as located in individual people, and to focus instead on repertoires in context, viewing them as a distributed set of resources that are chained together contingently in activities, in a process of 'repertoire assemblage' (Kusters 2021: 188). Here, spatial and semiotic repertoire thinking meet.

Yet another construct that points to the social patterning of linguistic repertoires is that of register. Specific linguistic and semiotic features and patterns, whether labelled or not, can be associated with specific social attributes, i.e. become enregistered (Agha 2003, Agha 2015, Agha & Frog 2015). Agha's definition of register encompasses 'cultural models of action that link diverse behavioural signs to enactable effects, including images of a persona, interpersonal relationships, and type of conduct' (2007: 145). These models often crystallise in language users' metalinguistic labels like 'slang' or 'polite language', which link semiotic features to (types or images of) speakers, speaker/interlocutor relationships, and typified social practices (Agha 2007: 145). Against this backdrop, speakers may draw on enregistered linguistic features to position themselves and signal their relationship to the interlocutor. For instance, the young participants in our research orient to different cultural models of action when interacting with their grandparents as opposed to cousins of the same age. With the notion of register, we can thus ask how a linguistic repertoire is perceived and deployed as a socially meaningful way of speaking (Pennycook 2018: 9). It is also a conceptual tool that steers attention towards what signs are in use and what they point to, rather than to what language is in use (Blackledge et al. 2014).

The complementary theorisations of repertoire discussed in this subchapter form a conceptual basis upon which to study the multilingual practices of Norwegian-Senegalese transnational families in this book. A repertoire approach does not rule out the meaningfulness of metalinguistic labels like Wolof, Peul, or French, by which participants in this study refer to parts of their linguistic repertoire. We, too, use them in analysis, but without taking the linguistic features they refer to for granted. The conception of language as a set of mobile resources that are acquired in various ways allows us to take into account participants' life trajectories, and the biographical approach to repertoires alerts us to the emotional aspects of these experiences. The spatial perspective reminds us that linguistic repertoires are not just to be considered as individualised, but as interaction in time and space, a point of departure for looking at family repertoires and heritage language repertoires. The understanding of registers as sets of linguistic features linked to cultural models of action enhances a fine-grained analysis of social meaning in interaction and offers leeway to consider semiotic resources other than just linguistic ones. We complement these ideas with explicit attention to digitally mediated communication below (Sections 2.3, 2.4, 2.5).

2.2 Family multilingualism

The study of family multilingualism has expanded and diversified within the field of FLP. Important developments here include a reconceptualisation of its constitutive elements: 'family', 'language', and 'policy' (2.2.1). 'Language' in family multilingualism studies is marked by the apparent contradiction between how families interact multilingually and how families talk about languages. Categorising and labelling languages is often at odds with what is actually going on when multilingual families interact, and still the labels have symbolic value for family members. A particularly important symbolic value is accorded to 'heritage language', and practice-based approaches combined with the language socialisation framework help study both communicative and symbolic or emblematic dimensions of these linguistic resources (2.2.2). Family multilingualism goes beyond linguistic complexity in a specific setting, it is also about 'practising family'. To understand how language and family mutually constitute each other, we consider the family as a space that is discursively constructed and negotiated through multilingual spatial repertoires (2.2.3).

2.2.1 Family language policy and beyond

The field of family language policy (FLP) has expanded and diversified since it was first defined by King, Fogle and Logan-Terry (2008) as explicit and overt planning in relation to language use within the home by family members. Both 'policy' and 'family' have been reconceptualised in this research, and lately also a less essentialising definition of 'language' has been adopted in the field. In this subsection, we look at current developments and how they inform our study before we discuss the research gap in FLP regarding families' digitally mediated interaction.

As discussed in detail by Lomeu Gomes (2018), Spolsky's tripartite model of language policy, which includes all language practices, beliefs, and management decisions of a community of polity (Spolsky 2004: 9), has been the premise for the way that FLP has been conceptualised. In FLP studies, Spolsky's focus on institutional context is brought together with child language acquisition research, which had often been based on detailed analysis of caretaker–child interactions (see King 2016), with the aim of identifying the impact of beliefs, practices, and conditions on child language outcomes. The emphasis on explicit and overt planning in the initial definition of FLP was extended to include implicit language policies in families, inferred through interactional data (e.g. Gafaranga 2010, Curdt-Christiansen 2013). The field thus turned towards an understanding of policy that encompasses language practices, also including literacy practices (Curdt-Christiansen 2009).

The ethnographic research that followed these developments has offered insight into the complexity of factors that affect family multilingualism. Drawing on Lave and Wenger (1991), Lanza (2007) considered the family as a community of practice to focus on language socialisation processes, i.e. learning through language and learning to use language (Schieffelin & Ochs 1986). Further language socialisation research in FLP studied children's language development in connection to social factors like the nature of intergenerational speech resources, parents' educational background and language learning experience, migration trajectories, and socio-economic conditions (Curdt-Christiansen 2018). In this book, we also draw on language socialisation as an interpretive frame to examine heritage language practices (see Section 2.2.2, Chapter 8).

Language socialisation research has been criticised for overlooking children's agency (e.g. Gafaranga 2010), as children have been found to play active roles in family language policy (Fogle 2012, Obojska 2019, Said & Zhu 2019, Johnsen 2021) and to act as co-researchers of their own FLP (Little & Little 2022). Furthermore, family language policy is not only about the nuclear family in terms of parents and their children. Other family members have also been shown to influence multilingual practices (Smith-Christmas 2014, Coetzee 2018), and the field has benefitted from studying various family constellations (Fogle 2012, Wright 2020, Kozminska & Zhu 2021, Vorobeva 2021). The diversification of research interests has put new factors integral to family multilingualism on the table, like parents' beliefs about family, childhood, and caregiving (e.g. Fogle 2013), changing family constellations (Vorobeva 2021), and the defining of selves and various family roles (King 2016). This, in turn, has led to a conception of 'family' as dynamic, an understanding of 'family-making' as a social practice that is tightly intertwined with language, and an interest in how families are constructed through their language practices (King & Lanza 2019, see Section 2.2.3).

While both 'policy' and 'family' have been redefined and oriented towards practice perspectives in FLP research, its notion of 'language' has remained more essentialist. In line with Fishman's (1991, 2001) conception of the family as crucial for language maintenance through intergenerational transmission in face-to-face situations, a typical FLP research question has been how macro-sociological factors and parents' ideologies impact on maintaining a (minority) language in the family. Consequently, the concept of language has been influenced by binary oppositions between societal language and home language, school language and heritage language, as well as between language shift and language maintenance. Such binaries are problematic in several ways; we here point out three issues addressed in recent research.

First, there is often more complexity in family multilingualism than what two named languages cover, in particular in other contexts than those represented by the white middle-class of the Global North (Kasanga 2008, Li & Zhu 2019a, Purkarthofer & Steien 2019). More complex linguistic repertoires call for more complex approaches. Second, there has been a tendency to view languages as systems rather than as social practice. Part of the problem, Lomeu Gomes (2018) argues, is the reference to Spolsky's model, which positions language and language varieties as bounded entities and reflective of sociocultural patterning, overlooking social categories like race, ethnicity, and class. Similarly, Hiratsuka and Pennycook (2020) locate the problem in the very definition of FLP, which links language to decision-making and not to practice as the basic organising principle of daily life (cf. Pennycook 2010). They argue that rather than looking at policy, family multilingualism research should promote expansive and dynamic understandings of the different elements at play in family interaction (Hiratsuka & Pennycook 2020: 749). Recent work seeks to do this, drawing on concepts like translanguaging and translingual practice. Several studies (e.g. Lee et al. 2021, Lindquist & Garmann 2021) draw on translanguaging to present the home as a translanguaging space (Li 2011), for instance presenting intonation as an aspect of translanguaging in FLP (Lee, Pang & Park 2021). An important aspect of these studies is the interest in multimodality and semiotic resources going beyond the linguistic resources (Kusters et al. 2021, Kozminska & Zhu 2021).

Third, the focus on language maintenance and language shift leads to dismissing other factors at play when individuals and families deal with languages (Zhu & Li 2016). To overcome this focus, Zhu and Li (2016) suggest studying families' and individuals' motivations for learning languages in terms of their imagination, looking forward, not backwards: Because different generations and individuals within the same family have vastly different sociocultural experiences, more attention needs to be paid to these experiences. Such consideration is found in

Purkarthofer and Steien (2019) and Purkarthofer (2021) who draw on linguistic repertoires in Busch's (2012) sense, as part of the individual's biography. Developing the notion of 'partially shared repertoires', Purkarthofer (2021) seeks to replace the idea of language as transmitted from parent to child and give room for different family members' agency and differing meanings attached to various linguistic resources. In sum, the developments referred to here suggest that essentialist notions of language maintenance or shift fall short and propose ways to overcome them. However, there are still gaps that need to be filled, notably regarding digital family interaction.

Until now, there has not been a substantial interest in digital practices within FLP, despite their importance in the family context (Lanza & Lexander 2019, Lexander 2021a). While the use of didactic digital tools for language learning in the home, alongside videos and computer games, have been studied to some extent (Little 2019, 2020b, Hatoss 2020), we also need to study interpersonal interaction with family members in transnational settings. If not, we lose important insight into how families draw upon their linguistic repertoire in everyday action, both in spoken and in written practices; the family members' use of certain resources may even go unnoticed. Referring to the definition of FLP, Palviainen and Kędra (2020) argue that digital interaction in multilingual families implies explicit and implicit language choices, just like any other interaction, and Palviainen (2020a: 87) furthermore suggests that the definition of FLP should be expanded to include digital practices. Curdt-Christiansen and Huang (2020: 188) suggest that 'networked FLP' could be a useful term to investigate digital cross-boundary connectedness and its influence on family language practices and policy. We return to the few existing studies of digital communication in the family in Section 2.4.4.

In this book, we draw on methodological and theoretical insights from FLP to focus on digital interaction in multilingual families, but aim to go beyond the frameworks associated with FLP research. We use the terms 'family multilingualism' and 'family language practices' to underline our practice approach to language and signal that we focus on interpersonal interaction rather than decision-making. We also draw on language socialisation theory (cf. Section 2.2.2 and Chapter 8), we consider families as constructed through linguistic practice (cf. Section 2.2.3 and Chapter 6), and we study participants' biographies as part of their repertoires (cf. Chapters 5 and 8).

2.2.2 Heritage language practices and heritage language socialisation

Heritage language is defined as 'the language associated with one's cultural background', which 'may or may not be spoken in the home' (Cho, Cho & Tse 1997: 106). Some studies choose to use other terms, such as 'home language' or 'mother tongue', to refer to minority languages spoken at home (cf. Schalley & Eisenchlas 2020). Even though the reference here to 'the language', in the singular case, is conceptually problematic, we nonetheless retain an understanding of 'heritage language' as linguistic resources associated with a family's cultural background(s). However, we prefer the term 'heritage language practices', following up on the practice-based approaches to heritage language developed by De Fina (2012) and Canagarajah (2019). These practice-based approaches offer insights that go beyond a focus on language maintenance and shift. De Fina (2012) studied interactional resources in a three-generation Italian American family. She found different ways of interactional engagement with heritage language in the family environment, including speech accommodation, translation, metalinguistic commentary, trying out, and performing. She concluded that even minimal heritage language use could have deep symbolic meaning in a family context. Canagarajah (2019) found that identities related to linguistic and cultural background can be indexed by fragmented and diversified practices. He contrasted the primordialist idea of heritage language, i.e. as autonomous, bounded, elaborated, and tied to a specific territory, with migrant Tamil speakers' practice-based view of heritage language competence. Their view of such competence included the strategic alignment of bits and pieces of Tamil 'with multimodal semiotic resources and spatial repertoires to accomplish social and cultural communicative activities' (Canagarajah 2019: 42). Canagarajah (2019) here refers to the spatial repertoire, which we also use as an analytical tool in this book to investigate digital heritage language practices (cf. Section 2.1).

Several factors affect how individual family members integrate heritage language(s) in their practices, and as Blackledge et al. (2008: 537) suggest, processes of passing on a heritage language can lead to intergenerational transformation of both linguistic features and the meaning of heritage language to a community. A dynamic notion of heritage language and a complex sense of belonging are therefore needed (Li & Zhu 2019a), thereby taking into account the 'complex interrelationship between access to the language, parental language skills, links to identity construction, and perceived usefulness' (Little 2020a: 207–208). To achieve this, and in order to examine heritage language learning through complex practices in digital space, we adopt a language socialisation lens, i.e. socialisation to use language, through language (Schieffelin & Ochs 1986). Learning language in this perspective implies not just lexico-grammatical forms, but also norms and expectations in specific cultural contexts, particularly salient in a heritage language perspective (He 2008). When children have contact with heritage language-speaking relatives, their interlocutors will often have a desire to assist them to become more proficient not just in the use of linguistic features, but also regarding the values, ideologies, identities, and stances and practices associated with language practices (Duff 2012: 566). In addition, language socialisation offers a framework for integrating interactional, ideological, and political aspects, providing insights into the construction of identity and belonging (Fogle & King 2008).

2.2.3 The discursive construction of multilingual family space

In her study of how prospective parents imagine multilingualism for their children, Purkarthofer (2019) made the participants use Lego building blocks in interviews to literally build the family language policy they envisioned. This methodology exemplifies recent family multilingualism research with an interest that centres more around how families construct themselves through language practices and less on what languages are used when (King & Lanza 2019, Lomeu Gomes 2020). Instead of looking at the family as a domain (cf. Fishman 1965), recent FLP work considers the family a space where meanings and relationships are negotiated through multilingual practices that embrace speakers' lived experiences (Lanza 2021). As Lomeu Gomes (2020) puts it, families are 'talked into being'. This family space can be conceptualised along the private–public continuum of social life (Lanza & Lomeu Gomes 2020: 165, Mirvahedi 2021), looking at aspects like the influence of public discourse on how people construct their private family space, for instance regarding kinship and kinterms (Wright 2020, 2022). This perspective thus enlarges earlier FLP approaches by considering a wider range of macro-sociological structures as influential factors for language use in the home and by examining other aspects than just language choice in analysis. Methods that can be applied to carry out such analysis are found in interactional sociolinguistics and discourse analysis, including intertextuality (Gordon 2009), power and connection manoeuvres (Tannen et al 2007), and moral socialisation (Ochs & Kremer-Sadlik 2015).

As Wright (2020: 3) points out, it is the family, not language, that comes first; families are interested in being and doing family more than they are interested in language, and family roles and relationships take priority over language choice. Instead of starting from language practices, we may thus start from kinship processes to look at multilingualism in the family. This can be carried out through building on Bakhtin's (1999) dialogicality in considering intertextual repetition as a fundamental means of binding families together (e.g. Gordon 2009). Intertextuality affirms interlocutors' shared history and membership in the same group, and shared meanings are created that construct the family as a unit. In a transnational and digital context, intertextuality interferes with differing cultural practices, differing understandings of migrants' lives, and differing norms across geographical spaces, and is communicated with different linguistic resources.

The construction of family identities is furthermore closely connected to the construction of intimacy and power relations (Ochs 1992, Tannen 2006, Tannen et al. 2007, Gordon 2008, 2009). Tannen's research (1994) departs from a view of power and solidarity as intertwined in conversational interaction. The negotiation of these two dimensions takes place through 'power manoeuvres' and 'connection manoeuvres'. Power manoeuvres establish or challenge status and hierarchy, and connection manoeuvres aim to manage intimacy and solidarity. These two types of manoeuvres are not necessarily distinguishable in interaction, as an utterance may create both at once. In their study of four American families' everyday talk, Tannen et al. (2007) look at speakers' utterances as complex interplays of both power and connection manoeuvres: Speakers aim to influence other's actions and determine their own, but also seek to reinforce their intimate connections as members of the same family (Kendall 2007: 14–15).

This connection between intimacy and power in US families is also central to Ochs and Kremer-Sadlik's (2015) work. They claim that children's routine expression of compassion with others conditions the viability of interpersonal relationships, family, and community. In routinised activities with intimates, children learn how to treat others, build relationships, and enact identities (Ochs & Kremer-Sadlik 2007a). In addition, the parents' wish to educate their children to become economically successful affects family communication, also in view of providing children with specific language skills. In the context of transnational migration, and multilingualism, the relation between linguistic resources, compassion and economic progress becomes more complex, and this also affects practices of family solidarity and morality. For example, research by Li Wei and Zhu Hua (2019a) in the UK describes how a father from Hong Kong had shifted from speaking Cantonese to Mandarin with his children, after they had acquired Mandarin from friends of Chinese origin in university. The authors also refer to a Hakka-speaking mother who encouraged her children to learn Mandarin because it would be important for them if they one day wanted to go to China to work and study. As a result, parents in these families promoted Mandarin, not the parents' first languages, i.e. Hakka and Cantonese, as cultural heritage. These examples show how transnational connections and aspirations guide heritage language conceptions and meaning-making in multilingual families in complex ways.

2.2.4 A 'digital turn' in FLP research

Transnational connections are enhanced by digital communication tools, and online space has become important for the language-mediated experiences of multilingual families (King & Lanza 2019: 718). It follows from the research reviewed above that digitally mediated communication, too, can provide space for heritage language socialisation in contexts of transnational mobility and connectivity. It supports children's and adolescents' independent interaction with transnational relatives, where they need to draw on heritage language resources to communicate. Through interaction with family members of different generations, these children can become familiar with various aspects of heritage language that may not be that easily accessible in the country of residence. As we show in Chapter 8, transnational interlocutors of different generations may promote specific linguistic heritage resources through explicit or implicit norms and expectations.

Work on heritage language socialisation points to social factors in speakers' physical environment that may affect heritage language learning, like negative societal and individual attitudes related to minority languages (Guardado 2018: 49), conflict with social acceptance, economic survival, and legal status (Canagarajah 2008). In digitally mediated communication, however, speakers can create and access spaces of communication that orient to other sociolinguistic values than those dominant in the physical environment (polycentricity, see Chapter 7). To study this movement, it proves fruitful to bring the concept of spatial repertoires (Section 2.1) in connection with heritage language socialisation (Section 2.2.3) in order to examine their construction of identity and belonging. In this understanding, families construct themselves through linguistic practices, including heritage language. An investigation of language practices as everyday social activities, from which language regularities may emerge (Hiratsuka & Pennycook 2020), should therefore include digital social activities. Children engage in family interaction both at home and in their parents' homeland, e.g. through holiday visits and transnational mediated communication (Haque 2012, Szecsi & Szilagyi 2012). They construct family roles and manage family relationships both off- and online. In this book, we therefore consider the family as a space that is discursively constructed through a wide range of both direct and mediated language practices. These practices, including power and connection manoeuvres and moral socialisation, are understood as collaboratively assembled among family members and shaped by transnational family activities (cf. Canagarajah 2018).

2.3 Multilingualism online

Multilingualism was one of the earliest topics of early linguistics approaches to interactive written discourse (Ferrara et al. 1991) or computer-mediated communication (CMC, Herring 1996) in the 1990s. This research covers a vast area (Androutsopoulos 2013, Lee 2017) with different theoretical underpinnings, which may be narrowed down for the purposes of this exposition to two main fields of inquiry, labelled 'multilingual internet' and 'multilingual practices online' for ease of reference. We begin with a brief outline of the first field, which covers statistical and distributional research on the use and status of different languages on the web. For example, global statistics of the distribution of languages online are compared with the distribution of languages across the world population (cf. Lee 2017: 15–22). Long before social media, the early internet was heavily skewed towards English, the language of most websites and discussion groups. With the localisation of the web (Danet & Herring 2007), multilingual user interfaces were developed for websites and social media platforms, sometimes drawing on crowdsourced translations (Lenihan 2011). The availability of online content in different languages has important implications for linguistic diversity, language maintenance, and sociolinguistic justice in the age of globalisation. An English-only internet would erase local and culturally particular sources of knowledge construction and diminish chances for smaller languages to remain important for the transmission of information. To exemplify this with reference to the sociolinguistic context of this study (cf. Chapter 3), the various Senegalese languages in our participants' repertoires differ in terms of online presence and language technology support. Wolof, our participants' main heritage language, has its own Wikipedia subdomain, wo.wikipedia.org, with currently 1.654 articles (for comparison, Norwegian Wikipedia has more than half a million articles). Bilingual dictionaries for languages such as French, English or German also exist for Wolof, though not, or to a much lesser degree, for other Senegalese languages such as Joola or Peul, which some of our participants also speak.[2] While there is evidence that the presence of a language in Wikipedia is not by itself a sufficient indicator of substantial content in this language (Deumert 2014b), these resources can obviously be useful for heritage language learning (a topic we turn to in Chapter 8).

However, relevant to this book is mainly the second area, multilingual practices online, more specifically delimited to interpersonal mediated communication in public or private digital spaces. The genealogy of research in this area, including earlier work by both authors, has been formative to this project and is also a site where the gradual transition towards theoretical frameworks that move beyond enumerative approaches to multilingualism may be observed. Taking a broadly chronological order, this chapter first reviews code-switching approaches to multilingual communication online (2.3.1). We then discuss research associated with terms such as networked multilingualism and digital translanguaging, and shaped by the attempt to develop a more fluid, semiotically inclusive approach to linguistic heterogeneity online (2.3.2). In a third step we examine the relationship between mediated interaction and digital affordances (2.3.3).

2.3.1 Code-switching approaches

The earliest attempt to chart multilingual practices online drew heavily on theory and methods from code-switching research. Paolillo (1996) was probably the first researcher to examine how linguistic repertoires including majority language (American English) and heritage language (Punjabi) are used in chatroom and discussion groups, and to empirically distinguish between code-switching patterns in synchronous and asynchronous online spaces. Later research charted patterns of multilingual interaction in a wide range of digital spaces with various types of population, including diasporic communities (cf. research overviews in

Dorleijn & Nortier 2009, Leppänen & Peuronen 2012, Androutsopoulos 2013, Lee 2017). These studies draw on linguistic and sociolinguistic frameworks of code-switching research. The first focus on structural complexities with a particular interest in whether switching and mixing online corresponds to syntactic constraints identified for spoken code-switching. For example, Dorleijn & Nortier (2009) argue that CMC data offer insights into authentic patterns of vernacular bilingual discourse. The second, discussed in detail below, take their cues from research on conversational code-switching (Gumperz 1982, Auer 1984, 1995) and examine contextual conditions for and functions of conversational code-switching, sometimes combined with a more ethnographic view on online communication. Leaving differences aside, both angles on code-switching offer ample evidence that code-switching is a communicative resource online, albeit with a different emphasis each.

An example for an interactional approach to code-switching is research by the second author (Androutsopoulos 2006, 2007, 2013), which has drawn on the bilingual interaction framework by Auer (1995, 1999, 2000). This approach is interactional, in that code-switching is understood as a sequential process between two or more interlocutors who draw on shared parts of their linguistic repertoire to accomplish interactional goals, thereby taking into consideration what participants consider to be a code. Auer's framework has three dimensions of analysis. First, code-switching is distinguished from code-mixing by a combination of formal and pragmatic criteria, the main point being that code-switching is by definition functional, whereas code-mixing is socially indexical as a whole rather than at the level of individual switches. Characteristics of code-mixing include a high proportion of intrasentential alternations and a high amount of ad-hoc lexical transference. Second comes the distinction between insertional and alternational code-switching. In the former there is a dominant code ('base language'), and features of one or more additional codes are inserted at the level of phrases or clauses, but the return to the base language is likely and predictable to the participants. This is what happens in many excerpts discussed in this study with French, acting as a base language, and Wolof, to which participants often switch for various discourse purposes (cf. Chapters 6 and 7). In alternational code-switching, turns may come in all relevant languages, and a return to the respectively other language is not predictable, but depends on participants' ongoing exchange. Third, Auer also distinguishes between participant- and discourse-related code-switching. In the former, speakers orient to the perceived or assumed competence (or lack thereof) and/or language choice preference of their interlocutors. Consider for example Rama's effort to speak Joola to her grandmother back in Senegal (cf. vignette in Chapter 1). The latter – discourse-related code-switching – can index several contextual dimensions, such as choice of addressee, shift or maintenance of topic, and agreement or disagreement to the interlocutor, thereby acting as a contextualisation cue.

All three dimensions of this framework are applicable to analysis of CMC data, showing that CMC is just as multifaceted as spoken verbal interaction in pragmatic-functional terms. Based on a research survey, Androutsopoulos (2013) discusses several documented discourse functions of code-switching in CMC that show pattern similarities to spoken multilingual communication, including:

- conversational routines, e.g., greetings, farewells, good wishes
- culturally specific genres, e.g., reciting poetry, singing, joke-telling
- reported speech (as opposed to the writer's own speech)
- repetition of message for emphatic purposes
- indexing a particular addressee
- contextualising a shift of topic or perspective, e.g., to distinguish between fact and opinion, or to contextualise what is being said as jocular or serious
- indexing conversational alignment or dispreference by taking up or rejecting the language choice of preceding contribution(s)

These discourse patterns are documented in both asynchronous modes (discussion forums, mailing lists) and synchronous ones (e.g., Internet Relay Chat channels). Some patterns, such as the first two ones on the list, have been found to favour a sustained use of minority or migrant languages. In the German-Persian and German-Greek web discussion forums studied by Androutsopoulos (2006, 2007), actions such as greetings, sayings, cracking jokes, and similar were often carried out in the respective heritage language, even though the bulk of the forum discussion was in German. In other cases, the metapragmatic meaning of code-switching is rather created through the situated contrast between the codes involved, as when for example a narrative is carried out in one code and punchlines or some reported speech come in a different code (see similar examples in Chapters 6 and 7). In view of the critical discussion above (Section 2.1) it seems again important to point out that 'codes' in this analysis are not determined in a decontextualised manner, but rather through contextual, often ethnographically grounded examination of the respective online communication in context.

Ethnographically informed analyses of digital multilingual communication have brought to the fore the value of linguistic diversity as an interactional resource. Code-switching online may index various interactional contexts and participants' social identities and interpersonal relations (Seargeant et al. 2012, Androutsopoulos 2014b). Research also shows that multilingual communication online is a site of linguistic creativity and language play (Danet 2001). For example, Fung and Carter (2007) study English/Cantonese bilingual discourse among UK students from Hong Kong and find a high level of wordplay and creative use of language, principally, but not exclusively, for the maintenance of interpersonal relations and the construction of social identities. Tsiplakou

(2009) examines how email writers draw on a range of dialects and languages in order to act out 'localised performativities', i.e. contextually constructed social identities, which participants playfully claim for themselves, stylise, or parody. Lexander (2012) shows how Senegalese texters draw on graphic features (quotation marks, spelling variation) and code-switching in the composition of messages, and Lexander (2018) analyses the performance of different voices by young Senegalese in multilingual text messages. However, bilingual interaction is not always welcome in digital environments, especially so in public spaces. Research shows that the use of minority and migrant languages may be banned, or pressure is exerted on users to switch to the majority language. The preference of minority/migrant languages for bracketing elements or speech genres ideologically tied to the minority culture can be seen as a response to such pressures. In this sense, publicness and indeterminacy of audience as well as the planning afforded by writing online have sometimes been considered inhibitors of code-mixing, though not switching.

2.3.2 Networked multilingualism and digital translanguaging

Research grounded on code-switching brought to the fore the value of linguistic diversity as an interactional resource online. Limitations of this research are, broadly speaking, related to the degree to which characteristics of mediated communication are taken into consideration, especially related to: the production of utterances and sequences in the written mode; the eminently reflexive character of writing and editing, which is inherent even to the most synchronous CMC mode; its distinct participation frameworks, including public and often anonymous participation; the wealth of semiotic resources available for combination with linguistic signs. In retrospect, it seems fair to say that code-switching approaches have tended to either underplay these characteristics or treat them as preconfigured contextual parameters, such as the binary distinction between synchronous and asynchronous modes of online communication that was common in early CMC research. Consequently, the '(often implicit) tendency to view language use in CMC as a reflection of spoken language choices' has sometimes erased 'the properties that make networked multilingualism distinct from and non-reducible to a written representation of spoken discourse' (Androutsopoulos 2015: 202). For example, treating CMC in direct analogy to spoken language cannot explain the ways in which multilingual practices online deliberately overshoot their supposed target in terms of intentionally 'fabricated', even artful mixtures of linguistic features from different origins, as described by several researchers (e.g. Fung & Carter 2007, Tsiplakou 2009, Vandekerckhove & Nobels 2010, Jørgensen et al. 2011, Lexander 2012, Deumert & Lexander 2013, Dovchin 2015, 2016). Returning for a moment to the legacy of multilingualism scholarship (Section 2.1), discussions of polylingual languaging (Jørgensen et al. 2011) draw on social media exchanges to explain polylanguaging as a process of selection and combination of features with different provenience and indexicality.

Drawing on this theoretical influence, Androutsopoulos (2015) developed the concept of networked multilingualism specifically for social media data in an attempt to remedy a straightforward equation of online to offline code-switching. Networked multilingualism posits that language practices by multilingual social media users are constrained in three ways: (a) the digital mediation of written language, (b) their access to network resources, and (c) their orientation to networked audiences. The first point draws attention to the asymmetry of spoken and written partitions of a linguistic repertoire, as observed in many speech communities worldwide, including migrated or minority populations. In Senegal, for example, speakers become literate first in French and then in a more limited range in Wolof and other Senegalese national languages (e.g. in literacy classes and in university), and the resulting predisposition for using French as a base language in interactive written discourse is well documented in our study. In some diaspora communities, a heritage language is spoken but not written or is written in vernacular Romanised characters because its original script has not been acquired (Androutsopoulos 2006). The complexities of literacy thus drive a wedge into the assumption that spoken multilingualism would be simply remediated into chatting online. The constraint of writing also applies to the emergence and deployment of visual contextualisation devices – such as innovative uses of punctuation or emoji (Busch 2021) – and to the opportunities for using script as an interactional resource (discussed below). The second constraint, access to network resources, emphasises the ability to draw on and recontextualise resources from the global mediascape of the web for one's own communicative purposes. For example, sharing and embedding digital content sometimes leads to people's own language production fusing with linguistic features from shared digital content, for example linking up online content and adding a caption that dialogises with this content. Another example is the creative interactional use of language technology resources, for example the use of machine translation to send good wishes in a heritage language. The point here is that the production of utterances online is not limited to one's own linguistic input, a point also corroborated by digital literacy practices such as remixing and subtitling (Lee 2017). The third constraint ('being networked') is essentially the dimension of audience design, including the variety of participation formats in CMC (Dynel 2014) and the indeterminacy of audience in social networks. In our study, the awareness of audience is pertinent to the distinction between dyadic exchanges and chatgroups (Chapter 3), but also to polymedia management for different types of addressees (Chapter 4). For example, communicating in a semi-public network of 'friends' with some degree of shared histories, cultural references, and semiotic repertoires may lead to predictable code choices, but may also give rise to 'context collapse', i.e. the co-presence of different social contexts in the same online network (Androutsopoulos

2014b) and to resulting attempts to manage this by means of 'context design' (Tagg & Seargeant 2021).

The 2010s also witnessed other approaches to multilingual CMC that gain inspiration from the theoretical debates discussed in Section 2.1. Heteroglossia has been taken up to emphasise the deliberate, even strategic character of composing multi-voicedness in CMC (Leppänen et al. 2009, Androutsopoulos 2011, Tagg 2016). In a rare study of non-public texting between a private user and multiple interlocutors, Tagg (2016) uses the notion of heteroglossia to analyse moment-to-moment shifts between indexing a regional voice as opposed to a more urban and sophisticated one, and how these are encased in specific interactional moves between the key informant with various interlocutors. Translanguaging has been repeatedly applied to interactive written discourse data. Remarkably, various theoretical approaches to translanguaging, other differences aside, are associated with writing and speech events that involve both writing and speaking (e.g. Canagarajah 2013a). The translanguaging approach by Li (2011, 2018) and García & Li (2014) explicitly advocates a semiotic and multimodally inclusive understanding of translanguaging that encompasses pictorial resources such as emoji and other visual signs, though without delving analytically into their use. Schreiber (2015) coined the term 'digital translanguaging' to examine the self-presentation practices of a Serbian university student of English who draws on Serbian and English combined with embedded videos and imagery to construct the persona of a Serbian hip-hop DJ on Facebook. Dovchin (2015) investigates personal networks of Mongolian young adults in social media as a site of 'translingual' practices that involve a fluid use of various languages, scripts, and intertextual references. Dovchin argues that

> online mixed youth language practices should be understood as 'translingual' not only due to their varied recombination of linguistic and cultural resources, genres, modes, styles and repertoires, but also due to their direct subtextual connections with wider sociocultural, historical and ideological meanings.
>
> (Dovchin 2015: 437)

In this approach, translingualism explicitly encompasses the fluid combination and recontextualisation of semiotic resources, which, as repeatedly argued in the literature, is promoted by a key condition of networked communication, i.e. planning for and performing in front of an audience. A second conceptual feature of digital translanguaging approaches (by this or other terms) is a heightened metalinguistic awareness with regard to the historical, social, and ideological underpinnings of translanguaging. In a similar vein to the 'polylingual norm' articulated by Jørgensen et al. (2011, see also Jørgensen 2008), Dovchin interprets translingual practices as resistance to determining a single language of communication (Dovchin 2015: 452).

However, it seems fair to ask how the critical dimension of translanguaging is empirically borne out at different settings. In the data for this study, resistance practices by mixing and recombining semiotic features are not documented, and this may be related to the fact that we examine private mediated interaction rather than public exchanges in social networks, which are perhaps more prone to drawing on semiotic bricolage to perform a stance to an audience. Nevertheless, the indeterminate relation of linguistic features to named languages and the deliberate, even strategic bricolage out of a wealth of semiotic resources, as afforded by the technological infrastructure for online communication, are underrepresented in the earlier code-switching scholarship reviewed above and explicitly brought out in translanguaging approaches. Both points are represented in our study. Take as an example the word *amin/amine* 'amen' (cf. Chapter 7, Excerpt 7.1), which is written in the same way in Romanised Arabic and Wolof, making it impossible to categorise it by language. Likewise, Urban Wolof includes many French-origin features, but classifying these as 'French' in analysis bears the risk of introducing analytical breaches between seemingly separated languages that might seem artificial to participants. At the same time, the layer of graphemic representation – spelling – may give additional cues as to how participants associate linguistic features to particular registers of language. For example, even though Wolof literacy is not taught at Senegalese schools, there exist different orthographic conventions for written Wolof (Lexander 2020b), each pointing to different social contexts of usage. In our data, spelling Wolof according to the standard indexes specific diaspora networks associated with a particular religious brotherhood (cf. Chapter 7).

The complexities surrounding the choice and alternation of orthographies and scripts in CMC have gained considerable attention in recent research (Hillewaert 2015, George 2019, Li & Zhu 2019b, Androutsopoulos 2020). Findings show that orthography and script, too, may be subject to interactional choice and negotiation (rather than being predetermined), and that script choice can be enregistered (Agha 2007) with socio-political groups and stances, which can be indexed in discourse in practices of script switching and mixing. For example, in a study of semiotic practices by Serbians in social media, George (2019), examines how 'Serbian youth mix languages and writing systems in complex ways, adhering to dominant ideologies of language and identity in some ways and flouting them in others' (p.1). George's analysis centres on memes that blend Western and Serbian frames of reference in their combinations of image and caption and their choices of language and script for the caption. This study, too, emphasises the ideological and political dimension of linguistic choices in social media discourse, though with emphasis on script: in this process, choosing English instead of Serbian for a status update (see also Schreiber 2015) is meaningful, and the same holds true for choosing Latin or Cyrillic script for the representation of either English or Serbian. By navigating these combinatory opportunities in their social media practices of posting and sharing, social media users evoke and blend different 'systems of semiotic meaning' by which to critically 'index fluency and assert participation in multiple spheres' (George 2019: 400), namely 'Serbian tradition and (Western) global popular culture' (George 2019: 414). This line of research draws more attention to languages with a script other than Roman, such as Chinese (Li & Zhu 2019b), Greek (Androutsopoulos 2020), Swahili (Hillewaert 2015), Mongolian and Korean (Dovchin 2015, 2016), or Serbian (George 2019), and shed light on the complexities and implications involved in their online representation.

Linking this discussion back to code-switching (Section 2.1), we see that the conceptual transition from code-switching to translanguaging is both theoretically and empirically motivated, with the relation between the two best understood as layered. Tensions between codes in online exchanges, as uncovered by code-switching research, have not disappeared. On the contrary, they are evident in many kinds of interactional data, including this study. What translanguaging theory adds on is a recognition of fluidity and indeterminacy regarding the seemingly unambiguous 'belonging' of features to languages and speakers to communities. It moreover brings to the fore the nexus of language use and metalinguistic awareness – a point prominent in heteroglossia and in Jørgensen's (2008) concept of a 'polylanguaging norm' that goes against the grain by anticipating and flouting expectations. And while most studies of code-switching online are empirically limited to threads of sequentially arranged messages in private or public settings, analyses of digital translanguaging encompass the multimodal complexities of communication online. Resources for translanguaging are not just distinct named 'languages', but all semiotic features available for digitally mediated communication. In this sense, a notion such as digital translanguaging pulls together in a new way the complexities of writing, the pictorial and visual affordances of digital communication, and participants' heightened awareness of audiences, indexicalities and expectations.

2.3.3 *Affordances for mediated interaction in the digital ecology*

Whether it is grounded on either code-switching or translanguaging, research on multilingual practices online has been shaped by two empirical constraints: an emphasis on public communication and a lack of consideration given to the expanding digital ecology. First, the emphasis on public CMC in spaces such as multi-party chat channels, forums, and social media platforms is well-justified at a practical level, but has left private settings of digital communication, including transnational families, far less considered. There are only a few studies on private multilingual practices in texting and emailing (Georgakopoulou 1997, Tsiplakou 2009, Lexander 2011, Tagg & Lyons 2017) or personal networks in social media (Lee 2007, Seargeant et al. 2012, Androutsopoulos 2015). Likewise, direct comparisons of multilingual behaviour by the same speakers on-and offline have been extremely difficult to carry out. Second, data collection and analysis has been largely limited to one site or platform at a time. Multi-channel datasets, which capture language use by the same individual on different platforms, as we do in this study, are very rare in the literature (Tagliamonte 2016, Tagg & Lyons 2017, 2021a). This single-platform bias is predominant in quantitative studies of social media language variation (e.g. Twitter), but also in studies of private data. While also justified from a practical viewpoint, this limitation does not address one of the key questions in this book, i.e., the interplay of channel, affordance, and audience.

Against this backdrop, a point of departure for this study is that the limitation of much CMC research to public data, often from a single domain of origin, is out of pace with current realities of mobile digital communication in transnational settings. Mobile devices and apps have brought digitally mediated communication to the centre of everyday life, and the expanding affordances of mobile devices for mediated interpersonal interaction by means of texting, talking, video connectivity, and combinations of the above is eagerly appropriated by transnational partners or family members. As illustrated with Rama, the many modes of digital interpersonal communication are not in a social void but selected for communication to specific types of interlocutors, each time patterning together with different semiotic selections at the level of modality and language style or register. Consequently, an aim of this study is to refocus on mediated interpersonal interaction rather than public online communication, thereby framing mediated interaction as an omnipresent and inconspicuous facet of everyday languaging. Indeed we view the transnational practices of our participants not as something that 'approximates', 'simulates', or 'compensates' absent speaking, but as a distinct type of mediation in interpersonal communication. A theoretical challenge here is to move beyond a conception of 'media' as a container for language – a view that has been quite dominant in linguistics – and towards a procedural and practice-oriented view of mediation as an interactional accomplishment (Arminen et al. 2016, Androutsopoulos 2021b). Following up on the above, instead of thinking of digital language use as something distinct (from everyday spoken interaction or other modes of communication) and homogenous (in terms of language style), it seems more productive to start with a contextual understanding of patterns of transnational communication by interlocutor and relationship type (cf. Chapter 6), and then to consider concomitant semiotic selections, including language choice.

Part of this endeavour is a heightened attention to affordances for digitally mediated interaction. Affordances is a multifaceted concept that found its way from perceptual psychology (Gibson 1986) to industrial design to communication theory (Hutchby 2001) and has been widely used in social media research in the 2010s (Bucher & Helmond 2019). Digital technologies offer a range of action possibilities to their users and at the same time set constraints on what actions are at all possible with a particular device or software. For example, Facebook affords communication by writing and posting digital content, but writing on Facebook does not afford extensive typographic manipulation, such as selecting fonts and font sizes. Affordances are continuously evolving in a feedback loop between industry and use, in which social media users indirectly influence how affordances develop over time (Bucher & Helmond 2019). Affordance is thus a notion that balances opportunities for and constraints on communicative action, thereby explicitly avoiding a deterministic perspective on digital communication. So, instead of assuming that digital technologies (e.g. the choice of a particular messenger) directly influence communicative practices (e.g. language choice), the assumption is that technologies afford actions (e.g. exchanging messages in almost-real time), which participants collate into practices (e.g. multi-party small talk in a chatgroup) by connecting afforded actions to interlocutors and semiotic choices.

Social media research distinguishes between high-level and low-level affordances (Bucher & Helmond 2019). High-level affordances (e.g. persistence, searchability, duplicability) create conditions of possibility for digitally mediated communication at an abstract and encompassing level. For example, the affordance of persistence is reflected in digital archives such as messenger protocols and social media news feeds, which can be searched up. The affordance of duplicability means that any digital content can be copied, duplicated, and transformed, thus giving rise to information flows and chains of semiotic transformation such as memes or mash-ups. By contrast, low-level affordances are situated at a more concrete, tangible level related to communicative actions. From a language analysis viewpoint, it seems useful to distinguish three subtypes. First, affordances that enable the production of communicative action. For example, we may say that a given software application affords sending personal messages in text or voice or video, attaching digital content, makes available certain kinds of emoji, and so on. Second come affordances that support interpersonal coordination, such as alerts to receiving new messages, indicators of production and reception status, indicators of caller or sender identity, and so on. Attending to these affordances can influence the course of mediated interaction (Meredith 2017). Third are affordances that enable the editing of digital content and complex forms of composition, such as remix (Lee 2017).

Empirical applications of the concept from a linguistic viewpoint differ in terms of whether they focus on available affordances or on how social media users perceive digital affordances. Lee (2007) focuses on affordances for the production of discourse in synchronous chat environments (ICQ and MSN) in a study that was carried out with 19 young adults from Hong Kong who use three distinct languages, i.e. Mandarin

Chinese, Cantonese, and English. Lee's emphasis is on how users perceive the affordances of these environments for communication (including the relative ease of inputting characters in different scripts). In a more recent study, Wikström (2019) examines affordances regarding the representation of reported speech on Twitter and identifies a range of typographic means for separating out reported speech from the poster's own speech. Other recent research examines how social media users deploy the affordance of producing both written and spoken messages in software such as Skype and WhatsApp (König &Hector 2019, Sindoni 2021). These studies examine whether participants in mediated interaction exchange spoken and written turns sequentially or simultaneously, how participants coordinate these affordances in their realisation of interactional moves, and how written and spoken utterances complement each other or open up distinct (but temporally overlapping) participation frameworks. This dual-mode affordance is particularly popular in the data for this study, and its implications for language choice are explored in Chapters 6, 7 and 8. The next section situates our analysis of affordances and multilingual practices in the context of polymedia, i.e. a digital ecology with multiple, even competing alternatives for mediated interaction.

2.4 Transnational families and digitally mediated communication

As discussed above, there is increasing research interest in language in mobility, linguistic complexity in transnational families, and digitally mediated language practices. However, although the bodies of research on multilingual families as well as on language in digital communication are substantial, these studies seldom cross each other. Language is crucial when families separated by geographical space create 'virtual togetherness' to stay in touch (Baldassar 2008). Still, digital communication is little researched within family multilingualism and FLP studies (see Lanza & Lexander 2019 for an overview), and transnational families are hardly ever examined in the field of CMC research (cf. Section 2.3). Therefore, we also consider research on transnationalism and transnational family ties from anthropology, sociology, and media studies in our study (2.4.1) and specifically focus on theories of mediated co-presence (2.4.2) and polymedia (2.4.3). We furthermore build on findings from the handful of existing studies on family multilingualism in digital interaction (2.4.4).

2.4.1 'Doing family' transnationally

The link of migrant and migrant-background populations to spaces of origin and heritage across national boundaries has been theorised in the notion of transnationalism, which created a shift in how international migration is researched (cf. Glick Schiller et al. 1992, 1995).

From an earlier focus on migrants' adaptation to, or social exclusion from, their place of immigration, attention thus turned to various kinds of global connectivity sustained by transnational individuals and communities (Vertovec 2001). Transnationalism is seen as a response to the global economy that makes full incorporation in the countries in which migrants resettle not desirable or not possible, because of social inequalities, racism, xenophobia, and discrimination (Glick-Schiller et al. 1995). The discursive construction of transnational diasporas is moreover supported by governments in countries with massive emigration, including Senegal (Diop 2008), which praise the migrants' financial contributions to their societies of origin. As a result, transmigrants settle and become incorporated in the economy, institutions, and patterns of everyday life of their country of residence, while still maintaining connections and conducting transactions in the countries from which they emigrated (Glick-Schiller et al. 1995: 48). With reference to Senegal, Kane (2011: 9) points out that 'transnationalism is the dominant mode of adaptation of the Senegalese in late twentieth-century America', and Riccio (2011) describes how Senegalese migrants in Italy who successfully integrate in the organisational structures of the receiving country are intensively engaged in development projects in Senegal. Family ties, too, are managed transnationally, mediated by available information and communication technologies (Hannaford 2017, Yount-André 2018). We consider implications of transnational mediation for practices of family-making, including the construction of identity, intimacy, solidarity, and power, at various points (cf. Chapters 5, 6, 8).

Against this background, transnational families can be defined as families that live some or most of the time separated from each other, yet hold together and create a feeling of collective welfare and unity, or 'familyhood' (Bryceson & Vuorela 2002: 3). Family members who are spread across multiple localities can constitute 'stretched families' (Porter et al. 2018) who maintain contact to retain a sense of collectivity (cf. Baldassar et al. 2007: 13). Transnational families sustain various inter- and intragenerational family relations, including practices of transnational parenting of children who are being cared for by kin (Vives & Silva 2017, Berckmoes & Mazzucato 2018, Meyers & Rugunanan 2020, Nedelcu & Wyss 2020). Communication, emotional support, and financial assistance are forms of transnational care, which sustain the sense of belonging (Baldassar 2007, Baldassar & Merla 2014a, Reynolds & Zontini 2014, Ahlin 2020). Wilding et al. (2020) argue that when emotions circulate, afforded by digital media, they give substance to and define the surfaces and boundaries of transnational families.

As described in Section 2.1, communication is increasingly shaped by global economic, political, and cultural flows (Appadurai 1996). Translocality refers to both local and global connections (Kytölä 2016), people do not only engage in 'sedentary' or 'territorialised' language practices, but also 'translocal' and 'deterritorialised' ones (Blommaert

2010: 4–5). On the interactional level, translocality is characterised by a reconfiguration of time-space and overlapping communicative frames, as people interact with physically absent others as if they were present (Deumert 2014a: 10). This is what mediated co-presence is about (cf. Section 2.4.2). Transnationalism and translocality bring migrants closer to political events and developments in their country of origin and thereby have consequences for language practices. As an illustrative example, Curdt-Christiansen and Huang (2020) demonstrate that new powers gained by China in recent years have raised the social status of Chinese migrants in British society, with implications for (among other things) lingua franca practices and language education in community schools. Translocal connections also contribute to the diversification of transnational communities. Through differences in the country of origin, migration trajectories, language attitudes, linguistic varieties, sense of belonging, and socio-political affiliation, these communities become sites of contestation for language and identities (Curdt-Christiansen et al. 2021). Family ties are central to migrants' transnational connections, and the management of these relationships is key to the negotiation of linguistic practices and identity work (e.g. Cuban 2014). If transnational communities become sites of struggle, caught between an urge to maintain loyalty to the past (home country) and a pragmatic need to integrate into the mainstream society (Curdt-Christiansen et al. 2021), this also takes place at the family level. In her study of visual and narrative constructions of young African descendants' translocal subjectivities, Evans (2020: 14–15) found that transnational connections with family members around the world were of crucial importance for pride in cultural heritage, multilingual identities and translocal place-attachments, which provide counter narratives to exclusionary discourses and experiences of racialisation.

2.4.2 Digital co-presence in transnational families

To manage transnational family connections, developments within information and communication technologies provide essential tools (e.g. Glick-Schiller et al. 1995, Vertovec 2004, Wilding 2006). As emphasised in media research, digital connectivity does not only enable post-migration contact maintenance, but facilitates processes of migration and transnational mobility in the first place (Madianou 2014, Leurs 2015, Marino 2019). In other words, people risk transnational leaps on the taken-for-granted condition that seamless connectivity to their homeland families and communities will be maintained. Several studies examine how families draw systematically on digital tools to create virtual co-presence (e.g. Wilding 2006, Baldassar 2008, Madianou 2016, Nedelcu & Wyss 2016, Greschke 2021). Baldassar et al. (2007), for instance, describe how the rise in the capacity for creating virtual co-presence with digital media leads to renewed expectations and obligations, for instance for transnational caregiving. Different ways of constructing co-presence are reflected in the family interactions studied in this book and motivate a theoretical perspective that shifts attention from media as channels to processes of mediation. As discussed in Section 2.2, discursive perspectives on family-making point to the importance of everyday routines like dinnertime homecomings (Kendall 2006) and walking together to school (Wright 2020). Families who are distributed across different households in different geographical areas or even time zones do not share these routines. However, they find other ways of creating co-presence, making use of digital media to 'produce and reproduce "family practices" in a transnational social space through the use of different types of virtual togetherness' (Nedelcu & Wyss 2016: 203). By creating digital co-presence, families produce spaces where solidarity and power can be contested, consolidated, and negotiated.

Researchers distinguish different categories of mediated co-presence. Licoppe (2004) coined the term 'connected presence' to refer to a communicative management of relationships between two parties, whereby mediated communication is interwoven with physical contact in different patterns. In one pattern, a continuous connection is established through frequent and brief 'communicative gestures' that draw on the affordances of mobile phone calls and text messages to establish mutual engagement. Licoppe distinguishes this from a second, less dense mode of relationship management, consisting of less frequent personal meetings and long telephone conversations. Following up on Licoppe's seminal research, Nedelcu and Wyss (2016) distinguish three main types of ordinary co-presence: 'ritual', 'omnipresent', and 'reinforced'. The two first relate to Licoppe's (2004) connected presence. More specifically, 'ritual co-presence' is made up of minimal signs of solidarity through e.g. short regular phone calls, whose significance lies in the fact that there is routinised connection and not in the content of the interaction. 'Omnipresent co-presence' is constructed through being in contact with and available for transnational family members throughout the day, especially via video calls. 'Reinforced co-presence' means an increase in the frequency of contact born out of a pressing need, for instance when health problems occur. These forms of co-presence imply different negotiations of power and solidarity. An example of exerting power through omnipresent co-presence is the use of frequent unannounced video calls to monitor family members, checking their outfits and whereabouts (Hannaford 2015).

Another variation on the same theme is the notion of 'ambient co-presence', i.e. the 'peripheral awareness' of activities and whereabouts by distant others, which is obtained not through interpersonal contact, but through browsing social media (Madianou 2016). Pictures and posts in social media as well as information provided by these media's locative services give off cues of people's mobility and social life, and an accumulation of such information over time may lead to an awareness of the daily routines of distant others and give rise to concern when these routines are not followed (e.g. when a person does not log on to Facebook at the usual time). Ambient co-presence can lead to a feeling of reassurance for one party, like a parent who wants to monitor children at a distance, but also to a feeling of being controlled or surveilled for the other party, as when confronted with questions of why there is a break of routines (Madianou 2016). While these types of co-presence are differentiated by intensity and frequency, Greschke (2021) categorises co-presence in terms of its focus of attention. In 'object-related co-presence', there is mutual attention towards a jointly focused third entity, like a game. In 'attention-oriented co-presence', the participating interlocutors are in the centre. Greschke views object-related co-presence as a preferred option for transnational video interaction with children, whereas in attention-oriented co-presence, the interlocutors recreate family rituals at a distance, for instance cooking and dining together during video calls (Marino 2019). Choices of media and semiotic modes are important for these options of constructing co-presence (Greschke 2021: 846). For instance, photo messaging is used to give access to different spaces and different intimacies simultaneously, to share place over distance, and to authenticate presence (Villi 2010, Villi & Stocchetti 2011, Lobinger 2016, Prieto-Blanco 2016). To understand how a given relationship is shaped by communication technologies, the entire available 'technoscape' ought to be considered (Licoppe 2004: 135).

These studies, mainly grounded in anthropology and sociology, show that media practices affect transnational 'doing family' (cf. Morgan 1996) in fundamental ways, which in turn may affect family multilingualism. Transnational families draw on digital media to create spaces of co-presence where power and intimacy are negotiated with complex semiotic resources. The various types of co-presence are also interesting from a sociolinguistic point of view, since they might come along with different language practices. For instance, heritage language practices will differ between ritual exchanges with the Senegalese grandparents in weekly phone calls, as opposed to multimodal interaction in hour-long video game sessions with Senegalese cousins. These differences open various possibilities of language socialisation. As a result, understanding digital ways of 'doing family' and their implications for language practices calls for a broad perspective towards different aspects of family life as well as different spaces created by technology.

2.4.3 Polymedia: An ecology of media choices

Our study also draws on polymedia theory, a qualitative media studies framework that focuses on conditions and consequences of media choice in transnational communication among migrants and their families (Madianou & Miller 2012a, 2012b, Madianou 2014a, 2014b). Polymedia theory investigates the impact of media choices on social and emotional aspects of transnational family relationships. Its innovativeness lies in a shift of focus from the study of discrete media to an analysis of available media for interpersonal communication within a family or other basic social group. A central premise of polymedia theory is that if preconditions of costs, availability, and media literacy are met, people treat the media at their disposal as an integrated 'environment of affordances' (Madianou & Miller 2012a). Media are thereby defined not by their semiotic capacities, but by their relationship to each other in the practices and awareness of particular (groups of) users. For example, Dang et al. (2019) study how a transnational family is jointly watching TV while simultaneously writing on Facebook. In an integrated environment of communication technologies, users exploit the affordances of available media to express emotions and manage relationships (Madianou & Miller 2012b: 172). Madianou (2017: 107) argues that 'choosing one medium or platform over another acquires emotional intent: the ways in which participants navigate the media environments they have access to become as meaningful for their relationships as the actual content that is exchanged through these platforms.' The concurrent choice of media channel and semiotic modality (e.g. voice message, voice call, video call, text message) may have social and emotional consequences. For example, while parents may choose to make phone calls or video calls to their children in pursuit of emotional immediacy, their children can choose to respond by email or text message in order to control the pace and distance of communication (cf. Madianou & Miller 2012a). Through continuous choices, communication technologies constitute environments in which transnational relationships are enacted, and over time these choices transform the relationships themselves (Madianou 2019). Sinanan's (2019) work provides a telling illustration of the differing roles played by diverse media choices. While Facebook affords families the opportunity to illustrate family relationships by posting for instance photos and videos and to project societal ideals (see also Pfeifer & Neumann 2021 for examples from the Senegalese context), conversations in private chat groups alleviate the pressure to maintain appearances, and tensions between ideals and practices emerge to reflect more of the everyday situations of family relationships.

Polymedia theory has been used in research on geographically dispersed families (e.g. Dang et al. 2019, Sinanan 2019) as well as to study family communication within the home (Nag et al. 2016, Stæhr & Nørreby 2021) or media use and social relationships in other contexts (e.g. Elul 2020). Some studies have challenged the polymedia premise of cost, accessibility, and literacy being equal to all participants. For example, Greschke (2021) suggests reframing this premise as a research question and thus enable analysis to consider the unequal distribution of accessibility or media literacy across participants, for example as determined by actors' living conditions (Greschke 2021: 836). Elul (2020) uses the term 'noisy polymedia' to acknowledge how people use digital media under unstable infrastructural conditions. In addition to polymedia, other concepts have been coined to analyse users' engagement with the proliferation of media, but without the broad uptake that polymedia has had. Tandoc et al. (2019) proposed 'platform-swinging' to describe the routine rotation among social media platforms as opposed to switching to one platform and abandoning another. Even though different platforms are associated with different affordances, they are still treated as a holistic social media environment, and through platform-swinging, users segment and balance diverse ways of self-expression and manage relationships (Tandoc et al. 2019: 27). Boczkowski et al. (2018) use the term 'social media repertoires' in their empirical investigation of how people perceive and evaluate different social media platforms and what kinds of audiences and discourses they associate with each platform. However, these studies do not consider linguistic and interactional dimensions of polymedia communication, which are crucial to our study and discussed in the next section.

2.4.4 Language and media in family-making practices

The few studies that consider the interplay of linguistic and media repertoires in transnational family communication can be split into two subfields: FLP research on digital media in family-making practices, and studies on transnational family communication from other disciplines. Starting with the first, FLP-oriented research on digital family communication has focused on heritage language practices. Various case studies show how family members – parents, children and siblings, grandparents, extended kin – participate in spoken and/or written multilingual exchanges on screen or around the screen (Kenner et al. 2008, Szecsi & Szilagyi 2012, Parven 2016, Li & Zhu 2019a, Zhao 2019). For example, mobile phones enhance the children's and adolescents' independent transnational interaction (Curdt-Christiansen 2021, Kędra 2021, Lexander 2021a), and online conversations with peers in a heritage language can be experienced as 'fun', in contrast to the 'chore' of speaking the same heritage language(s) at home (Marley 2013). Families are also found to enhance their capacities in the societal language through family-internal interaction (Al-Salmi & Smith 2015, Kheirkah & Cekaite 2017, Lexander 2020a).

Parents play a pivotal role for children's interaction with other family members (Szecsi & Szilagyi 2012, Zhao 2019). Palviainen (2020b) examined video-call contact in two single-mother family constellations. The interaction between the pre-school aged children and their interlocutors relied on the mothers' facilitation and organisation, and enhanced family multilingualism. When it comes to facilitation, children can lead the way, too, for instance when it comes to digital competence and skills in the societal language. Several studies point to complex multilingual practices in (intergenerational) interaction in front of the screen, with parents, children, grandparents, and siblings shifting between roles as 'teachers' and 'learners' (Kenner et al. 2008, Al-Salmi &

Smith 2015, Parven 2016, Kheirkhah & Cekaite 2017). Zhao (2019) presents an interesting case where a child in the UK enters his mother's transnational WeChat conversation to chat with a group of her friends in China. The child draws on his Chinese language skills and on emoji to communicate, thereby expanding his access to heritage language speakers (Zhao & Flewitt 2020: 278).

Even though we focus in this book on interpersonal interaction and not educational tools for language learning, studies of language learning through games, apps and other online content reveal interesting connections with transnational family-making. The studies of learning in multilingual homes through digital play and through consuming online content, like YouTube videos or films, show that children's use of educational games can replace some of the functions of more formal structures of heritage language teaching (Eisenchlas et al. 2016). The use of digital games and apps for learning in the home evidently relies on the availability of resources and technical 'know how', but also on the attitudes of parents and children towards both heritage language and online gaming (Little 2019). Parents' negative views of technology may change as they experience children engaging in heritage language learning online (Said 2021).

Together, these practices have an impact on language, media, and family-making practices of multilingual families (Palviainen & Kędra 2020, Palviainen 2020b, Lexander 2021a). Languages are embedded in digital media activities and interwoven in daily family life (e.g. Palviainen & Kędra 2020, see also Palviainen 2020c). This research also supports the recent emphasis in FLP studies on extended family members' importance for family multilingualism (e.g. Vorobeva 2021). Furthermore, it is worth mentioning an even less studied online phenomenon with relevance to family multilingualism, namely blogs and other similar discourse that address and/or are produced by multilingual families (Bello-Rodzen 2016, Lanza 2020). These can be studied as narratives about family language policy, which multilinguals can relate to in various ways, for instance to seek advice for practice in a specific family context, and they also contribute to turning family multilingualism into a commodity (Lanza 2020: 185).

Since specific language practices are needed to stay in touch with relatives in the country of origin, it comes as no surprise that studies of media and transnational families that only mention linguistic issues in passing still see language as an important dimension. For example, sociologist Ducu (2018) described how a Latvian woman in the UK talked with her mother on Skype daily, often with her 7-month-old daughter present, to ensure the virtual presence of the grandmother in the girl's life *and* to facilitate learning of Latvian. The woman used other languages and other media to stay in touch with her Romanian mother-in-law, as they sent messages to each other on Facebook, first translated, via English, by Google translate. In an example from Germany (Ducu 2020), a Romanian grandmother who had recently migrated used WhatsApp when she looked after her grandchildren so that their parents could translate for her. The parents refrained from using Romanian with their children in order to facilitate their integration into German society, and the grandmother had not learnt the societal language. In the field of education and migration studies, Cuban (2014) found that transnational families built new vocabularies and interaction styles, including non-verbal means, to express their emotions in digital communication. Thereby, they managed family relationships as well as a changing sense of self, as a mobile learning community, 'caring and language sharing'. Another sociologist, King O'Riain (2015), focusing on practices for expressing emotions in the long Skype sessions of transnational families, mentions language competence as an important aspect. The grandparents in her study would observe their grandchild watching TV and ask for translations to enhance his conversation skills in Italian.

Given the importance of digital media for multilingual families, this area deserves serious investigation in a way that integrates language and media practices, since media ideologies and family language policies are intertwined in practice (Lanza & Lexander 2019). Through the combination of family multilingualism and polymedia, we can study not only patterns of media use as related to language practices, but also how interlocutors draw on both media and language to negotiate family roles, family relationships, and family identities, that is, how they 'do' the multilingual family. If we want to achieve this, we should not look at heritage language in isolation from other linguistic resources or within just a single medium while blending out its connections with other media practices. Such an isolationist approach would lead to missing how language and media choices are part of broader practices of doing family.

2.5 Conclusion: Towards the study of mediational repertoires

In conclusion we draw together the research strands reviewed so far to establish some basic assumptions for our study of transnational families in a digital age. In so doing, we emphasise the inseparability of linguistic resources from other semiotic resources and channels of mediation that are afforded by digital technologies and selected by interlocutors to maintain transnational relationships. Differently put, we argue against decontextualising linguistic practices from the media channels and resources that people mobilise to participate in mediated interaction, and instead suggest that 'digital speaking' is accomplished by drawing on a wide range of resources – characters on keyboards, emoji, GIF images, photos, videos, memes, machine translation chunks – and mediated through keyboard-and-screen technologies. Therefore, our epistemological interest is in understanding how transnational communicative practices are constituted through patterned co-selections from reservoirs of linguistic, pictorial, genre, and media resources.

Working towards developing an adequate framework to this purpose, we consider repertoire to be an important theoretical and analytical tool and explore ways to adapt it to the conditions of digitally mediated interaction. As discussed in Section 2.1, the linguistic repertoire has been reconceived in a sociolinguistics of globalisation perspective as individualised, subject to constant development, interacting with continuous processes of language learning, extending beyond linguistic structures, and linked to digital technologies of communication. From an interdisciplinary viewpoint, this discussion intersects with polymedia theory (Section 2.4). From a sociolinguistic perspective, the growing reception of polymedia theory leads to an exploration of parallel lines between linguistic and media repertoires and of implications of polymedia practices for language (cf. Androutsopoulos 2021b and papers in Androutsopoulos 2021a). Indeed, polymedia theory shows some striking similarities to languaging and repertoire theory in sociolinguistics. Just as recent theoretical debates in sociolinguistics challenge the perception of languages as bounded entities, polymedia shifts the focus from studying the medium in itself towards considering media as an integrated environment for interpersonal communication. In addition, it promotes thinking about how continuous linguistic and media choices shape the accomplishment of mediated interaction. Elements of polymedia theory – relationship management, emotional communication, multimodality, media ideologies – therefore constitute theoretical lenses through which to study transnational family language practices, including family multilingualism. The relevance of a polymedia environment in the context of this study is evident in the vignette on Rama at the opening of this book, where a range of conversations on different platforms, each drawing on different linguistic resources, were handled on the smartphone, considered a polymedia environment in its own right (Madianou 2014b).

At this interdisciplinary intersection, Tagg and Lyons (2021a) propose the concept of 'polymedia repertoire' as a multi-level scheme of nested choices that range from devices over environments (subdivided into interfaces, platforms, and channels) to modes and signs (semiotic resources). A digital device or social media platform is a resource into which other resources are embedded, conceptualising the polymedia repertoire as a 'polymedia nest'. The notion of nest is significant in several ways. One linguistic sign, like an emoji, can have varied meaning depending on its embeddedness and on how users position themselves in different ways to different interlocutors when moving between different platforms and channels (Tagg & Lyons 2021a: 749).

Our own notion of 'mediational repertoires' (Artamonova & Androutsopoulos 2019, Lexander & Androutsopoulos 2021) draws on additional inspiration from ethnomethodological research on mediated interaction (Arminen et al. 2016) and from the concept of 'mediational means', which originates in Ron Scollon's mediated discourse analysis. Scollon (2001) posits that all communicative action is mediated, and that 'mediated action is carried out through material objects in the world (including the materiality of the social actors – their bodies, dress, movements)' (Scollon 2001: 4). The crucial point here is to focus not on digital technologies as such, but on mediated communication as practice. A meditational tool is not a piece of hardware or software as such, but rather the integration or adaptation of technology into social practice. For example, Rama uses a certain app in conjunction with a specific language and modality choice in order to carry out interaction with a particular interlocutor. She regularly uses French and English to do texting exchanges with her mother (see examples discussed in Chapter 6), but Joola and her smartphone's phone app to speak to her grandmother. It is in these practices that the various smartphone apps selected by Rama become mediational tools to her connecting with her transnational family.

Against this background, we use the term 'mediational repertoire' to refer to the close and complex relationship of language and media repertoires for digitally mediated interpersonal interaction. We define 'mediational repertoire' as a socially and individually structured configuration of semiotic and technological resources that are deployed for mediated communication. Mediational repertoires are 'repertoires-in-use' (cf. Androutsopoulos 2014a, Tagg 2016). They represent the attested deployment of resources brought along by participants *and* afforded by the technologies of mediation they select. The elicitation and visualization method developed in this study, mediagrams, is presented in Chapter 4. In structural terms, a mediational repertoire can be examined in terms of selections on several hierarchical levels, including modalities of language (speaking, writing, or signing), various sets of pictographic and multimedia signs (e.g. emoji, memes, animated gifs, videos), and sets of software applications (e.g. WhatsApp, SMS, Signal, and so on). As in research by Tagg & Lyons (2021a), the aim is to chart how patterned co-selections of resources for digital communication differ depending on particular (types of) addressees. A mediational repertoire can thus be thought of as an augmented, or extended, repertoire that brings to the fore the interdependence of language to its mediational environment. However, it seems important to avoid an exclusively distributional analysis. Understanding who selects which language *and* media channel to communicate with whom – paraphrasing here Joshua Fishman's fundamental sociolinguistic question – needs to be complemented by an understanding of how digital media users build up an awareness of how media and semiotic choices match each other in their communicative practice. In other words, it seems useful to distinguish between the 'augmented' or 'enriched' semiotic repertoires afforded by digital ecologies ('repertoires of mediation') on the one hand, and the ideological connections between various repertoire elements ('registers of mediation') on the other. Following the notion of enregisterment introduced in Section 2.1, these connections are ideological in the sense that they are formed in a population's perception and metadiscursive activities. No doubt such enregisterment also takes place regarding polymedia interaction, as identified by Busch (2018). In this process, media choices are reflexively associated with typical addressees and domains of communication, on the one hand (e.g. professional vs. private communication), and typical linguistic choices, e.g. concerning spelling, punctuation, vocabulary style and pictorial choices (for example to use emoji or not, and what kinds of emoji), on the other.

Overall, our approach to the study of mediational repertoires starts with distributional analysis (reconstructing 'repertoires of mediation') and moves on towards exploring speakers' reflexive awareness and the language and media ideologies that underpin it. This two-step approach is reflected in the structure and findings of this study. Our participants' mediational repertoires are reconstructed and compared in detail (cf. Chapter 5), and there is evidence for their reflexive awareness of how certain language and media choices are connected to certain (groups of) interlocutors. However, the notion of mediational repertoires is best understood as still explorative, and this is for two reasons. First, we do not have comprehensive evidence for all participants' awareness of their mediational patterns. We can show that such awareness does exist, but cannot claim that all distributions observed in the compilation of mediagrams are subject to metasemiotic reflexivity on the part of speakers and addressees. Second, the enregisterment of mediational choices with (types of) interlocutors is a dynamic, fast-paced process whose understanding would require a more extensive multi-sited ethnography than we were able to carry out in this study. Still, the basic idea of a mediational repertoire, in which polymedia and multilingual resources fuse together in socially and emotionally meaningful combinations, fits well the experiences and practices of our multilingual participants who use several smartphone apps to communicate with translocal family members. The remainder of this book explores this idea and its sociolinguistic implications.

Notes

1 However, we do not deal with a number of (contested) theoretical claims associated with translanguaging, especially concerning the joint or separate processing of linguistic features.
2 These are examples for online dictionaries for Wolof and French: www.lexilogos.com/wolof_dictionnaire.htm, Wolof and English: www.lexilogos.com/english/wolof_dictionary.htm, Wolof and German: https://glosbe.com/de/wo, and Peul and French: www.lexilogos.com/peul_dictionnaire.htm

3 Media and language use in multilingual families

An ethnographic study in Norway

In our introduction, we described how Rama, one of the adolescent family members in our study, uses different aspects of her linguistic and media repertoire to communicate with family and friends in Norway and elsewhere. In this chapter, we introduce the broader sociolinguistic context of these observations (3.1). We then present the families whose practices are studied in this book (3.2) and the resources of their linguistic repertoires (3.3).

3.1 Sociolinguistic research with Senegalese migrants in Norway

The repertoires and practices of our participants have been shaped by the main aspects of the sociolinguistic contexts of Senegal and Norway. We briefly present a description of these before turning to factors that influence the lives of Senegalese migrants in Norway.

3.1.1 Language and society in Senegal

Like other West African countries, Senegal is linguistically diverse. Senegal's linguistic complexity is formed by ethnic diversity, interethnic marriages, and a long history of geographical mobility (Diop 2008). Spoken practices are fluid even in rural areas (Watson 2018, Weidl 2018). They are shaped by repertoires acquired through interaction with family members and neighbours of different ethnic and geographical background, and by mobility that includes shorter or longer stays in different places (Dreyfus & Juillard 2004, Weidl 2018). In 2020, there were 16.7 million inhabitants in the country (Agence Nationale de la Statistique et de la Démographie, 2020), speaking a total of 26 national languages. About 80–90% of this population speak Wolof (Cissé 2005, Mc Laughlin 2008a), while the estimated figure of speakers of the official language, French, is much lower at around 10% (Mc Laughlin 2008a).

Through a 'wolofisation' process (Diouf 1994) that started in the 19th century and has been bound up with social, political, religious, and historical factors, Wolof has become a primary marker of national identity

DOI: 10.4324/9781003227311-3

in Senegal and is often referred to as *notre langue nationale* ('our national language'). In this process, a rising number of ethnically non-Wolof Senegalese adopt Wolof as their main language of communication and/ or refer to themselves as Wolof (Diouf 1994: 24). Wolof is thus regularly spoken in families that do not identify as Wolof (Swigart 1990, Dreyfus & Juillard 2004: 64) and it is also used alongside Arabic in mosques and in churches (even though very few Wolofs are Christian). Some therefore consider the progress of Wolof as a nation-building process (O'Brien 1998, Diouf 2001).

There are different registers of Wolof (Thiam 1998). An urban identity is associated with a register which is often referred to as 'urban Wolof'(e.g. Mc Laughlin 2022), incorporating a wide range of French language material, but also features from other Senegalese languages, like Joola and Peul, as well as Arabic and English (Swigart 1992, Thiam 1994, Dreyfus & Juillard 2004). Mc Laughlin (2001) argues that the Wolof spoken in Dakar has had a profound effect on the notion of ethnicity in the Senegalese context and has contributed to a de-ethnicised urban identity. This urban register is not a recent sociolinguistic phenomenon; Wolof-French speech styles were documented already in a phrase book from the middle of the 19th century (Descemet 1864, see Mc Laughlin 2008b). A different identity is indexed by *Wolof piir*, 'pure Wolof', considered to be free from French influence, and (positively or negatively) enregistered with the countryside (Mc Laughlin 2001). Within the Muslim Mouride brotherhood, the dominant sufi order in Senegal, there has been a call for a return to a purer Wolof (Ngom 2002).

The informal status of Wolof as 'the national language' is not uncontested. Important minority language groups, like Joola and Peul, resist the building of the Senegalese nation on *le modèle islamo-wolof* (Diouf 2001, Fagerberg-Diallo 2001, Gasser 2002). The resistance towards Wolof dominance was fuelled by the replacement of French colonial functionaries by Wolof speakers after independence (Diouf 2001: 78), and recent initiatives aimed at formally raising the status of Wolof are met with strong protest (Mc Laughlin 2008a). In particular, speakers of Joola, a language cluster that covers 20–30 varieties spoken mainly in Casamance, Senegal's south-western part, show resistance towards Wolof, which they call language of the *Nordistes*, 'people of the North' (Juillard 2005: 33, Mc Laughlin 2008a: 82). Different Joola varieties are associated with a specific village or polity through a process of patrimonial deixis (Lüpke 2021), and the use of a particular variety can thus index a speaker's regional belonging, while the entire Joola cluster has a strong ideological connection with the people and land of Casamance (Goodchild 2016, Lüpke et al. 2020). Casamance is different from northern Senegal not only in terms of language, but also in religion, since it does not share the long history of Islamisation of the north, as well as geographically, as the state of Gambia separates Casamance from northern Senegal. However, Wolof is nonetheless considered as indexing an urban, modern identity in Casamance (Juillard 1990: 68), where it has replaced Creole as lingua franca in the main city, Ziguinchor (Juillard 1995). Peul[1] is the most significant minority language in Senegal in terms of number of speakers and it is spoken in different varieties across West Africa. Opposition to wolofisation is expressed by speakers of this language. The '*Movement pour la Renaissance du Poular*' has promoted literacy in this language for cultural and linguistic defence (Mc Laughlin 1995, Fagerberg-Diallo 2001, Humery-Dieng 2001). Wolof, Peul, and Joola can be studied as subjects in university. They have a 'national language' status alongside the other codified Senegalese languages, like Mandinka, Sooninke, and Hassaniya, some of them only recently standardised, making up a total of 22 languages in 2021 (Sall 2021). Senegal's national language standards are written in the Latin script, but there is also a longstanding tradition of Ajami, i.e., writing in Arabic script, which continues to be associated with informal literacy practices (Lüpke & Bao-Diop 2014). With 96% Muslims in the country, Arabic has a long history of importance and influence in Senegal. However, both Ajami and the codified Roman orthography and grammar of the national languages that are taught in literacy classes for adults are still considered less valued when compared to French, since they don't have the same official status.

French is Senegal's former colonial language, its present official language and only language of instruction in formal schooling. It is considered the language of social mobility and factually serves as the language of formal functions and the written news media. Language attitudes towards French are ambiguous, however. It is the language of the coloniser, but also a language that Senegalese are proud to have appropriated as their own. In speech, Senegalese French is indexed through lexical and phonological features, e.g. rolling [r] instead of uvular [R] (N'Diaye Corréard et al. 2006, Lüpke & Storch 2013, Sow 2016). Francophone Senegalese often have a positive view of their skills in standard French, and Kébé and Leconte (2020) relate this to the figure of Léopold Sedar Senghor, first president of the country, first African member of l'Académie Française, and poet of the Francophone canon. Despite the dominance of French in writing, multilingual literacy practices are also common in both public contexts (e.g. publicity posters) and private ones (e.g. text messaging, cf. Lexander 2012). In several ways, the status difference between French and Wolof is decreasing. On the one hand Wolof has entered formal contexts in speech, while also being frequently used in informal digital writing, and on the other hand French is acquired informally *dans la rue* (Dreyfus & Juillard 2004).

On these grounds, it comes as no surprise that Senegalese migrants value linguistic diversity. In research with West African youth (from low-income families) in New York, Sall (2020) observed that being able to connect with co-ethnics over a shared African language put people at ease and reinforced their sense of belonging. Smith (2019: 129) documents how Senegalese parents in the USA make sure their children speak

Senegalese languages as well as English, because such multilingualism builds symbolic capital in the global Senegalese community. It enables speakers to claim a kind of 'global Senegality', a set of character traits that Senegalese migrants in Paris, Rome, and New York identify with, like being mobile, speaking multiple languages, and being able to use them in practising hospitality, *teranga*, as talking to someone in their language is considered hospitable (Smith 2019). The vignette on Rama's practices at the beginning of this book nicely illustrates this kind of multifaceted multilingualism.

Smith's (2019) comparison of Senegalese migrants in different localities illustrates the way geographical setting, demographic concentration and cultural and linguistic practices as well as ideologies are interrelated and affect language transmission. In New York, people in Harlem's 'Little Senegal' are expected to speak Wolof; it has become synonymous with Senegalese identity and is the lingua franca of 116th Street, the heart of Little Senegal (Smith 2019: 56). The host country's immigration policies affect family lives and constellations, too (Mbodj-Pouye & Le Courant 2017), which in turn affect language practices. For example, even though Senegalese migrants in Paris live more disparately, some nonetheless speak more Wolof after migration than before in order to maintain a link with their cultural background (Smith 2019: 60–62). Leconte (2001) even finds that minority languages like Manjak and Sooninke are transmitted to children to a greater degree by Senegalese migrants in France than by parents in the Senegalese capital Dakar. This language maintenance among West African migrants in France is enhanced by a migration pattern whereby people originating from the same village live in the same locality (Leconte 2001), making various combinations with French in bilingual interaction the unifying code in migrant families (Leconte & Kébé 2013). A specific level of French language competence is required to obtain citizenship in France, while at the same time excellent skills in the language do not prevent the racialisation of Senegalese migrant speakers with reference to their accent (Smith 2019: 72–75). There are furthermore conflicting norms of 'correct French' between emigrants returning from France and the educated elite who have not lived in the metropole (Kébé & Leconte 2020). In Italy, the Senegalese migrants' work and residence conditions are often temporary, family reunification is rare (Hannaford 2017), and the return to the country of origin is a goal (Riccio 2002). This affects Italian language learning to some extent (Smith 2019: 103). Emigration to the USA has contributed to a rising importance of English in Senegal, especially with young people, through influence from American linguistic features and popular culture (Auzanneau 2001, Lexander 2011). In sum, this discussion of Senegalese and Senegalese migrants' linguistic repertoires exemplifies how language ideologies vary with transnational mobility. For Senegalese migrants in Norway and their children, the languages of Senegal are still available, but their status and value shift as Norwegian enters their repertoires.

3.1.2 Language and immigration in Norway

During the last 50 years Norway has become more linguistically diverse due to immigration (Kulbrandstad 2020). Multilingualism is, however, not a recent phenomenon in the country; it encompasses the languages of the indigenous population and a long history of national minorities, including Norwegian sign language users. We do not know how many languages are spoken in Norway as we are writing, since population censuses do not include questions on language. Estimates from Statistics Norway indicate the number of languages to be around 300 (Wilhelmsen et al. 2013), and in a review of research, Kulbrandstad (2020: 214) evaluates the number of potential users of minority languages to be 1 million, i.e. almost 20% of Norway's population.

Like many other European states, Norway has a history of oppression of linguistic diversity. Norwegianisation policies were directed at the Sámi, since 1990 recognised as Norway's indigenous population, and groups that are now recognised as national minorities, such as Kven (also called 'Norwegian Finnish People'), Forest Finns, Taters/Romani people, Jews, and Roma. The long-term effects of harmful and violent measures of assimilation are still felt, even though the Norwegian state has made concessions to make up for some of the damage done. Legislative actions concerning languages are part of these actions. In the 1990s, Sámi obtained status as an official language alongside Norwegian, and later Kven, Romani, and Romanes gained national minority language status as Norway signed the European Charter for Regional or Minority Languages. In 2018 'The commission to investigate the Norwegianisation policy and injustice against the Sámi and Kven/Norwegian Finnish peoples (The Truth and Reconciliation Commission)' was established.[2]

Norwegian has two written standards that are mutually intelligible. Bokmål ('book language'), based on Danish, which was the official language during Dano-Norwegian union (1537–1814), is by far the most prominent standard variety, while Nynorsk ('new Norwegian') is based on dialects spoken in different parts of the country and used by a minority. Dialect use makes up an accepted and valued aspect of linguistic diversity in Norway (Kulbrandstad 2007), hence the term 'the dialect country' (Skjekkeland 2010). 'Polylectal' (Røyneland 2017) communication is common, as people are expected to keep the dialect of their place of origin. Dialect is spoken across domains, including school, official settings, and mass media, and there is no spoken standard taught in school. In written digital interaction, young people, but also adults and politicians, write in dialect (Rotevatn 2014, Røyneland 2018, Strand 2019).

Immigration was rare in Norway until the mid-1960s, when particularly Pakistani work migrants started to arrive (Vassenden 1999). Figures from Statistics Norway (2021) show that 18.5% of the Norwegian population of 5,4 million consists of immigrants or persons born to immigrants.

About half of the migrants come from Europe, with Poles and Lithuanians as the two biggest groups, while 14% come from the African continent. Immigration affects urban areas in particular, where heteroglossic youth practices have emerged, comprising linguistic material from different immigrant languages, and specific prosodic and syntactic features (see Svendsen & Røyneland 2008, Opsahl 2009, Røyneland 2018). This multiethnolectal speech style is an important means to express a specific social youth identity. It is to a certain extent being legitimised by the uptake of hip-hop lyrics in school textbooks (Opsahl & Røyneland 2016) and popular TV series (e.g. series named *17*, *18* and *19*), and by the positive reception of novels that include multiethnolectal features (Skaranger 2015, Shakar 2017).

Even though linguistic diversity is viewed as an asset in Norway's Core Curricula (Ministry of Education and Research 2017), the migration policy in Norway represents Norwegian language competence as the key to integration and inclusion (Kulbrandstad 2017). In 2019, the government increased the level of Norwegian competence required to get citizenship.[3] In White Papers on immigration policy since the 1980s, the Norwegian language is viewed as the main means of accessing economic, social, and cultural capital in Norway (Kulbrandstad 2017). This, along with the political and media discourse, is summed up in a statement by one of the project participants, Oumou, mother in the Diagne family: *Alt avhenger av norsk* ('Everything depends on Norwegian', interview data).

3.1.3 Senegalese immigrants in Norway

There are very few Senegalese in Norway. According to Statistics Norway (March 2021), 317 of 800,094 registered immigrants in Norway are Senegalese, which corresponds to 0.01% of the immigrant population. There are another 108 citizens who were born in Norway to Senegalese parents (with Senegal as place of birth), 16 citizens born in Norway to Norwegian-born parents of Senegalese origin, and 144 citizens with one parent born in Senegal and one parent born in Norway. The Senegalese share cultural and linguistic practices with the Gambians, who are more numerous in Norway (1252 immigrants plus 623 citizens born to Gambian parents (with Gambia as place of birth) (Statistics Norway 2021). Little is written about Senegalese in Norway, apart from a couple of postgraduate theses on Senegalese football players (Lawrence 2009) and on social networks of Senegalese in Oslo (Diallo 2013). Our research thus provides empirical findings about a group of migrants whose language practices and digital communication has not been studied in the Norwegian context. On an international scale, while other studies of Senegalese migrants examine transnational families where only one household member has migrated (Hannaford 2017, Vives & Silva 2017), our study is concerned with families where migrant-background children and one or two immigrant parents live together. In fact, our participant families stand out from most Senegalese migrants in Europe who only tend to achieve family reunification to a low extent (12–18% according to the MAFE (Migration between Africa and Europe) project, cf. Beauchemin, Caarls & Mazzucato 2018).

Most Senegalese migrants live in the Greater Oslo Region (Statistics Norway 2022). There is, however, no 'Little Senegal' in Oslo like the one in New York, where Wolof and other Senegalese languages are regular means of communication (Smith 2019). Indeed, the physical contexts where Senegalese languages can be used in Norway are far fewer when compared to France and Italy, let alone the USA. The families' location within Norway also affects their language practices, especially considering the varieties of Norwegian in their repertoires (cf. discussion in Section 3.1.2). Speaking a Norwegian dialect with strong regional connotations is likely for families who live outside the Oslo region, whereas using a Norwegian multiethnolectal style is more likely for those who live in low-status urban districts. However, indexing a local Norwegian identity through language style is not straightforward for the participating family members. Many adolescents with migrant backgrounds do not feel accepted in Norway and cite their skin colour as a reason for this lack of acceptance (Frøyland & Gjerustad 2012, Røyneland 2018). For most Senegalese migrants in Norway, there is a double set of prejudice: on the one hand, they make up a minority of colour, and on the other, they are Muslims (Diop 2020). Being born in Norway does not necessarily lead to being considered 'Norwegian' (Ali 2018, Joof 2018). Against this background, digital communication may work as a 'safe black space' (Mainsah 2014) for the connection with linguistic and cultural practices related to peers in Norway or elsewhere in the world, including the (parents') homeland.

3.2 Presentation of participants

The participants in our study were recruited through the friend-of-a-friend principle from the first author's personal network. Access was facilitated by her competence in Wolof and the experience of several long stays in Senegal. Parents from two of the families had already accepted to be followed on Facebook for research purposes a couple of years before the project started, and one family familiar to the researcher volunteered to take part when asked if they knew of other families who could be interested. In collaboration with this family, several potential participants were invited to a dinner where information about the project was given. This led to a fourth family accepting participation. These four families differ slightly when it comes to language use and household composition, see Table 3.1. In three of the families, both parents were born in Senegal, and in the fourth, the mother was born in Norway. The 'Languages' column presents the participants' own perspective on their linguistic repertoire, as it includes all languages mentioned in interviews. Some participants only reported languages they used regularly, others

Table 3.1 Overview of participating families

Family members are listed from oldest to youngest. Country of birth: N= Norway, S = Senegal. Fictitious names have been adopted and individual age is not disclosed to avoid identification of the families. The languages are those that were reported in interviews and/or attested in digital data. In the Bâ family, an 'Asian language' linked to a family member's biographical background has been anonymised; 'Languages of the Middle East' refer to other languages, of which bits and pieces are used in the workplace.

Family	Family member by age (country of birth)	Languages (reported and/or attested)
Diagne family	Ousmane, father (S)	Wolof, French, Arabic, Norwegian
	Oumou, mother (S)	Wolof, French, Norwegian
	Momar, son (S)	Wolof, French, Norwegian, English
	Marième, daughter (N)	Wolof, English, Norwegian
	Abdou, son (N)	Wolof, Norwegian
Bâ family	Sara, mother (N)	Norwegian, [Asian language], English, French, Wolof, Arabic, Spanish, [Languages of the Middle East]
	Cheikh, father (S)	Peul, Joola, Wolof, French, Arabic, Italian, Spanish, English, Norwegian
	Nabou, daughter (N)	Norwegian, Wolof, Arabic, English, French, [Asian language], Peul
	Mamadou, son (N)	Norwegian
Sagna family	Felipe, father (S)	Joola, Wolof, French, English, Spanish
	Rama, daughter (S)	Wolof, French, English, Norwegian, Peul, Seereer, Japanese
Coly family	Astou, mother (S)	Joola, Mandinka, Wolof, French, Arabic, Norwegian, English, Spanish, Italian
	Awa, daughter (S)	Wolof, French, Arabic, Norwegian
	Ibou, son (S)	Wolof, French, Arabic, Norwegian, Spanish, Turkish, Urdu, German
	Aida, daughter (N)	Wolof, French, Arabic, Norwegian, Spanish, Italian, Swedish, Berber, German, Farsi
	Issa, son (N)	Wolof, French, Arabic, Norwegian, English, Spanish

also included more peripheral parts of their repertoire. Ibou and Aida, for instance, mentioned languages they know bits and pieces of, through their friends of migrant backgrounds (Turkish, Urdu, German, Berber, Farsi); Aida and Rama listed languages they only encounter in online content and discussions (Italian and Japanese, respectively). The languages spoken by the family will be discussed after a brief introduction to the four families.

3.2.1 The Diagne family

The Diagne family consists of two parents born in Senegal, Oumou and Ousmane, a son born in Senegal, Momar, and a daughter, Marième, and a younger son, Abdou, born in Norway. Ousmane came to Norway some years before Oumou and their oldest son Momar. When the research was being carried out, both parents worked in the public sector as skilled workers, and Ousmane had a university degree from Senegal. The children were at school.

The family is Wolof, from a dominantly Wolof-speaking area, and the parents and the oldest son thus spoke this language as their first language. Everyday conversational interaction in the home included some Wolof, but was carried out mostly in Norwegian, with Marième and Abdou using Wolof less than their parents did. The parents were worried about the Wolof competence of the two youngest children. Marième had been reluctant to use this language, but after she gave a presentation in school about Senegal and got very positive feedback from her classmates and teachers, she seemed to have become more interested in her background, including the Wolof language, the parents said (see Chapter 8, Section 8.2). Abdou said he preferred Norwegian, which he called 'real language', as opposed to Wolof, the 'Senegal language'. However, he did speak to his parents in Wolof during fieldwork meetings. The oldest son Momar expressed reflections along the same lines as his parents, as he wanted to 'remember' his first language (see Chapter 8).

The main concern of the Diagne parents regarding Wolof was communication with their families in Senegal. Momar communicated digitally with Senegalese family members on a regular basis, most frequently with his cousins with whom he lived until he moved to Norway at primary school age. During holidays in Senegal, Marième also got along well with her peers using Wolof. When Kristin visited the family towards the end of the project (our fifth meeting), Marième said that after their last visit in Senegal, she had started communicating digitally with a cousin of her age, exchanging greetings and sometimes videos, from activities like cooking. Abdou, who was still below primary school age at the time of data collection, did not interact with family members in Senegal to the same degree, either digitally or during holidays. The Diagne family had contact with another family of Senegalese origin that lived close to them, but apart from this, the main contact with Senegalese languages and culture was online.

3.2.2 The Bâ family

Sara, the mother, was born in Norway and had multilingual parents. The father, Cheikh, grew up in southern Senegal in a trilingual context. The Bâ family members had a rich linguistic repertoire, which had been further extended through schooling, work, and mobility. The two children, Nabou and Mamadou, of primary school age and below at the time of data collection, were born in Norway and engaged with the family's linguistic resources in different ways, through songs, prayers, films, books, and cultural events, in addition to conversations with relatives and

Media and language use in multilingual families 55

friends of the family. Sara had a university degree and worked in the public sector at the time of the data collection, Cheikh was receiving professional training to become a skilled worker while also running his own business.

Both Sara and Cheikh spoke Wolof, French, and English, in addition to Norwegian, and used the three languages when talking to each other. Cheikh was Peul, and spoke this language, while Sara spoke the first language of her father to some extent (the language has been represented as 'Asian language' in Table 3.1, to preserve anonymity). They also had some knowledge of Arabic related to their Muslim faith. Being members of the Mourid brotherhood, Wolof was important to their religious practices as well (see Chapter 7). Through mobility and studies, they had acquired Spanish (Sara) and Italian (Cheikh). During data collection, Norwegian was the main language of communication in the family. The father suggested that French might be the 'best' language for his daughter to learn, if she was to 'feel Senegalese', while the mother thought it was important for her to learn Peul, because the husband's family was 'typically Peul' (see Chapter 8, Section 8.1).

The Bâ family engaged in digitally mediated communication with Cheikh's family in Senegal and in France. Cheikh preferred WhatsApp and did not use Facebook, while Sara had a Facebook Messenger account, but logged off in periods, finding Instagram to be a better channel for managing relationships, for instance with her in-laws (see Chapter 5, Section 5.1). Together with Cheikh, she facilitated her children's interaction with their grandmother in Senegal (see Section 3.3.3). Sara was also happy that Nabou, who got her first mobile phone during the project, had occasional contact with cousins in Senegal through the application Musical.ly (which later was bought up by TikTok), using English and emoji. The daughter otherwise used her mobile phone to interact with her parents and friends, in Norwegian. The Bâ family could use their extended linguistic repertoire in their contact with other Senegalese background families in Oslo, one of them being the Sagna family.

3.2.3 *The Sagna family*

Rama, introduced at the beginning of this book, was born in Senegal and came to Norway to join her father, Felipe, who had already lived in the country for ten years. Felipe also had a Norwegian-born daughter who lived part time in the household. Felipe had studied for one year in university in Senegal and worked as an unskilled worker in Norway at the time of the data collection.

Felipe and Rama were Joola – an ethnolinguistic origin they share with the Coly family – and grew up with Wolof and Joola used in fluid ways in the local community, and then acquired French and English at school. Felipe had also studied Spanish. When Rama lived with her mother and stepfather in Senegal, she went to school with French as the language of instruction. Rama furthermore learnt Seereer from living for a while in a Seereer-speaking area in Senegal, and she also spoke a little Peul during the interview, claiming she knew very little of this language. After two years in Norway, Rama spoke Norwegian very well and the father praised her skills in acquiring new languages: 'I believe she's very good with languages' (original: *jeg tror hun er veldig flink med språk, jeg*, interview data). Rama had attended Koranic school in Senegal and therefore knew some Arabic, while her father, of Christian faith, had not learnt Arabic. Felipe thus represented a minority within the already small group of Senegalese in Norway. Being a Christian, the mosque and Muslim ceremonies were not natural meeting points for him as for the majority of the Senegambian migrants.

Rama expressed a fascination for languages as she described her linguistic repertoire in the language portrait session (see Chapter 4, Section 4.1.1). She was interested in Japanese, having learnt some of the language from watching anime movies, and said she would like to go to Japan to study the language in the future. She communicated online with her mother and other relatives in Senegal in Joola, Wolof, French, and English. Both father and daughter expressed a translanguaging attitude towards their practices. In their interaction with each other, they claimed to use 'all languages'. Felipe commented that what some criticised as language mixing had in fact become one language, and this was a good thing (see Chapter 4, Section 4.5). On the other hand, named languages were described as important resources in themselves. For instance, Felipe wanted to use more French with his daughter in text messages in order for her 'to build up' her command of the language. And because Joola was considered 'our language' and Wolof 'our national language', 'it is a little bit embarrassing when you go there [to Senegal] and don't sp... do not know your language' (original: *det er litt flaut når du går dit og ikke sn... å ikke kunne ditt spark*, interview data). Felipe therefore wanted to be better at speaking Joola and Wolof with his daughter. He otherwise managed a complex network of friends, relatives, and business partners online, using Joola, Wolof, and French to this purpose.

3.2.4 The Coly family

Three of the Coly family members were born in Senegal: the mother Astou, the oldest daughter Awa, and the oldest son Ibou. The younger daughter and son, Aida and Issa, were born in Norway. During the data collection period, Awa moved out of the flat for studies. Ibou also finished high school during this time, but continued to live with his family, while Aida and Issa were still at school. Astou worked in the public sector. Two of the children's uncles lived in Norway as well, while their father lived in Senegal.

Astou, the mother, spoke Wolof, Joola, French, English, some words of Spanish and Italian, in addition to Norwegian. She said she really loved Mandinka, another of the Senegalese national languages, spoken by her parents and relatives in Gambia. With her children, she used Wolof and

Norwegian, and the children also used Wolof in written and spoken digital interaction with friends and relatives in Senegal. The four children agreed upon a hierarchy of Wolof competence among them, corresponding to their age hierarchy, where Awa was on top, which is not unusual for older siblings when it comes to minority language use (Smith-Christmas 2018). There followed Ibou and Aida, with the youngest, Issa, at the bottom. But Aida claimed that Issa learnt fast, since he was a child, and Issa himself said in the interview that when he got his own phone, this made a difference because it allowed him to speak more with people in Senegal.

The Coly family's neighbourhood was well-known, even stigmatised, for its cultural and linguistic diversity. When talking about their linguistic repertoires, the Coly children mentioned languages acquired through their friends from different backgrounds: Aida claimed to understand Farsi, Ibou some Urdu and Turkish. Many neighbours were Muslims, and Arabic had a wider presence beyond its specifically religious usage. Momar, the oldest son in the Diagne family who lived in a different city during fieldwork, explained that he was the only 'dark-skinned' child at school (original: *eneste mørkhuda*, focus group data), but Issa, the youngest Coly child, said he was happy to live in an area with great diversity: 'We're lucky here, you know. There is like 95%, for instance all the way from primary school to high school, 95% are not from Norway' (original: *Ja vi er heldige ass. Det er sånn nittifem prosent, for eksempel hele ungdomsskolen, fra barneskolen, barnetrinnet, helt til ungdomsskolen nittifem prosent er ikke fra Norge*, focus group data).

Although diverse with regards to parents' geographical and ethnic origin, the four families' linguistic repertoires largely overlap. All families speak Norwegian as the main language in everyday family communication, with Wolof as the second most used. They all include French in their repertoires; even some of the children who have not learnt French in school mention it as one of their linguistic resources. When it comes to other languages, there is variation in terms of individual life trajectories with regard to national languages used (Joola, Peul) and with regard to competence in languages learnt in school and in the neighbourhood.

3.3 The families' linguistic repertoires

As discussed in Chapter 2, Section 2.1, the perceived values of people's linguistic resources change as people move from one space to the other. Senegalese migrants coming to Norway usually have some competence in French, a language with a much higher number of speakers than Norwegian on an international scale, but they also speak languages that are minorised in Norway. In this section, we take a closer look at the families' linguistic repertoires, describing the usage and status of these languages in the various spaces of communication that the family members inhabited during the period when we were doing this research. Looking back to our discussion in Chapter 2, Section 2.1, we would like to point out that our reference to single languages like 'Norwegian' and 'Joola' does not mean we view these languages as homogenous and bounded entities. Quite the contrary, all metalinguistic labels used here index diverse registers and heterogenous language practices, much in line with current sociolinguistic approaches to multilingualism (cf. Chapter 2, Section 2.1) as well as in studies of small-scale multilingualism in the Senegambia (cf. Lüpke & Storch 2013, Juffermans 2015, Lüpke 2016, 2021, Weidl 2018). We start with Wolof, the language most closely associated with the Senegalese nation, and end with Norwegian, the main language of the families' living environment when they participated in our research project.

3.3.1 Wolof

In line with its status in Senegal as the main national language, Wolof was used by all participants in the study regardless of ethnic origin, albeit to varying extent, with generation as an important factor. All Senegal-born adults spoke it as a first language, sometimes together with other first languages, and Sara Bâ had studied Wolof in University and could therefore both speak it and write the standard orthography. There was more variation in the children's use of Wolof. Rama, Momar, Awa and Ibou were all born in Senegal and learnt Wolof as a first language. While Rama had only lived in Norway for a couple of years when data collection took place, Momar, Awa and Ibou claimed that they spoke Wolof less well after many years in Norway. Digital data in our corpus shows that these adolescents, born in Senegal, communicate in the language in complex ways, and sometimes with what could be termed 'second language features'. Wolof thus appears as the most used language of Senegalese linguistic heritage in all families, including the three families where parents have a different ethnolinguistic background. Wolofisation (cf. Section 3.1.1) was particularly reflected in the Coly family, where the children spoke Wolof, not Joola or Seereer, despite their mother's Joola and their father's Seereer ethnic origin. Indeed, Astou Coly, the mother, grew up in Dakar, mainly using Wolof with her siblings, while Joola was reserved for her parents. She still spoke Wolof with her siblings in video calls and phone calls, but her text messages to them were mainly in French. However, Astou Coly never spoke Joola to her children, and they in turn said they wanted their future children to learn Wolof. Cheikh Bâ, too, claimed he spoke more Wolof than Peul, and that if he would think in an African language, that would be Wolof. Mirroring Astou Coly, he reported he used mainly Wolof with his siblings, especially in playful exchanges. Rama and Felipe Sagna also used Wolof with each other.

The Norway-born family children had at least receptive competence in Wolof. Marième Diagne said, 'they talk Wolof to me, but I answer in Norwegian' (original: *dem sier wolof til mæ, men æ svare på norsk*, interview data). Observed communication at home during fieldwork took place in both Wolof and Norwegian. The Coly children said that in the beginning when they had moved to Norway, their mother talked to them in Wolof, but as they answered in Norwegian, she, too, switched to Norwegian. Still, at the time of data collection, the children claimed that they used more Wolof within the nuclear family than before, due to more use of the language in digitally mediated interaction. They also spoke Wolof with an uncle who had just arrived in Norway due to onward migration, and Awa watched TV series in Wolof on YouTube. For Nabou Bâ, Wolof was one of several languages in the family repertoire in which she knew some words and greetings. By contrast, occasions to use Wolof outside the home were few. Momar Diagne, an adolescent during fieldwork, said: 'Wolof, I almost only speak it at home and I am more out than at home' (original: *wolof, da, det æ snakker jo det nesten bare hjæm og e e mer ut enn hjem*, interview data). The Coly children did not like the potential Wolof language space of cultural events, like Muslim feasts, which Gambians also attended, since there were not many participants of their own age, and the Diagne family lived in a part of Norway where there were no organised feasts like this. Even though Norwegian was dominant and Wolof more or less invisible in their society of residence, Felipe experienced that his language skills were appreciated. Sometimes he was hired to do interpreting between both Wolof and Norwegian and French and Norwegian for public social services.

Wolof was an object of value judgement and appeared in different registers. Rama claimed that her mother and grandmothers in Senegal preferred to communicate with her in their ethnic language. Her mother, Rama told us, did not like so much that the children spoke Wolof, because she thought there were too many bad words in Wolof (original: *mamma likte ikke så mye at vi barna snakket wolof fordi at wolof-språket så er det litt sånn mange stygge ord*, interview data). Rama played several voice messages (recorded in the interview) in typically urban Wolof style with various family members of her own age and of the parents' generation. In our digital data, the language appeared mainly in its urban Wolof form, too, i.e. with features usually associated with other languages, mainly French among the adult family members, but also English in message threads by the family children. Momar reported that a Wolof register with little French influence was in use when he interacted with his grandparents in video calls, and Felipe had a friend that he claimed wrote 'real' Wolof in terms of vocabulary. As mentioned in Section 3.1.1, there has been a call for a return to 'pure Wolof' within the Mouride brotherhood (Ngom 2002). Cheikh, who was member of this brotherhood, was part of a WhatsApp group chat for Mourides in Norway, where Wolof was spoken and written in accordance with these norms (see Chapter 7, Section 7.3.3). These exchanges also included some instances of Wolofal, i.e. Wolof written in the Arabic script. This Wolofal was marginal in text message threads, but also Wolof written in the Latin script appeared overall less often in messaging than French, reflecting the dominance of the latter in Senegalese literacy. On the other hand, Wolof seemed to predominate in spoken online communication, much in line with its status as Senegal's dominant spoken language. In a telling example, when Kristin asked Oumou Diagne if she communicated with her brother in Senegal in writing, Oumou answered: 'I write, yes, write French, and speak Wolof'(original: *jeg skriver, ja, skriver fransk og snakker wolof*, interview data). This division of labour was also confirmed by other adults who referred to their lack of literacy education in Wolof, and the family children, too, claimed they understood spoken Wolof better than written and it was easier for them to speak than write it. Issa explained that he did not speak Wolof fluently but described his competence as 'enough' (*nok*, interview data). However, in writing, he said he could only write the common greeting *nanga def*, so, if he wanted to say more than that, he would record and send voice messages.

In sum, Wolof had a unique position in the linguistic repertoires of all the families. It appeared as the language that linked them the most to Senegal and it was the most commonly used Senegalese language in the home. However, its use was restricted to communication at home and online, with a somewhat stronger presence in spoken communication.

3.3.2 Joola

While Wolof had a similar role in all four families, Joola was used by only four participants (Cheikh Bâ, Felipe and Rama Sagna, and Astou Coly), but played a different role for each of them. Felipe used Joola the most. He grew up with Joola-speaking parents in a small village in Casamance, a region with strong ideological connection to Joola languages (cf. Section 3.1.1). However, Felipe told us that there were not many contexts for him to use Wolof in Norway, and even fewer to use Joola.

INTERVIEW DATA 3.1: FELIPE SAGNA

Felipe   *Joola, det er morsmål, wolof er nasjonalspråket det er de to språkene. Her er det vanskelig å snakke når ikke... eh, ja, jeg bruker når jeg møter folk fra Senegal, så da snakker vi, men det er veldig sjelden. Siden vi er ikke mange her og vi har ikke så mange venner fra Senegal.*
Joola, that's the mother tongue, Wolof is the national language, those are the two languages. Here it is difficult to talk when we don't ... eh, yeah, I use when I meet people from Senegal, so then we talk, but it is very rare. Since we are not so many here and we don't have so many friends from Senegal.

The limitations of written usage discussed above for Wolof are likewise valid to Joola. Felipe said it was equally difficult to write in Joola or Wolof due to his lack of literacy in either, and he therefore used what he called 'French thoughts and letters' to write these languages. He nevertheless could 'proceed for a long time with text messages in Joola', for instance in exchanges with another Joola-speaking participant, Cheikh Bâ. They would greet each other in Joola and sometimes speak it as a secret language.

Felipe described Joola as part of his multilingual practices, usually spoken in interactions that included Wolof and French linguistic material. When interacting with people of higher age, he would seek to use Joola only. This was in line with his daughter Rama's experience. She grew up in Casamance like her father did, but also lived in other parts of Senegal where other languages were dominant. She recounted how her grandmothers refused to answer if she spoke to them in a language other than Joola. One of her relatives had told her she had to 'keep the other languages back' when talking to her grandmother, and just stick to Joola. Other people she met in Senegal during holiday, too, ignored her when she was not speaking Joola, Rama reported, or even confronted her for forgetting Joola: 'I kind of forgot Joola, so it was a little difficult to talk every time when they say [how are you in Joola] [Rama], then I said *Salam maaleykum*, so they started saying you have forgotten' (original: *jeg glemte sånn joola så det var litt vanskelig å snakke hver gang når de sier kasumay [Rama] så sa jeg salam maaleykum, så de begynte å si du har glemt*, interview data). This example is interesting, in that the feature that triggered other people's reproaches in Rama's narrative is not her use of French or English, but an Arabic greeting that is very frequent in Senegal, but at the same time associated with Islam, a faith that is less predominant among Joola speakers.

The mother in the Coly family, Astou, spoke Joola with her parents who were from Casamance. She still used it to some extent in digitally mediated interaction, especially voice messages. However, as mentioned above, Astou grew up in Dakar and communicated in Wolof with her siblings, and eventually spoke Wolof with her children when building her own household. Her oldest, Awa, said she felt she should speak Joola since her mother spoke it, but she knew only a little, and mentioned a couple of greetings as examples. For Cheikh Bâ, Joola had become less important due to mobility. When growing up in Casamance, he learnt it as one of his first three languages, but he did not use it in the home with his children and compared it to Spanish and Italian, other languages that he had learnt but did not use any more.

INTERVIEW DATA 3.2: CHEIKH BÂ

Cheikh   *Joola det er et språk som jeg snakker men jeg praktiserer det ikke så mye. Det er som spansk eller italiensk språk som jeg trenger også å høre en eller to dager for å komme inn, for jeg snakker, jeg snakker spansk og italiensk, men jeg blander så mye til å snakke det og høre det så og så mye for å komme inn til språket.*

> Joola, that is a language that I speak, but I don't practise it so much. It is like Spanish or Italian language that I also need to listen to for one or two days before I get into it. Cause, I speak, I speak Spanish and Italian, but I mix so much to speak it and understand it and so much to get into the language.

Felipe was fond of using Joola features in digital interaction. When communicating with his nephew, Joola was spoken in voice messages, and when text messaging with a friend from childhood, Joola appeared in bits and pieces of outrageous banter, as common in social interaction among close friends of Joola origin (see analysis in Lexander & Watson 2022). However, Felipe's WhatsApp diaspora group, discussed in Chapter 7, Section 7.3.1, featured little use of Joola.

INTERVIEW DATA 3.3: FELIPE SAGNA

Felipe   *Det kommer an på hvem jeg snakker med, med vennene mine, eller folk som jeg…, ja…. Det er… det er mest blanding. De, vi skriver litt mer fransk, noen har vært på skole og de kan fransk. Ok. Da bruker jeg mest sånn, da bruker jeg fransk. Og hvis det er vennene mine i samme universen, da vi, he, he, he, he, vi, he, he, skiller når vi prater. Når jeg skal tulle, da bruker jeg joola, og, ha, ha, eller wolof, da.*
It depends on who I talk to, with my friends, or people that I…, yeah…, it's… it's mostly mixing. They, we write a little more French, some have been to school and they know French. Ok. Then I use mostly, like, then I use French. And if it's my friends in the same universe, then we, ha, ha, ha, ha, we, ha, ha, make a difference when we talk. When I'm going to joke, then I use Joola, and, ha, ha, or Wolof.

In sum, Felipe, Rama, Astou and Cheikh shared Joola as one of their first languages, but its role and value to them differed, related to their individual language-biographies as well as to factors such as mobility and ethnic belonging.

3.3.3 *Peul*

While Joola is associated with southern Senegal, Peul is associated with specific parts of northern Senegal, particularly the Senegal River valley area. However, the only Peul speaker in the study, Cheikh Bâ, was from Casamance. He grew up with Peul in the home and Joola in the neighbourhood, in addition to Wolof. His wife, Sara, wanted to learn more than the few Peul words she already spoke and used when reaching out to her in-laws, who she qualified as 'very Peul'. In a comment to a video Sara had posted on Instagram, one of her in-laws referred to this Peul background when she called her daughter, Nabou, *une vraie princesse peule* ('a real Peul princess', digital data). Sara said she would often listen to the language when Cheikh communicated with his contacts, and she had once obtained textbooks and started learning Peul vocabulary. However, assistance from her husband had not been overwhelming, Sara said, and Cheikh explained this by his lack of formal schooling in the language: 'It's not just me, but we are many to talk, I talk Peul or I talk Wolof, but we are not good at teaching it' (original: *det er ikke bare jeg, men det er mange som kan snakke, jeg snakker peul, eller jeg snakker wolof, men vi er ikke flinke til å lære det [bort]*, interview data).

Cheikh spoke Peul to his daughter, Nabou, when she was a toddler, but moved on to Norwegian when she started answering. Nabou said: 'I learnt it when I was younger, then, then dad asked me in Peul and I answered in Norwegian, not Peul!' (original: *jeg lærte det når jeg var liten, da, da spurte pappa meg på peul, og så svarte jeg på norsk, ikke peul!*, interview data). Cheikh explained the move from Peul to Norwegian by a lack of occasions to practice Peul in Norway and by his focus on learning Norwegian.

INTERVIEW DATA 3.4: CHEIKH BÂ

Cheikh   *På begynnelsen jeg snakka på peul med [Nabou], men på en måte så konstaterte jeg at det blir vanskelig, jeg snakker ikke peul med ingen i Norge, jeg kan være her to-tre måneder, hvis jeg ringer ikke på telefon jeg snakker peul, jeg tenker, okay, jeg har ikke fine bøker og sånn og sånn, og jeg må lære meg språket.*
In the beginning, I spoke Peul with [Nabou], but in a way I concluded that it will be difficult, I don't speak Peul with anyone in Norway, I can stay for two-three months here, if I don't make phone calls I don't speak Peul, I thought, okay, I don't have nice books and that stuff, and I have to learn the [Norwegian] language.

Cheikh Bâ's reflections on the use of Peul in the home will be further discussed in Chapter 8.

The Bâ children named their grandmother by the Peul term, *pati*. Sara reported that Nabou would sometimes talk to *pati* on the phone and use Peul. Then, after thinking it over, Sara corrected herself: 'Or – we try to make you say it, ha, ha' (original: *eller vi prøver å få dere til å si det, he, he*, interview data). This was confirmed by Nabou, who said her mother would tell her what to say on the phone. When Nabou had a school task to interview a grandparent, she interviewed *pati* in a WhatsApp phone call, with her father acting as an interpreter.

During fieldwork, Cheikh Bâ reported using Peul in online interaction, particularly in voice messages and phone calls with his mother and using

French and Wolof with family members and friends in Senegal and France. With his sisters and brothers, Cheikh spoke and wrote Peul and Wolof. When Sara reminded him of friends with whom he communicated in Peul, he said: 'Yes, we speak Peul too, but with friends I think I mainly speak Wolof' (original: *Ja, vi snakker også peul, men med venner jeg tror at jeg snakker mest wolof*, interview data). With a Seereer friend with whom he communicated regularly, Cheikh used Wolof in a fluid way that also included Peul features like *a jaaraama*, 'thank you'. Peul thus had a marginal, but salient presence in the linguistic repertoire of the Bâ family, both in terms of its actual use and its value as a symbol of Peul identity.

3.3.4 French

French is another language that was used more by the parents than the children in the families. All adults spoke it, having learnt it in school. The adolescents Awa and Momar, who had spoken French in Senegal in their early infancy, followed French second language classes in secondary school in Norway, while Ibou and Aida were not offered this option in their schooling. Momar said that when he started to learn French in school, he was surprised to learn that what he had thought of as ordinary (Norwegian) language was in fact French.[4] Awa and Ibou had also attended pre-school in Senegal before coming to Norway and according to their mother, they spoke French fluently because of that. Awa regretted that this was no longer the case. Aida said she had learnt some French through the presence of French features in Wolof discourse: 'I don't know any French, I don't know, only because of Wolof, we mix in French words' (original: *jeg kan ikke noe fransk, jeg kan ikke noe bare fra på grunn av wolof vi blander inn franske ord*, interview data).

Momar, too, said he learnt French through urban Wolof. For Momar, French was so closely linked to Wolof that he described it as 'a backup if I forget Wolof a little, then I have the word in French' (original: *en backup for hvis æ glæmme wolof, litt, da så har æ ordet på fransk*, interview data). Skills in the one language would complement the skills in the other.

INTERVIEW DATA 3.5: MOMAR DIAGNE

Momar   *For dem kan jo fransk og, ikke sant, det e jo på en måte en slags blanding mellom wolof og fransk, da, at hvis æ ikke kan ordet på fransk, så kan æ det på wolof, og hvis æ ikke kan det på wolof, så kan æ det på fransk*
For they know French and, right, it is kind of a mix between Wolof and French, then, so if I don't know the word in French, I know it in Wolof, and if I don't know it in Wolof, then I know it in French

Ousmane Diagne claimed that relatives in Senegal expected their children to speak French since they had emigrated. This was, however, not a language that they used much with the children, but Momar watched Senegalese TV and sports channels in French together with his father. For Abdou Diagne, one of the youngest participants, French was a language of the future: 'No, I'm not able to [speak it], but I can practise it when I get older.' (original: *nei, e klare ikkje de, men e kan øve meg på det når jeg blir stor*, interview data). The parents in the Bâ family, Sara and Cheikh, mainly talked French together in the home, sometimes with Wolof. Sara said that they had started out with more use of Wolof, moving to more French after their children were born (see Chapter 6).

Rama attended both primary and secondary school in Senegal, with French as the language of instruction. In addition, her mother and stepfather in Senegal were both teachers and supported her learning of the language through reserving one day per week for exclusive use of French in the home. Rama even called French 'a little mother tongue in a way' (original: *litt morsmål på en måte*, interview data). Felipe said he wanted to build up his daughter's French through using it at home, and Rama agreed on the importance of developing her French skills. Rama's skills in French proved to be an advantage for her when she came to Norway. Since she could not get a place in the introductory class for immigrants, she instead started directly in a regular Norwegian school class, and a French-speaking classmate, also with migrant background, served as a language broker. This furthermore helped her integrate socially with the other pupils. Similarly, with French being available as an option for second foreign language learning in high school, the French competence of the parents could be of help when assisting their children with homework. Otherwise, French was of little practical use in the Norwegian context.

Overall, the parents, who learnt to write in French, preferred French to Wolof for writing online, whereas the family children used French to varying degrees in their transnational communication. Momar Diagne said he found it easier to speak French than to write it. Still, when receiving written messages in French from his uncle (on Facebook Messenger) and as comments to his Facebook posts, he replied in written French.

Like Wolof, registers of French were the object of value judgement. Astou, for instance, criticised her brother for his French spelling, and when Aida asked why, she explained that she did not approve of the potential changes this could engender:

INTERVIEW DATA 3.6: ASTOU AND AIDA COLY

Astou   *Broren min som bor i hjemlandet nå, han skriver slang, for at jeg liker ikke det jeg skriver ordentlig*
My brother who lives in the homeland now, he writes slang, I don't like it, I write properly

Aida	Hvorfor liker du ikke det?
	Why don't you like it?
Astou	Fordi jeg vil ikke glemme hvordan man skriver ordene, jeg vil ikke glemme det, synes jeg, jeg synes det er dumt at folk driver og forandrer
	Because I don't want to forget how you write the words. I don't want to forget it, I think, I think it's stupid that people are modifying

Unconventional French orthography also figured in Felipe's messaging with young football players in relation to his football academy project in Senegal. Felipe claimed that these players would 'write in a code so that it takes some time to understand', a code which included not only French unconventional spelling, but also some Wolof vocabulary.

Overall, the role of French in the participants' linguistic repertoires can be summed up as important, but secondary to Wolof and Norwegian. It was, however, important as a written language in transnational interaction, mirroring its position in Senegal. It was more useful in Norway than Wolof, but still marginalised when compared to Norwegian and English.

3.3.5 Arabic

As mentioned above, the great majority of Senegalese are Muslims. This implies the presence of Arabic, both in speech and writing, which provides a transnationally shared frame of religious reference. It is common for Muslim Senegalese to attend Koranic school, and all of the Muslim participants had some knowledge of Arabic, either through schooling or other religious practices. Rama, too, whose father was Christian, had attended Koranic school in Senegal, and Awa, Ibou and Issa received similar education in Norway. Issa had stopped 'when it started getting too difficult', while Awa and Ibou still followed classes in their spare time during fieldwork. Ibou demonstrated his familiarity with the script as he wrote his name in Arabic on his language portrait but claimed that Awa was more skilled in the language than him. Ibou called Arabic the 'English of the Muslim world' and said he used it with friends in both Norway and Senegal, providing examples of this. Aida had not attended Arabic classes, but still used the language with family and friends.

Arabic appeared in various ways in the participants' digitally mediated communication, including chain messages, shared memes, videos, prayers, and other religious content that will be discussed in more detail in Chapter 7. In Cheikh's Mourid chat group, voice messages with religious (Mourid) speeches started with a prayer in Arabic, then continued in Wolof. There were pictures with Arabic script, and Arabic script was used to write in Wolof. In the participants' own digital writing, Arabic was not used to produce longer stretches of texts, but mainly appeared in the form of inserted words and expressions in Latin script.

3.3.6 English

Most participants had acquired English in the school setting but evaluated their competence differently. Felipe Sagna learnt English in school and seemed to be comfortable using it. Ousmane Diagne, older than Felipe, did not seem comfortable with English, but this did not stop him from using it at times. English appeared more important for the children's generation than the parents'. As mentioned above, English expressions work as youth identity markers in Senegal, and English is also popular with youth in Norway (Rindal 2015). In the Norwegian education system, English is taught as first foreign language from the first grade of primary school, and in Senegal it is compulsory from the first year of secondary school (*sixième*). Several young project participants experienced that their peers in Senegal valued the English competence they were acquiring in Norway. Rama reported she had improved her English skills in Norway: 'In English, I knew a little bit, like 1% at school in Senegal. When I came here, I learnt a little more, so now I know around 50, I think' (original: *på engelsk, da kunne jeg litte grann som 1% på skolen, i Senegal, da jeg kom hit, så lærte jeg litt mer, så jeg kan 50, tror jeg*, interview data).

Rama communicated in English with two of her Senegalese relatives online. In addition, English expressions like 'hello my baby' and 'good night' appeared in written messages she exchanged with her mother. Other family children, too, regularly used English to communicate digitally with peers, aunts, and uncles in Senegal. Rama and Momar even supported the English learning of their peers, and also Awa appeared to have higher competence in English than her transnational interlocutors. In line with its status as an identity marker, English appeared in Facebook content and interpersonal interactions, often limited to singular expressions and greetings.

3.3.7 Norwegian

Norwegian language was used in most social spaces relevant to the participants: at work, at school, at leisure. They had attended Norwegian language education and training when they came to Norway and all spoke Norwegian at work during fieldwork. Ousmane said he had studied Norwegian for three months, had taken the Norwegian test, and had then started working. The family children spoke Norwegian at a first-language level, except for Rama, who had only recently migrated. Ousmane's oldest son, Momar, had started in a primary school introductory class when he arrived, while Rama started directly in a regular secondary school class.

68 *Media and language use in multilingual families*

The registers of Norwegian that were relevant to participants included multiethnolectal speech, so-called 'Kebab-Norwegian' in popular discourse, a term also used by Ibou, who claimed that he always wrote text messages in this register. Momar and his parents also both spoke and wrote the local dialect of their region. Norwegian was, moreover, predominant in communication at home for all families, sometimes in patterns where parents spoke Wolof and children answered in Norwegian. Astou found this to be a common practice in the neighbourhood:

INTERVIEW DATA 3.7: ASTOU AND AWA COLY

Astou   *Det gjør alle barna her, alle barna som kommer fra andre land, selv om foreldrene snakker eh, ja*
All the children here, all the children who come from other countries, even though the parents speak, eh, yeah

Awa   *Morsmål*
Mother tongue

Astou   *Morsmål, de snakker bare norsk, de svarer på norsk*
Mother tongue, they speak only Norwegian, they answer in Norwegian

---

Overall, Norwegian dominance was accentuated in household-internal communication in all families (see Lexander 2020a), and Norwegian also appeared in Facebook status updates and in comments on Facebook (cf. Chapter 7). Ousmane Diagne reported that texting in Norwegian was a conscious practice to help his wife, Oumou, learn new Norwegian words, and Aida Coly explained her choice of Norwegian in text messages to her newly arrived uncle by his need to learn the language (Lexander 2020a). In SMS exchanges with a Senegalese friend in Norway, Ousmane included features from Norwegian, Wolof, and French, and a similar practice could be observed with a Senegalese friend who had moved from Norway to live in Italy. Astou even said she would regularly, albeit unconsciously, introduce Norwegian words into her group-chat messages in Wolof, despite the lack of Norwegian competence on the part of her Senegalese interlocutors. However, the dominance of Norwegian was also perceived as a challenge against maintaining a high level of heritage language competence. Felipe, for instance, said that he and Rama used too much Norwegian and was concerned that they would forget Joola and Wolof – a discourse examined in more detail in Chapter 8.

Notes

1 We use the term 'Peul' here, as used by the participating family that speaks this language. Other names for the same language cluster are 'Pulaar' and 'Fula' in English.

2 See uit.no/kommisjonen.
3 The competence requirement was increased from A2 to B1 (Common European Framework of Reference for Languages (cf. *Aftenposten* 28 August 2019, www.aftenposten.no/norge/i/EWq2mo/urealistisk-hoeyt-krav-til-norskkunnskaper-for-aa-faa-statsborgerskap)
4 'Because there were some items that I thought like, this is not French, but then it was in fact French, this is ordinary, kind of' (original: *For at det var non ting som æ tenkte, sånn, det her e ikke fransk, mens så va det egentlig fransk, det her e helt vanlig, liksom*, interview data).

4 Visualising languages, modalities, and media

From language portraits to mediagrams

In designing the project methodology, we aimed for a combination of eliciting participants' reflections ('subjective data') and communicative actions ('objective data'). Given our focus on linguistic repertoires (cf. Chapter 2, Section 2.1), our aim was to investigate the ways Norwegian-Senegalese families use digital media to enable participation and social interaction, and the linguistic resources they mobilise to this purpose. We made use of ethnographic techniques by which to elicit both 'subjective' and 'objective' data, thereby drawing on discourse-centred online ethnography (Androutsopoulos 2008, Androutsopoulos & Stæhr 2018) and family multilingualism studies (Curdt-Christiansen 2013, King & Lanza 2016, Zhu & Li 2016). As already discussed in Chapter 2, Section 2.4, we also took inspiration from polymedia research to examine participants' choices of media channel depending on their relationship with different interlocutors and the specific demands of particular communicative situations. To document these different facets of transnational connectivity and their implications for multilingual practices, our data collection made use of a wide range of methods, including visual techniques, interviews, focus group discussions, media diaries, nonparticipating observation, and collection of digital textual data. In this chapter we first outline various types of visualisation applied in our study, namely language portraits, media maps, and mediagrams (4.1). We then discuss the process and outcome of our multi-sited data collection (4.2) and the collaborative development of mediagrams (4.3). We subsequently outline our methods of analysis (4.4) and conclude by reflecting on ethical considerations and challenges encountered in the research (4.5).

4.1 Visualising repertoires

Visualisations have proved useful in the study of linguistic repertoires and to a certain extent for research on multilingual digital communication as well. We discuss methods we used (language portraits) and considered using (network graphs), and methods we developed in the project, i.e. media maps and mediagrams.

4.1.1 Language portraits and network graphs

Language portraits are part of an ethnographically grounded, language-biographical approach to multilingualism pioneered by Brigitta Busch (Busch 2012, 2013, 2017, Purkarthofer 2018). Busch's understanding of a linguistic repertoire focuses on how speakers associate certain linguistic resources with particular socio-biographical experiences and communicative spaces (cf. Chapter 2, Section 2.1). As people's habitual linguistic choices are not necessarily conscious, it is a methodological and analytical challenge to bring them to the fore (Busch 2017), and language portraits are a technique developed to this aim. The speakers are provided with a body silhouette and multi-coloured pens and are asked to map the codes and languages that mean something in their lives. This yields two sets of data: the visualisation itself and a narrative that is 'elicited by the image' (Busch 2012: 518). Busch argues that this narrative enables speakers to articulate what meaning they 'attach to their linguistic resources, their language practices, and their language attitudes in particular, and what significant lived experiences underpin these constructs of meaning' (Busch 2012: 518–519). Furthermore, the participants themselves have the power to define what they consider a language or way of speaking and the labels they attach to their linguistic resources (Busch 2016: 54). The visual mode offers other ways of telling than spoken narrative; contradictions, fractures, overlapping, and ambiguities can be represented in the drawing, whereas the verbal mode favours diachronic continuity and synchronic coherence (Busch 2016: 55).

In our project we used language portraits in initial interviews to elicit linguistic repertoires and language use. The portraits drawn by father and son in the Diagne family (see Images 8.2 and 8.3 in Chapter 8) demonstrate the value of the method for the study of digital communication as well. In addition, language portraits preluded the collaborative drawing of media maps during fieldwork. Our media maps and mediagrams (discussed in the next sections) were also inspired by previous attempts to visualise the interplay of language and media choices in individual communication (Brandehof 2014, Nemcová 2016). These visualisations are couched in language and superdiversity research and aim 'to unravel the social structure of superdiverse diaspora networks through analysing sociolinguistic repertoires' (Brandehof 2014: 28). More specifically, Brandehof's study of Cameroonian migrants in Belgium draws on interviews and ethnographic observation to explore linguistic and media choices towards various interlocutors and to various purposes. Nemcová (2016) draws on interview data to study the personal networks of three students with different geographical and migrant backgrounds who study in the Netherlands and in China. In the example given in Figure 4.1 (from Nemcová 2016), the informant's interlocutors are grouped together by geographical location (Netherlands, Russia), in part subdivided by region or city (Eindhoven, Tilburg). Icons are used to represent languages and

72 *Visualising languages, modalities, and media*

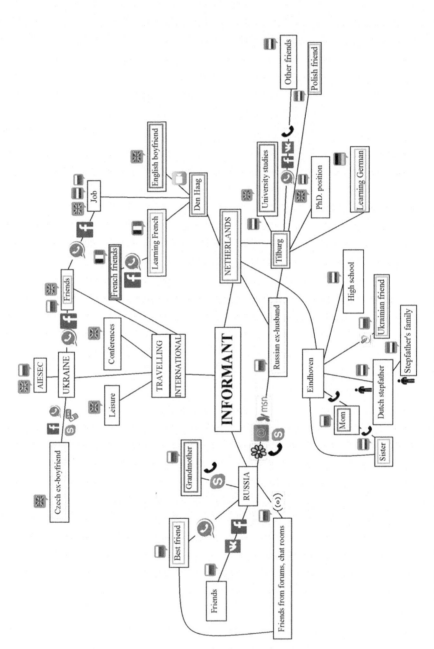

Figure 4.1 Visual representation of Nadya's network (Nemcová 2016: 20)

media applications. Domains of communication are placed in boxes and frequency of contact is indicated by colour-coding. (For further discussion of these graphs, see Lexander & Androutsopoulos 2021)

Both language portraits and network graphs offered inspiration to the method we developed. Mediagrams resemble language portraits and communication graphs in that they visualise one individual's language choices to relevant partners rather than representing the distribution of linguistic features across an entire social network. They differ to language portraits not only in the obvious sense of including distinct modalities of language and media choices, but also by representing media choices directed to specific interlocutors. While both mediagrams and network graphs are based on interview data and ethnographic observation, mediagrams are also compiled on the basis of digital data samples.

4.1.2 Media maps

Media maps are visualisations of an individual's mediated communication, considering their addressees and choices of media channels and languages. While language portraits start with a body silhouette, media maps are drawn on a blank page. Participants were given colour pens and crayons and invited to draw out a diagram of their transnational family communication, using any shapes and colours they would like to. In accordance with these open instructions, the results varied considerably. Some drawings focused on the use of colours, others foregrounded named interlocutors, languages, and media. Some participants let the researcher make the drawing, while providing information they wanted to see included, others did the drawing collaboratively with the researcher. The range of outcomes is illustrated by three examples below (Images 4.1, 4.2 and 4.3). These differences aside, these handmade maps become a reference point for the rest of the narrative interview. In analogy to a language portrait, a media map invites and shapes a metalinguistic narrative, for example by enabling a participant to use shapes and colours as an occasion for sharing language-biographical and techno-biographical stories (Barton & Lee 2013), thereby also providing a point of departure for the collection of digital data samples in a further process (cf. Sections 4.2 and 4.3). Like language portraits, then, media maps used the affordances of visualisation to prompt metalinguistic reflexivity (Busch 2013: 36ff.). The mere process of drawing offered participants opportunities to reflect on and distance themselves from their own practices.

Image 4.1 shows the media map of Aida Coly, who let the researcher make the drawing on her instructions. Her point of departure was the various media channels she used, and then she named groups of interlocutors for each channel, like 'friends' (*venner*) and 'friends and family Senegal' (*venner/fam Senegal*), further dividing between 'siblings' (*søsken*) with whom she used Snapchat, and 'Issa' ('S4.2') and

74 *Visualising languages, modalities, and media*

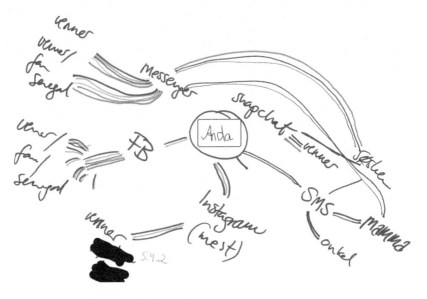

Image 4.1 Media map of Aida Coly

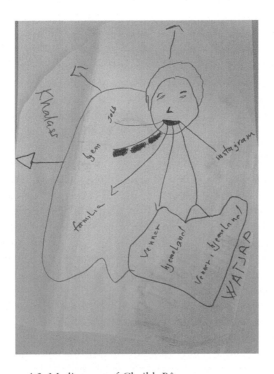

Image 4.2 Media map of Cheikh Bâ

Image 4.3 Media map of Mamadou Bâ

'Awa', two of her three siblings, with whom she used Instagram 'mostly' (*mest*). The coloured lines indicate languages used, with more colours for exchanges with family and friends on Facebook and via Facebook Messenger, and fewer for SMS interaction within the household and with the newly arrived uncle. In later interviews, Aida reported more (groups of) interlocutors and media apps, which were added to her mediagram.

The media map by Cheikh Bâ (Image 4.2) presents his mediated communication as coming out of his mouth and head. A line encapsulates his interlocutors and activities to the left of the head. Closest to his mouth, the names of his wife and two children are lined-up along a vector that starts from the mouth. A bit further to the left come more vectors with the items *jobb* ('work'), *hjem* ('home'), the latter on the same vector with family members, and *familia* – we do not know why he chose this Italian-sounding variant of the word. To the left of the line, delimited from the family space, is the Wolof name of a radio show, *Khalass*, written down by the researcher to represent information provided by Cheikh in the course of the drawing. To the right, three more vectors connect the figure's mouth to certain social spaces and media apps. The items *venner* ('friends') and *hjemland* ('homeland') are framed with a line, followed to the right by the word WhatsApp (in capitals), while Instagram stands somewhat separated.

In Image 4.3, the youngest son in the Bâ family, Mamadou, has drawn a picture of himself, with the lines to his interlocutors coming out of his head, where the researcher has written the names of his sister (blurred here), *Mamma* ('mum') and *Pappa* ('dad'). In fact, the entire Bâ family drew pictures of themselves, either represented by the head or the entire body, probably as a result of it being a collective activity where they inspired each other (they were drawn at the same time, on one single large sheet of paper).

The role of media maps in anchoring the participants' attention and keeping them focussed on the topic of discussion is also consonant with research with participant-generated sociograms (Hogan et al. 2007, Tubaro et al. 2014), which points out the advantages of including a visual depiction of a participant's social network into the data-gathering process. In our experience, this was particularly useful with interviews that were carried out in the family home amidst constant interruptions, such as ringing doorbells.

Overall, visualisation tools like media maps enhance participants' empowerment and agency by letting them choose how to visualise themselves. Other researchers who use similar techniques for the study of family communication report similar experiences. For example, Prieto-Blanco (2016) used a 'circle of reference' to illustrate participants' perspectives on photo-sharing practices of Spanish families living in Ireland. Prieto-Blanco asked participants to divide their network into colour groups based on the intensity of the photo-sharing (share daily life with/do not share daily life with), but some disputed the researcher's categorisation, arguing that it did not correspond to their reality. Kędra (2020, 2021) used an 'interactive collage' to investigate how Polish families in Finland defined family and communicated with those they considered as family members. Kędra distinguished women from men with a silhouette on the colour cards, but the participants did not always adhere to this distinction, as they would for instance use a female silhouette to represent a husband, or group random silhouettes together to indicate a specific number. These two studies illustrate that while the methodology applied by the researcher affects what data participants bring to the table, participants themselves also execute agency when actively working with visual techniques.

4.1.3 Mediagrams

The mediagram idea and term are inspired by sociograms, a key method for the visualisation of social network data (Huang et al. 2006) that is widely received and adapted for the study of linguistic variation and change in sociolinguistics (Milroy 1980, Sharma 2017). The design of mediagrams orients to sociograms for personal networks, which represent social relationships between a core participant (*ego*) and relevant partners (*alter*). We adopt the circular layout and the 'ego star' graphic pattern that is common in sociograms in sociolinguistics scholarship (Sharma 2017). Similar to the use of sociograms in social-scientific research, mediagrams are a graphic representation of qualitative data aimed at making patterns visible and at presenting information during the data-gathering process (cf. Drahota & Dewey 2008, Hogan et al. 2007, Tubaro et al. 2014; see also Hepp et al. 2016 for a similar procedure in communication studies). Differences between our mediagram design and sociolinguistic network graphs concern the kind of represented information and the graphic modalities deployed. Shape, layout, and colour represent different languages, language modalities, and media tools, and the making of the graphs relies on subjective as well as objective data (interviews vs. samples of digital interaction).

Mediagrams resemble language portraits in that they visualise one individual's linguistic repertoire and practices rather than representing the distribution of linguistic features across a social network. However, unlike language portraits they also represent mediational choices directed to specific interlocutors, including the choice of both media and language modality. Mediagrams also enable the analyst to relate single interactional episodes to the broader context of digitally mediated communication in a family, taking different generations, geographical locations, and communication strategies into consideration. In this analysis, we focus on the linguistic and media choices by various family members towards a range of interlocutors – members of the nuclear family in Norway, relatives and close friends, in Senegal and elsewhere – thereby paying close attention to the diverse language experiences of individual speakers. Overall, mediagrams have a more central function in our study than language portraits or media maps because they constitute a pivotal point for data collection, management, and analysis during as well as after fieldwork. The creative process that led to the compilation of mediagrams is a collaborative endeavour that started at the first meeting with participants and continued throughout the data collection phase.

4.2 Data collection

Even though a lot of the data analysed in this book are excerpts from online conversations, our data collection is grounded in the everyday lives of the four families ('offline-first approach', cf. Androutsopoulos 2021b, Tagg & Lyons 2021a). Data collection was carried out by the first author from 2017 to 2019. It included three to five individual meetings with each family and one gathering of all participants for focus group sessions. In addition to the visualisations, interviews, and collection of interactional data, we collected media diaries, carried out observations, and interacted digitally with the participants in order to ask questions that came up during analysis and to keep them updated on the project's progress.

Data collection sessions took place with all members of each family present (if not unavailable for some reason). Even though the term 'interviews' is used for convenience throughout this book, the meetings with the families were not arranged as semi-structured interviews, but rather consisted of a series of conversations organised around the visual input discussed above, which acted as a prompt for narratives and the exchange of ideas. While the main focus was on one participant at a time, other participants contributed to the discussion by commenting, adding information, and asking questions. It seemed important not to confront participants with questions and concerns about 'correct' or 'incorrect', 'good' or 'bad' answers, and equally to avoid having the researcher talk too much and dominate the speech event. Following the portrait-drawing activity, participants were invited to visualise their mediated communication in media maps themselves (discussed above). The rest of the encounter focused on the media map, and some excerpts of digital data were collected on the spot, if possible. We asked for samples of mediated interaction between the participant and interlocutors represented on the drawing, or participants offered such examples themselves. In this process, the participants actively took part in the collection of interactional data and defined themselves boundaries of shareability by deciding which excerpts to disclose and how to share them, e.g., by means of a download or screenshot. In addition, participants were invited to fill in a media diary that came with prefabricated columns for various languages, types of media apps, and interlocutors. Ousmane Diagne, Astou Coly, and her three oldest children did this, and they talked about their notes in the interviews.

The visits to the family homes offered the possibility of observing language practices between the household members as well as their digital interaction with others. Observation was in particular facilitated in meetings with the Diagne family. Since they lived outside Oslo, meetings typically took place during weekends and included family activities to which the first author brought her own family. Observation and several interview sessions were continued when the Diagne family visited the researcher's home for a week during summer holidays. As a consequence, the data set collected with the Diagne family is more extended than data from the other families. The focus group discussions also took place in the first author's home as part of a *Tabaski* (*Id al-adha*, the Muslim feast in memory of Abraham's sacrifice) celebration for all project participants. During the focus group sessions, the participants were given a list of topics for discussion and organised it themselves without a researcher present, adolescents and adults separately. The aim of this procedure was to diminish the influence of the researcher's and the parents'/children's co-presence on the conversation.

As a consequence, the collected data is quite heterogeneous in terms of its production processes, modalities, and materiality. Interactional digital data were produced independently of and mainly prior to the project. It consists of text, audio and visuals, including videos, and comes in the form of screen shots, downloads, and recordings (of voice messages). The rest of the data was produced for the project by participants and

Table 4.1 Overview of collected data

The first column includes the length of recorded interviews per family. The second column features digital interaction data per media channel and respective number of message threads. The other columns state the particular types for data collected by participant. Due to technical issues, one interview with the Bâ family did not get recorded, resulting in less recorded data; it was replaced by extensive fieldnotes.

Family (interview recordings in total)	Family member	Digital interactions (no. of threads)	FB timeline	Language portrait	Media-gram	Focus group	Media diary
Diagne (4h 42min)	Ousmane	SMS (6) WhatsApp (8) Messenger (5)	x	x	x	x	x
	Oumou	SMS (4) WhatsApp (7) Messenger (3)	x	x	x	x	
	Momar	SMS (2) WhatsApp (1) Messenger (1)	x	x	x	x	
	Mariême	SMS (2)		x	x		
	Abdou	---		x			
Bâ (1h 26min)	Sara	SMS (2) Instagram Messenger (4) WhatsApp (1)	x	x	x	x	
	Cheikh	WhatsApp (4)		x	x		
	Nabou	SMS (2)		x	x		
	Mamadou	---		x	x		
Sagna (3h 5min)	Felipe	SMS (1) WhatsApp (7) Messenger (4)	x	x	x	x	
	Rama	SMS (1) WhatsApp (2) Messenger (5)		x	x	x	
Coly (2h 43min)	Astou	SMS (1) WhatsApp (2) Messenger (1)	x		x	x	x
	Awa	SMS (1) WhatsApp (2) Messenger (3)	x		x	x	x
	Ibou	WhatsApp (2) Messenger (5)		x	x	x	x
	Aida	WhatsApp (1)	x	x	x	x	x
	Issa	WhatsApp (1) Messenger (1)		x	x	x	

80 *Visualising languages, modalities, and media*

researcher. It comprises discussion recordings, media diaries, fieldnotes, language portraits, media maps, and mediagrams. These, too, come in different modalities. Table 4.1 provides an overview over the type of data collected from each participant. Because of the participatory research design outlined above, the distribution of collected data across the families is uneven. Quantifying the digital data is problematic due to considerable variation in the ways it was collected (screenshots, downloads, copy-paste), the length of messages (from a single written word or emoji to long voice messages), and the number of messages per thread. Table 4.1 features the number of different conversations in various interactional threads, i.e. the exchange of messages mediated by a specific tool with specific participant(s). These are of different lengths, from one or two messages to long multimodal conversations covering several years of interaction.

Table 4.1 shows that SMS, WhatsApp and Facebook Messenger were the most used media channels for digital interaction. These include both dyadic chats, limited to one particular interlocutor, and group chats, connecting a group of people with a shared purpose, origin, or interest, for instance family group chats or a group for old classmates. Facebook timelines were open to larger audiences, typically a few hundred 'friends' per profile in these families, and shaped by the presence of different social relationships in the audience, e.g., relatives from Senegal as well as work colleagues from Norway. They thus constituted a public arena for a wide array of topics and discourses (cf. Chapter 7 for further discussion). In addition to the recorded interviews of the families, quantified in the table, there was WhatsApp and Messenger contact in between the meetings to discuss and clarify issues that arose during data management and analysis.

4.3 Developing mediagrams

Figure 4.3 shows the first version of the mediagram of Awa, oldest daughter in the Coly family, as compiled after the first fieldwork meeting. It is based on the interview and shared SMS messages between Awa and her mother. Awa is in the centre circle, and her different interlocutors as well as their geographical location are placed in satellite circles, with lines indicating language (colour) and modality (line style). The various media channels are represented by icons (see legend, Figure 4.2).

Awa's mediagram features Norwegian (red), Wolof (green), French (blue), and English (black). A continuous line indicates written, a dotted line spoken language use, and a mixed-type line indicates the use of both modalities in communication with a distant interlocutor (e.g. phone calls and text messaging). Media channel choices for each interlocutor are represented with distinctive icons next to each interlocutor circle.

At this stage, Awa's mediagram was unfinished. All interlocutors she mentioned during the map-drawing task were included, but her language and media choices were incomplete. For example, no data was

Visualising languages, modalities, and media 81

Icon	Media channel
	WhatsApp
	Messenger
	Phone Call
	SMS
	Facebook
	Viber
	Skype
	Snapchat
	Facetime
	Email
	Imo
	Instagram

Line style	Modality
	Written
	Spoken
	Written & spoken

Colour	Language
	Wolof
	Joola
	Peul
	French
	Arabic
	English
	Norwegian

Figure 4.2 Legend mediagrams

Figure 4.3 Mediagram of Awa Coly, compiled after the first meeting

yet available on her language choices towards her aunt in Senegal. These missing bits were identified while compiling the mediagram and discussed at the next fieldwork meeting, where the first author presented the graph to her. Each of the participants was invited to discuss their mediagrams and to comment on selected excerpts collected at the first meeting (for similar procedures see Androutsopoulos 2008, Nemcová 2016). The new information obtained in the follow-up interview was added to the spreadsheet and the mediagram was modified accordingly. The procedure of modifying the mediagram through new interview data can be repeated to the extent the fieldwork schedule allows for it, leading to iterative additions to the data collection and improvements of a mediagram. This way, on-going changes in the mediational practices of a participant can be captured. For instance, Awa already mentioned at the first meeting that she used English and Wolof with a peer living in Germany (also discussed in Chapter 8). At the second meeting she provided a long Facebook Messenger thread from the communication with this peer, revealing that she also used French and Norwegian features and received messages with German features in their texting exchanges.

Once the first version of a mediagram had been presented in a follow-up meeting, it was jointly examined by participant and researcher in order to be ratified, corrected, or complemented. We illustrate this with an example from the second meeting with the Coly family, where Kristin presented to Awa the first version of her mediagram (cf. Interview data 4.1). Awa confirmed the media she used with her friend in Germany and added Snapchat, which she reported they had just started using:

INTERVIEW DATA 4.1: AWA COLY

Kristin   *Og der er både WhatsApp, Skype, Viber og Messenger, stemmer det?*
          And there is both WhatsApp, Skype, Viber, and Messenger, is that right?

Awa   *Jepp. Nå har vi begynt å bruke Snapchat.*
          Yup. Now we have started using Snapchat.

Similar additions were made in interviews with other families. While the first version of Awa's mediagram was based on the media map she drew at our first meeting and on SMS messages she shared with us, this was extended after the second meeting to include additional relatives from Senegal and more smartphone apps (Figure 4.4). These additions were based both on the interview and additional excerpts from digital interaction that Awa shared with the first author. The excerpts can confirm information obtained in the interview and/or lead to changes in the display of language, modality, or media choices in a mediagram.

Visualising languages, modalities, and media 83

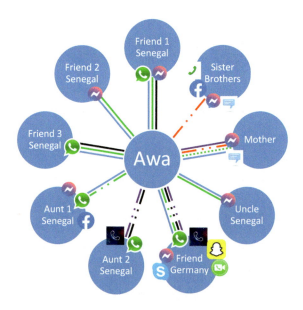

Figure 4.4 Mediagram of Awa Coly, compiled after the second meeting

Working together with a participant to identify missing data and potential oversights by the researcher runs more smoothly when reference is made to a visual representation. Mediagrams can also be used to discuss frequency of interpersonal contact and elicit details on the selection of languages and media applications.

Figure 4.5 summarises the collaborative process of mediagram compilation and use in six steps. At Step 1, participants draw maps in the interview setting and comment on them. At Step 2, textual data is collected. At Step 3, the data for each participant is organised in a calculation sheet with codes for language, modality, media channel, etc. This calculation sheet serves as basis for compiling the mediagram (Step 4), thereby taking note of points that were not clear and/or interesting interactions that the researcher would like to explore further. The mediagram is presented to the participant at the next data collection session (Step 5), where questions are discussed and new digital data that exemplify specific relationships represented in the graph are collected. This new data is used to modify the mediagram, which can be taken back to the participant again at the next meeting. This cycle of data collection, visualisation, ratification, and optimisation can in principle be repeated. At the end of the cycle (Step 6), a mediagram can be used for analysis.

Mediagram analysis draws on contextual information collected during fieldwork, as discussed in the next section. Mediagrams themselves cannot reveal the various motivations and circumstances that shape speakers' mediational choices. These must be disclosed in interviews that focus on

84 *Visualising languages, modalities, and media*

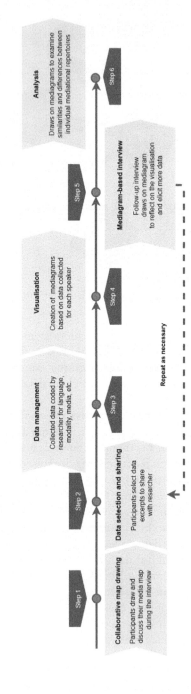

Figure 4.5 The mediagram research process step by step (based on Lexander & Androutsopoulos 2021)

the graphs. Moreover, each version of a mediagram provides insight into a person's mediational repertoire at a specific point in time. A sequence of mediagrams, then, may reveal changes in a person's mediational repertoire. Since mediagrams rely both on objective and subjective data (i.e. message threads and participant reports), they are perhaps more useful for representing repeated, even routinised language and media choices for mediated interaction with specific interlocutors, which have reached a certain level of metacommunicative awareness on the part of a participant. Unusual or even unique choices of mediational resources are represented to the extent they are visible in participants' shared extracts or explicitly discussed by them. In other words, mediagrams seem to work best by setting up a background against which nuances and situated exceptions may be revealed in follow-up exchange with a specific participant. Being part of a digital ethnography approach, mediagrams are not conceived of as a stand-alone tool. They represent equally an outcome of information elicited in interviews (and through collection of digital data) and an input into a subsequent exchange between participant and researcher, which may result in a mediagram being verified, modified, or contextualised.

4.4 Data analysis

The process of data analysis extended throughout the project and took its cues from several research fields, including interactional sociolinguistics, linguistic ethnography, sociolinguistic approaches to computer-mediated communication, and polymedia analysis (cf. Chapter 2). Given the particularities of fieldwork (outlined above), we see the project as especially committed to linguistic ethnography with its emphasis on emic perspectives, the careful investigation of various layers of communicative contexts, the back-and-forth oscillation between data analysis and theory (Barton & Hamilton 1998), and an overall 'openness to complexity, contradiction and re-interpretation over time' (Tusting 2020: 1).

All interviews and focus group discussions were transcribed. Also, voice messages were transcribed, translated, and in some cases discussed with the assistance of our colleague, literary scholar and Africanist Samba Diop. Interactional data and interview transcripts were first subjected to repeated close reading, sometimes leading to questions asked to the participants for clarifications. The analysis of threads of digitally mediated interaction took into consideration ethnographic insight and participants' metapragmatic reflexivity, i.e. the speakers' cognitive and discursive attention to their own and others' communicative conduct (cf. Androutsopoulos & Stæhr 2018). After the analysis of one interaction, we sought other bits of data with similar or opposite findings in order to identify and then double check patterns of language use. To gain an overview over the heterogeneous data set (cf. Section 4.2), a coding system was devised. This featured codes for language, interlocutor, modality and media channel, and various kinds of data were coded. This way, a quote from the interview data was coded in a way that made it comparable to a piece of interactional data or a media diary entry. The coded data was subsequently used to compile mediagrams. We analysed mediagrams comparatively, comparing individual mediagrams within a family and between families, as well as comparing language and media use with various interlocutors represented in one individual mediagram (see Chapter 5). The language portraits were analysed as visuals and as support for, and supported by, the interpretation of interview data (Chapter 8).

In addition, each of the following analytical chapters brings a set of more specific interests, concepts, and analytic categories to the fore. In Chapter 5, our comparative analysis of mediagrams is influenced by polymedia theory and typologies of mediated co-presence, thus leading us to examine carefully the selection of media apps for particular interpersonal contacts and its relation to the choice of linguistic resources. From Chapter 6 onwards, the analysis of digital data samples comes to the foreground. Taking our cues from sociolinguistic approaches to (family) multilingualism, we examine the semiotic resources drawn upon in specific interactions and delve into the family-making processes that surface in specific interactions. For this purpose, we also draw on frameworks on language socialisation, framing and intertextuality, power, and connection manoeuvres as well as morality practices (e.g. Lanza 2004, Tannen et al. 2007, Ochs & Kremer-Sadlik 2007). In Chapter 7, we adapt the concept of polycentricity (Blommaert et al. 2005a) to identify practices of digital diaspora participation. And in Chapter 8, we draw on interactional sociolinguistics and discourse analysis to investigate the role of digital communication in the families' heritage language socialisation and their discourse on linguistic heritage.

4.5 Ethical considerations and other challenges

Working with a minority group and including children as participants pose several ethical challenges. The collection of interactional data, which includes third party material and potentially sensitive information, is also an important concern.[1] Further ethical issues relate to interviewing families together or apart (Voltelen et al. 2018). We now briefly discuss these concerns and how we tackled them in the project.

When doing research with a very small minority group, like the Senegalese migrants in Norway, there is a risk of disclosing the identity of the participants even though they are anonymised through the use of pseudonyms and by withholding information about age, work, and family composition. For example, if we presented one of our female participants as, say, a mother of five, born in 1967, married to a Norwegian-born man, and working as a teacher in primary school in a named district of Oslo, all of this information would make it easy to identify this participant. On the other hand, some personal information needs to be disclosed to the reader, such as ethnicity and religious beliefs, in order to ensure a well-founded contextual analysis. We therefore sought to establish a balance where the level of details revealed allows the reader to evaluate the analyses, while at the same time information such as an participant's exact age and location remain undisclosed. Careful considerations of omitting material that is sensitive, even when shared by the participants, were made to protect them if identified. This is particularly important since the participants met each other at the focus group sessions and can therefore identify each other in the anonymised data.

Another concern lies in the risk of labelling participants as members of a minority group ('Norwegian-Senegalese', 'migrant families') and making generalisations about it, which could, in a worst-case scenario, enhance stereotypes and prejudices. However, a qualitative study like the present one sets the focus on individual practices and attempts to integrate participants' own viewpoints and voices in the representation of the material. Few Norwegians have a Senegalese background, and Norwegians generally know little about Senegal and the languages spoken there. For this reason, the participants seemed to take pride in the scientific interest in their practices and linguistic resources.

The process of recruiting participants affects data collection in terms of participants' expectations and motivations. Using the researcher's personal network for recruitment may increase a feeling of pressure to participate (cf. Staksrud 2019, 'social pressure consent'). It was therefore important to underline the contact persons' freedom of choice to refuse participation at any point of time. No compensation was offered for the participation. Some families approached within the first author's network did indeed turn down her request. It was further important to make sure that the children's participation was voluntary and did not follow automatically from that of their parents. Some children in the families did not take part, without the researcher asking why, and some were not present at the first meetings, but showed up to join the research at a later stage. Both parents and children/adolescents selected themselves which interactional data to share with the project, thus exerting agency in defining the extent and borders of their participation. The use of visualisations in the interview setting was another way of creating an environment where the family members could express their opinions freely. The first author brought up her own experiences from her stays in Senegal and her Wolof studies in the interview setting to create a communicative context for reflections and exchange on cultural and linguistic dimensions.

To make sure the consent was fully informed, also for the children, the consent form consisted of two pages, one with information about the project aimed at the adults and one with information adapted to the children, that could be read out aloud when necessary. Each participant, adult and child, signed an individual form. A central concern in collecting digitally mediated interactional data is the third-party interlocutors, that is, interlocutors who are not research participants but who are important contacts of the participants. It is not necessarily possible for the researcher to build relationships with all of these and make sure their consent to collection of interactional data is fully informed. In accordance with the Norwegian Centre for Research Data (*Norsk senter for forskningsdata*, NSD), the participants themselves got in touch with their interlocutors to ask whether it was okay to share their interactions with the researchers or not. For example, Awa Coly presented an interesting conversation at our first meeting, and before the second meeting she asked her interlocutor for permission to share it with the project. He accepted, and a long thread of messages was then added to the corpus. When Momar Diagne contacted his cousin to the same purpose, the cousin requested to speak to the researcher, in order to obtain the relevant information first-hand. The cousin then agreed that their interaction be shared on the condition of deleting some of the content.

Norwegian was the main language of the interviews, in accordance with everyday language practices in the families, while other linguistic resources were also drawn upon. This choice effectively favoured the first author, whose first language is Norwegian, and potentially increased her discursive power vis-à-vis the participants. However, it also offered to all participants the most favourable conditions for understanding each other. French could have been used for the interviews, especially considering that all adult participants speak French alongside Norwegian. Indeed, the parents in their focus group session would sometimes turn to French in their discussion, but extensive use of French in family interviews would have made it difficult for their children to follow and actively contribute to the conversation. Likewise, Wolof would have had a similar effect on both the children and the researcher, as the latter experienced when Oumou Diagne's sister visited from Senegal and a 'bonus interview' was carried out with her in Wolof. The families' linguistically diverse repertoires were still brought to the fore through their explanations of text and voice messages. For instance, when the Coly children played a love song that Awa had received from a friend of hers in Senegal, they asked the first author to try translating the Wolof words.

In addition to these ethical considerations, other questions of 'microethics' (Kubaniyova 2008) came up throughout the process of data collection, management, analysis, and dissemination, but cannot be discussed in detail, for reasons of privacy and harm reduction. These concern among other things what questions *not* to ask, what topics not to pursue, what data not to include in the corpus, and what data not to publish. As researchers and authors, we need to reflect on these issues at all levels and make informed decisions about what may minimise the harm and maximise the benefit for the participants (Flewitt 2019).

In qualitative research, data collection is seen as influenced by the relationship between participants and researcher (Blackledge & Creese 2010: 86) and the participants' assumptions of what the researcher is looking for. The first author's Wolof competence and cultural knowledge from several long stays in Senegal facilitated the establishment of relationships, but may also have led participants to consider her as particularly favourable to Wolof at the expense of other languages (French, Norwegian) in the family. However, due to the first author's first language competence in Norwegian, and to the societal pressure on Norwegian language learning, participants may also have had expectations regarding the use of Norwegian.

The information given to participants about a project also impacts on how they frame their statements. As an example, while the project aim was to explore mediated language practices, our use of language portraits and mediagrams could potentially have created the impression that the goal was to include as many languages as possible. Felipe presented a reflection on how he interpreted the project as being in favour of multilingual communication:

INTERVIEW DATA 4.2: FELIPE SAGNA

Felipe   *Jeg synes det er, jeg ha'kke tenkt, men jeg har hørt før folk som ... noen kritiserer når man snakker, tar litt av hver av de forskjellige språkene, men, jeg vet ikke men, etter jeg møtte, etter jeg hørte om din prosjekt, jeg synes det er, det er verdt å, jeg støtter det for det er ... det har blitt et språk! Det har blitt et språk. Så jeg synes det er veldig fint.*
I think, I hadn't thought, but I have heard people who... some criticise when you talk, take a little of each of the different languages, but I don't know, but after I met, after I heard about your project, I thought it was, it is worth to, I support it because it is... it has become one language! It has become a language. So I think it is very nice.

Although this was not the explicit intention of the project presentation, Felipe interpreted the project as being opposed to the critique of fluid language practices. His statement above led to a conversation about linguistic resources that probably also affected further interpretation by both participant and researcher. While it is probably not possible to entirely avoid signalling stances towards various questions raised by a study, it is not necessarily undesirable either, as long as there is awareness of the influences the interpretations may have on the research.

Moreover, a goal in ethnographic research is to create a space where participants feel safe and free to share their own reflections. This necessitates building a relationship of trust. In the context of transnational families, it is important to be conscious about the sometimes sensitive and emotionally difficult issues that may come up when family relationships are in focus. One measure we applied to create trust and a safe space was to arrange for the participants to have as much control over the data collection as possible, so that they were not forced into uncomfortable situations. The interviews with the families were therefore carried out mainly in their homes. The methodology in itself was also aimed at building trust and equity in the data collection relation. As discussed in Section 4.1, the interactional work of enhancing trust and reducing the power differential between researcher and participant was supported by using mediagrams as tools for collaborative data elicitations and analysis. It is our impression that the participants found it interesting to be part of the study. After data collection, publication drafts and conference presentations were discussed and shared, and the participants expressed positive attitudes about the fact that their practices would be presented in this book. Marième, daughter in the Diagne family, simply said: 'I want that book'.

The relationship between the researcher and the research participants is not only important for how participants frame their discourse and what kind of data is provided. In the analysis, the researcher's positionality will also affect how the data is analysed. While we cannot liberate ourselves from our background, we can bring in an awareness as to how this might affect the questions we ask, the answers we formulate, and the ways we understand participants' practices. Meeting the participants with respect in conversations with them and in writing about their practices is equally important. We commit to fostering equity not only in our personal and professional relationship with the participants, but also in how we present and use the findings. When Marième Diagne gets this book, we hope she will experience this respect as well as our gratitude for sharing her reflections with us.

Note

1 In accordance with national rules for the processing of personal data (*personsopplysnings-forskriften* §7–27), details of the project were submitted to and approved by the Norwegian Centre for Research Data (Norsk senter for forskningsdata, NSD). From 1 January 2022, NSD has become part of the broader Sikt – Norwegian Agency for Shared Services in Education and Research.

5 Analysing mediagrams

Mediational choices in polymedia environments

Following up on the presentation of mediagrams in the previous chapter, we now explore the mediational repertoires of family parents and children based on an analysis of their mediagrams. Mediagram analysis helps us explore the main questions of this book: how is family multilingualism being transformed in a digital age, how do people engage in digital literacy practices to maintain and develop family relationships, and how do digital affordances impact on the linguistic repertoires of transnational families? The chapter is organised into three case studies. The first focuses on two mothers, Oumou Diagne and Sara Bâ, and examines how they try to balance the pleasure of transnational communication with the pressure to communicate (5.1). The second compares the oldest daughters in the Sagna and Coly families to find out how they manage their social networks through written and spoken communication of a multilingual nature (5.2). The third takes a close look at the fathers of the Diagne, Bâ, and Sagna families, at their media, language, and modality choices, and compares patterns in their transnational connectedness (5.3). We then sum up what the cases tell us about media choice (5.4) and finally, we conclude with reflections on mediagrams as a method of data analysis (5.5).

5.1 Pleasure and pressure: Balancing co-presence

The mediagrams of Oumou Diagne and Sara Bâ exemplify a well-known dilemma: how do we manage our own constant transnational availability to others (Tazanu 2012)? This case study draws on the two women's mediagrams, and additional information gathered in the interviews, to examine their accessibility for transnational communication in terms of different types of co-presence (Nedelcu & Wyss 2016, Greschke 2021).

The parents in the Diagne family maintained close connections with Senegal and relatives in different countries in Europe, Asia, and America. They both described the ambivalence of internet-based transnational communication, which made their lives easier while also complicating them. For example, if something happened to their ageing parents in Senegal, they immediately knew and could provide care at a distance. Moreover,

DOI: 10.4324/9781003227311-5

92 Analysing mediagrams

the internet helped their children maintain skills in the Wolof language through communication with Senegalese peers (see Chapter 8). However, this connectivity also meant they got to know in detail problems of distant relatives and friends that they would prefer not to have awareness of while in Norway. And while long-lasting phone calls in the evening made sure that their children heard Wolof at home, it also blocked the parents from having a conversation with their children. Each family developed their own solution to this dilemma. In the Diagne family, both parents nurtured relationships in Senegal while also seeking to keep that communication from interfering too much with their life in Norway.

Oumou Diagne's account of her lived experiences shows how the increased possibilities of mediated contact can lead to a balancing exercise between the pleasures and pressures that come with transnational participation in family issues. Oumou interacted with her Senegalese family and in-laws on a frequent basis and with a range of smartphone apps (Viber, Skype, WhatsApp, Messenger, Facebook, SMS, phone calls), drawing on both Wolof and French, as illustrated by her mediagram (Figure 5.1, page 95).

Oumou's media choices depended in part on her interlocutors. For example, she used to talk to her older sisters in regular phone calls. She bought phone cards to cover these calls since her sisters were not yet able to go online. Later, they moved on to WhatsApp, a cheaper solution whose affordances for multimodal interaction had an impact on Oumou's relationship with her sisters. She noted that the lack of time pressure when talking to people in internet-based communication, as compared with regular expensive phone calls, had led to less conflict and misunderstanding (see Chapter 6). Oumou's brother in Senegal had internet connection at work, which allowed him to stay in touch with Oumou via Facebook timeline and Messenger. With her brother who first resided in China and then moved to the USA, Oumou used Skype and Viber before they eventually turned to WhatsApp, an app she also used with her nephews and her sister-in-law. These media choices contrast with her Norway household interaction, where texting and mobile phone calls were the main means of mediated communication.

As already mentioned in Chapter 3, Section 3.3, Oumou said she preferred speaking Wolof and writing French. The mediagram demonstrates to what extent this preference affects her interactions. Oumou reported using spoken Wolof to all ten (groups of) interlocutors displayed in her mediagram, and written Wolof with only two of these interlocutors. French appears in written form in messages to six addressees. Oumou's overall preference for the spoken mode, whenever afforded by messenger apps, is evident for example in her exchanges with her brother-in-law, her nephews and her relatives in France. The modality affordances of different media channels were important for Oumou's participation in a wide range of social activities in Senegal. She described how, through the combination of audio and video, she could take part in a family wedding digitally, observing bride and groom on the screen with the feeling of participating, through 'phatic co-presence' (Greschke 2021). Furthermore, she talked about the pleasure of seeing the people she talked to, observing new-borns and children growing up through photos, videos, and calls. She also discussed her transnational exchange with one of her nephews who wanted to marry a woman his mother did not accept. Through 'reinforced co-presence', i.e. increased contact for a specific need (Nedelcu & Wyss 2016), she was able to help the nephew to change his mother's mind about the marriage.

An important event in Oumou's life further illustrates the importance of the polymedia environment and the affordances associated with different media: her father's passing away. One day she received a phone call from her husband's brother. He asked her to hand the phone over to her husband, which she could not, since he was not present. Her in-law refused to tell her why he had called and asked her to tell Ousmane to call when he got back. Oumou got puzzled and anxious. When Ousmane got back, he called from a separate room and was told that Oumou's father had passed away and he, Ousmane, was now responsible for transmitting the message. Oumou was supposed to hear the news directly from her husband, not mediated by the mobile phone. Her grief, Oumou said, felt even stronger because of the distance, and she wanted to be physically with her family in Senegal. She immediately organised her trip, using her mobile phone to contact her manager at work and to buy tickets. As she left, she used the mobile to create virtual co-presence to share her feelings and experiences with her children and husband who could not join her on the journey. The youngest son did not understand what was going on, and why his mother had to leave so suddenly. Every day she made video calls to talk to him. She said that when her son's uncles and aunts showed up on the screen, he calmed down. She felt lucky being able to go to Senegal to see her family members and her father's grave. By contrast, her brother could not come from China and kept making expensive phone calls every day, engaging in practices of reinforced co-presence (Nedelcu & Wyss 2016).

Not only interpersonal interaction, but also social media were important in framing Oumou's experiences and emotions around her father's passing. Just after receiving the news, Oumou discovered that her sister-in-law had shared a Facebook post with a picture of him and a text in Wolof, Arabic, and French to inform about his death. Oumou reacted negatively to this. She thought it was too early to spread the news, as condolences should usually take place after the funeral, and that her sister-in-law should not be the one to share this, certainly not without alerting close relatives, like Oumou herself. Ousmane, however, found the Facebook post an efficient way of letting people know, even if the timing was a bit bad. He shared the post, tagging his wife, and this led to a long list of transnational condolences in the comment section, addressed to Oumou and her family in Wolof, French, and Norwegian. Through the social media sharing, Oumou lost control over the information flow, but at the same time received emotional support from a broad audience in a condensed timespan.

This example shows the extent to which transnational family life takes place in polymedia (cf. Madianou 2019), and the way various channels complement each other in the process of expressing grief and condolences (Giaxoglou 2015). Different media were used by Oumou and her environment to communicate the news, organise the trip, and stay in touch with the family back in Norway. These media choices indicate how different types of presence are constituted and managed in important moments of life. On the one hand, family members' communicational choices had an emotional impact on Oumou. While her closest relatives in Senegal wanted her to receive the message from someone close and physically present, her sister-in-law shared the news in a social media post. Through this post, Oumou's transnational contacts received the news without her contacting them personally, that is, in an instance of 'ambient co-presence' (Madianou 2016). Ousmane increased this effect by sharing the relevant post to make the news available to the family's Norwegian network as well. On the other hand, Oumou made her choices in accordance with her feelings. She wanted to be with her family in Senegal to share the mourning, while also staying in contact with her husband and children in Norway. She chose video calls for this purpose, observing that her son calmed down when he could see the environment in which she found herself. The example illustrates how people strive to enact and control the expression of emotions through exploiting differences in affordances, while also seeking to monitor other's emotions (Madianou & Miller 2012a). This leads to a preference for specific types of presence according to the situation. Here, there was preference for physical presence for the bad news and the funeral, substituted by reinforced co-presence for the brother in China. Reinforced co-presence also was constructed in Oumou's communication with her children and husband while away. Many contacts were informed through ambient co-presence, something that Oumou felt happened too quickly after the father's passing.

While media enable transnational participation in important life events, there is also a downside to always being connected. Oumou had to manage her availability to protect herself from pressure to engage in conflicts and problems in Senegal. For this purpose, she avoided answering specific incoming calls, and delayed or skipped responses to text and voice messages. During a field visit to the home, her sister had come from Senegal for a holiday. As she had constantly incoming, long-lasting calls from relatives who needed advice or wanted to discuss different issues, Oumou commented: 'It's too much'. Through her management of availability, she had avoided some of the solicitation that her sister experienced.

The transnational interactions of the Bâ family differed from those of the Diagnes in terms of media, language, and modality choices (see also Chapter 5, Section 5.3), and the situation for Sara Bâ was different

Analysing mediagrams 95

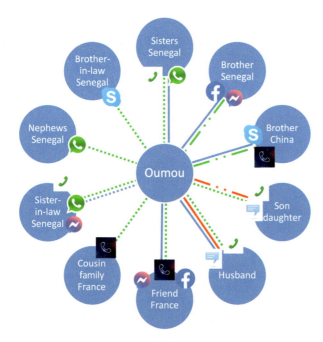

Figure 5.1 Mediagram of Oumou Diagne

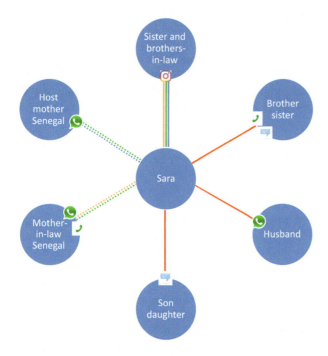

Figure 5.2 Mediagram of Sara Bâ

from that of Oumou, as her family members mainly lived in Norway. Still, Sara shared some of the same concerns as Oumou with regard to her Senegalese in-laws, and her strategy for managing her digital communication involved the choice of media channels. As Sara's mediagram (Figure 5.2) shows, she did not use Facebook Messenger much, although she had a Facebook account. Instead, she preferred to stay in touch with her Senegalese in-laws on Instagram where she posted photos, and her Senegalese in-laws posted comments in Peul, Wolof, French, and English. The reason for choosing Instagram, beside the fact that her in-laws had Instagram accounts too, was that their communication focused on sharing and commenting on photos rather than engaging in long conversations, thus aligning with a typical Instagram practice.

Unlike Oumou, Sara preferred exchanging written messages with her sisters-in-law and brothers-in-law. The fact that she spoke and wrote just a little Peul, the language she considered most important to them, perhaps contributed to her preference for pictures and short comments. Together with her choice of writing rather than speaking (i.e. sending voice messages), this can be viewed as a way of maintaining distance through ritual co-presence (Nedelcu & Wyss 2016). Sara's regular posting of photos of her and Cheikh's children shifted the focus to the in-laws' identities as aunt and uncle and thereby invited a more 'object-related' than 'attention-oriented' co-presence (cf. Greschke 2021). Like Oumou, Sara also expressed concern with regard to being constantly available, explaining that she did not like to be available online all the time. This way, she protected herself from some of the potential intrusiveness that can follow up on ambient co-presence. However, media choices also depend on the interlocutor's media preferences. Instagram was not an option for Sara's communication with her mother-in-law and other Senegalese elders. Their exchanges were only in speech, mediated by WhatsApp and phone calls. Sara also liked Facebook Messenger and used it with the researcher during fieldwork.

In conclusion, both Oumou and Sara navigated their polymedia environments to keep 'the right distance' (cf. Hernandéz-Carretero 2015) with their families in Senegal. Both women had a desire to stay in touch while controlling the frequency and intensity of contact, and each of them developed a different strategy to achieve this. As outlined by Madianou & Miller (2012a), their relationships were framed by the communicative environment constituted by the available media repertoire. Their continuous media use was constitutive of their relationships in Senegal, and their media choices depended on the relationship they wanted to manage rather than on a general preference for specific apps. As discussed in Chapter 2, Section 2.4, communicative choices and choice of modality are important for the construction of co-presence. Sara's preference for practices that can be qualified as 'ritual co-presence' – frequent, short exchanges of the same kind – rather than 'omnipresent co-presence' – being available throughout the day (cf. Nedelcu & Wyss 2016) – may explain why she mainly used an Instagram account to post photos and

Analysing mediagrams 97

exchange comments and messages with her in-laws. Through the choice of Instagram, she balanced the closeness and distance she wanted to keep in these relationships. However, interlocutors' access to media also came into play, leaving no other possibility than a phone call when contacting elderly people in Senegal. In conclusion, the management of mediated co-presence is a complex endeavour. Media channels, languages and languages modalities constitute a pool of resources that participants draw on in order to manage relationships at a desired pace.

5.2 Multilingualism and multimodality: Managing a network of generations

The children's generation, too, is under pressure to stay in touch. They are not expected to contribute financially, but may experience a pressure to comply with linguistic and cultural expectations of their relatives in Senegal. We now consider the mediagrams of Rama Sagna (Figure 5.3) and Awa Coly (Figure 4.4, see Chapter 4), the oldest daughters in the respective families, to examine how they managed their repertoires of mediation as they engaged in transnational family relations. The young women's transnational communication differed from that of Oumou Diagne and Sara Bâ regarding the range of languages, the range of media, and their patterns of correspondence. Rama and Awa used a greater variety of linguistic resources and used several languages in both written and spoken form, and there was less correspondence between linguistic codes and modes. Their range of media, too, was different. For example, they both used Snapchat, unlike their parents.

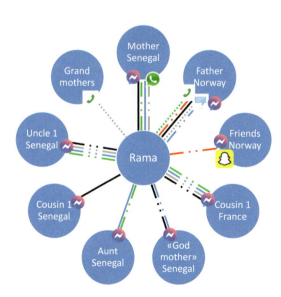

Figure 5.3 Mediagram of Rama Sagna

Both Rama and Awa engaged in transnational communication with people in several generations. The age difference between them and their transnational interlocutors was sometimes matched by differences in language practices. Rama interacted with grandmothers, uncles and aunts, and peers (cousins), in addition to the communication with her mother. Awa interacted with two aunts, an uncle, and a family friend of her own age. They were both expected to stay in touch, and not doing so could lead to negative reactions, as noted by Aida, Awa's sister: 'Yeah, sometimes I forget to answer to messages, then she [the aunt] usually says "you are forgetting me"' (original: *ja, det er noen ganger jeg glemmer å svare på meldinger, så pleier hun å si at du glemmer meg*, interview data). It is not necessarily an expression of disappointment when a speaker in Senegal blames the interlocutor for forgetting or abandoning them, as it is a rather common greeting when time has passed since her last contact. Nevertheless, it is a way of underlining the importance of staying in touch.

Rama reported that she spoke seven languages. Five of these featured in her digital exchanges: Joola, Wolof, French, English, and Norwegian. Rama's mother lived in Senegal, and they were frequently in contact via WhatsApp and Facebook Messenger. They communicated in Joola, Wolof, and French, in texting and voice, and also used some English in writing. Rama's communication with her father took place in 'all' languages, as Felipe said, but with a preference for Norwegian. With her grandmothers, Rama used only Joola, since, as she explained in the interview, they refused to answer if she addressed them in another language. Moreover, she used Joola together with Wolof, French, and English with her uncle and her cousin in France. The cousin in France benefited from Rama's English language skills, while Rama drew on his knowledge of French: the two interlocutors helped each other advance their respective language skills. Another cousin in Senegal saw his communication with Rama as an opportunity to improve his English. Various interlocutors implied interaction in various languages.

Awa's exchanges with her aunts and an uncle, as well as with male friends of the family, all took place in spoken and written Wolof, French, and English. Awa also wrote some Arabic, but preferred Norwegian with her siblings and mother. Not only did Awa have many contacts in and from Senegal, but also communicated quite frequently with many of them in several media and languages. Both Rama and Awa experienced pressure, connected to positive and negative sanctions, to use Wolof and Joola in digital communication, and this led them to draw on parts of their linguistic repertoires that were not otherwise extensively used in their Norwegian everyday life. We observed a rather rigorous distribution between texting in French and speaking Wolof with Oumou, but this was not the case for Rama, who wrote and spoke Joola Wolof, French, and English, nor with Awa, who wrote and spoke Wolof, French, English, and Arabic.

In Awa's case, intensive social contact seemed characterised by linguistic and media diversity. Her digital data shows that she regularly switched between media channels for consecutive speech events with the same interlocutor, and that this often implied a shift in mode. For example, her Facebook Messenger interactions with a peer in Germany features Awa's text messages such as: 'See you on viber' or: 'Can we Skype in 30 mins?' (English in original). This appeared as creating some kind of 'omnipresent co-presence', i.e. constant mediated availability for a particular addressee (Nedelcu & Wyss 2016). Awa's media multiplication strategy was different from that of Rama, who organised her social network by assigning specific media channels to specific addressees and thereby took relationship quality and geographical proximity into consideration. For example, Rama reserved WhatsApp for her closest relationships and Facebook Messenger for more distant ones, whereas Snapchat was only used with friends in Norway (cf. also Chapter 6, Section 6.4).

To sum up, Rama and Awa had diverse transnational networks that comprised several generations and differing language preferences. Compared to their parents' generation, they seemed to draw on a wider range of linguistic resources, even if they claimed that their language competence was limited. The diversity of their family-related networks appeared as potentially important for their feeling of being part of a larger transnational family, especially considering the lack of relatives in their everyday life in Norway, and their use of several Senegalese languages contributed to their feeling of belonging to a transnational Senegalese community, something that could potentially increase their motivation for using heritage languages.

5.3 Media, language, and connectedness: A comparison of three fathers

The two previous case studies demonstrate how micro-practices of everyday digital languaging are constrained by people's individual biographies. Although all connected to family or family-in-law in Senegal, Sara, Oumou, Rama and Awa have different backgrounds for these connections. Sara was born in Norway and got to know Senegal and Senegalese languages as an adult, while Oumou had lived most of her life in Senegal before coming to Norway. Rama grew up in Senegal and came to Norway as an adolescent, while Awa was born in Senegal, but had lived most of her life in Norway. Their mediational repertoires and the differences between them were obviously influenced by this.

Our third case study focuses on the three men who came to Norway as adults and had lived there for more or less the same number of years. We examine their mediagrams and complementary information to uncover similarities and differences in their transnational communication. We first consider variation in their media choices with the groups of interlocutors that they identified, we then turn to language and modality, and finally to their transnational connectivity.

100   *Analysing mediagrams*

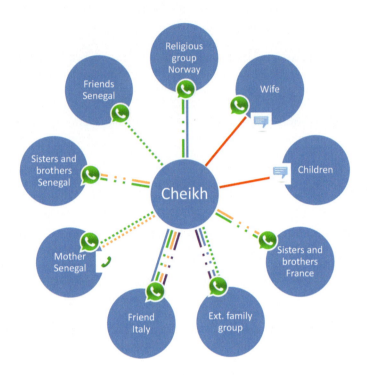

Figure 5.4 Mediagram of Cheikh Bâ

A first finding relates to differences in media choice. Cheikh Bâ used mainly WhatsApp in addition to phone calls and SMS messages, but Ousmane and Felipe had a wider range of media channels. Felipe used nine different channels and Ousmane used seven channels. Ousmane and Felipe used WhatsApp, Viber, Skype, and Facebook Messenger. They also used Facebook to communicate with relatives and friends and to participate in Facebook groups related to the Senegalese diaspora (cf. Chapter 7, Section 7.3.1). Sometimes one media channel was used to organise interaction in another. For example, Ousmane had a brother in Senegal who took care of his house there and he distributed remittances on Ousmane's behalf. To contact him, Ousmane sometimes sent him an SMS to arrange a meeting on Skype. Cheikh did not have a Facebook profile by choice: 'Others check Facebook when they get up in the morning, I check WhatsApp', he said in our second meeting (fieldnotes). Cheikh participated in various WhatsApp groups related to the Senegalese diaspora, and so did Felipe. Felipe also engaged in various projects related to his region of origin in Senegal and was the only participant who also reported email communication with Senegalese contacts. He thus used a variety of channels to manage his extensive transnational network.

Analysing mediagrams 101

Figure 5.5 Mediagram of Ousmane Diagne

For all three men, interaction with their mothers had been mediated in basically the same way, i.e., by synchronous voice communication, since they had emigrated from Senegal. Cheikh mainly used WhatsApp voice messages with his mother, and Ousmane Diagne called his mother once a week on the phone or on WhatsApp. The calls via WhatsApp were facilitated by relatives. Felipe stayed in touch with his mother through phone calls. They all spoke their ethnic language with their mothers, Peul (Cheikh), Wolof (Ousmane), and Joola (Felipe). The Peul voice messages that Cheikh exchanged with his mother also showed features associated with French, like '*âllo*'. With interlocutors of their own generation or younger, communication took place by both voice and text messages for all three participants. Cheikh communicated with his sisters and brothers in Senegal and France in a fluid use of Peul and Wolof, while Felipe interacted with friends, cousins, a nephew, football players, and his daughter with a range of linguistic resources (mainly Joola, Wolof, and French), both spoken and written. His email interaction with business partners was in French.

Ousmane's data showed a clear-cut difference between spoken and written interaction when it came to language use. His patterns were similar to those observed for Oumou (see section 5.1). In spoken interaction, Ousmane used an urban Wolof style that includes French features (cf. discussion in Chapter 3). In written messages, he usually preferred French, with some instances of Wolof linguistic material. In contrast,

102 *Analysing mediagrams*

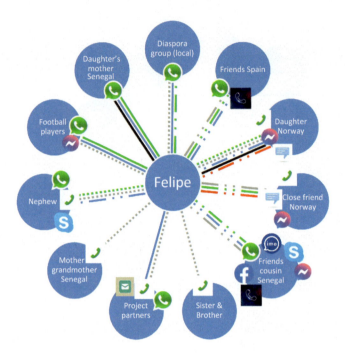

Figure 5.6 Mediagram of Felipe Sagna

Felipe and Cheikh wrote more Wolof than Ousmane did. For example, most written messages in the religious WhatsApp group chat that Cheikh was part of were in Wolof (cf. Chapters 3 and 7). Felipe wrote Wolof and some Joola in his written messages in different media channels. All three men usually communicated with their interlocutors in both writing and speaking, with the exception of older addressees, such as their mothers and older siblings or cousins, with whom they communicated in speech, a choice mainly motivated by the lack of digital literacy on the part of their older addressees. Within their Norwegian households, Cheikh reported that he only wrote in Norwegian to Sara and his children, whereas Felipe and Ousmane wrote and spoke in various languages in digital exchanges with their children. The communication between Felipe and Rama involved a wider range of language resources than the communication between Ousmane and his three children. However, in their communication with close friends, these two men often drew on an even wider range of linguistic resources than in the interaction with family members. Felipe referred to 'friends in the same universe' when talking about interaction which involved several linguistic resources (cf. Chapter 3, Section 3.3.2). All three fathers reported little use of English, a language that was much more prominent in the digital practices of their children.

The three men's mediagrams thus index differences in their degree of connectedness with relatives and friends in Senegal. Cheikh Bâ maintained less contact with people in Senegal when compared to the two other men, but still had important indirect relations, especially through the religious chatgroup he participated in, a close friend of his in Italy, and his sisters and brothers who lived in different countries. Ousmane Diagne had many contacts, but prioritised just a few, especially his mother and his brother who organised remittances for him and looked after his house in Senegal. Felipe Sagna had the most extensive contacts and also expressed their emotional importance. We see, then, that these participants lived their transnational lives by navigating polymedia environments in highly personalised ways. Ousmane, Cheikh, and Felipe had many things in common in socio-demographic terms. They had a comparable level of education, they had been migrants in Norway for a comparable number of years, they were employed, they were fathers with a family, and they communicated with relatives in Senegal and elsewhere in the world. However, their digital language practices differed considerably with regard to media choices, correspondences between modality and language, and their degree of connectedness in terms of interlocutors and frequency of contact.

5.4 Media choices

If we compare all seven mediagrams presented in this chapter, we see an overall divide between media choices in transnational interaction on the one hand, and interaction within the home and with contacts in Norway on the other hand. In transnational interaction, WhatsApp was important for all participants. Indeed, during the course of the project, we observed that WhatsApp progressively became a dominant media choice across all families at the expense of Viber and Skype, and our participants claimed this was due to their interlocutors' preferences. More generally, their media choice was related to general trends in application preferences of the Senegalese community. WhatsApp allows for phone calls, text messages, voice messages, video calls, and the sharing of pictures and videos, just like Facebook Messenger. It differs from Messenger in that users must provide their mobile phone number to be able to interact with others. Interlocutors on WhatsApp therefore frequently tend to be connected by strong transnational ties (Pérez-Sabater 2018: 164). This echoes with Rama's organisation of different media for different interlocutors, namely her use of WhatsApp with closer relatives. WhatsApp was, however, rarely used within the household, while Facebook Messenger was used across all connections. Phone calls were used more restrictively within the household and with older relatives. The costs of making phone calls within Norway are obviously lower than calling Senegal, while for (older) people in Senegal who struggled with digital media, phone calls were the only option for regular contact. SMS occurred almost exclusively in domestic interaction, with the exception of Ousmane's communication with his aforementioned brother in Senegal. This can be related to their messages often being of an urgent nature, as SMS transfer does not depend on internet connection. This finding shows that not only is transnational distance of importance, but also the nature of engagement in Senegal, and the same holds true for Felipe's email communication for business and project purposes in Senegal.

Media choice and media practices were also related to age. Simply put, different generations engaged in different practices with different media. As already mentioned, phone calls were made to elderly relatives, while Snapchat was only used by the children's generation, either exclusively with friends in Norway (Rama) or in transnational communication as well (Awa and Ibou Coly).

A cross-generational similarity in the findings concerns the comparatively higher number of media channels involved in close relationships. This is in line with findings from media multiplexity theory (Haythornthwaite 2005) and polymedia (Madianou & Miller 2012a: 122). Awa, for example, communicated with her friend in Germany on Facebook Messenger, Skype, Snapchat, WhatsApp, Facetime, and Viber. Similarly, Oumou reported using three different channels with her friend in France; Felipe used five media channels with friends and with his cousin in Senegal; Ousmane used four different ones to communicate with his Senegalese friend in Norway. This proliferation of choices within one dyad seemed to contribute to an 'omnipresent co-presence' (Nedelcu & Wyss, 2016), i.e. a feeling of continuous availability towards relatives and close friends. This variety of media was often accompanied by a variation in linguistic resources, another characteristic of close transnational relationships.

5.5 Conclusions

In this chapter, we focused on mediagrams as a method of analysis. As a form of visual representation, mediagrams help the analyst identify at a glance similarities and differences across individual mediational practices. In this regard, their advantage over the textual and numerical data on which they rely is conciseness and practicality. Mediagrams offer various opportunities for comparative analysis of the mediational repertoires of individuals, families, and generations, their changes in time, the social meaning of particular media choices, and implications for heritage language maintenance.

The three case studies illustrated this, showing similarities and differences across different individuals' mediational repertoires. The comparisons of the two adolescents and the three fathers show that regardless of apparent socio-demographic similarities, individuals develop quite individualised mediational repertoires. The case study of the two mothers (Section 5.1), in particular, shows that in coping with expectations of contact, various strategies may be employed. Each participant makes their own choices when it comes to media, modalities, and linguistic resources for relationship building. Through these practices, they construct identities as members of transnational multilingual families. The issues of digitally building transnational family relations, constructing various belongings, and enhancing language development will be further discussed in the following chapters.

6 'Doing family' online

Translocality, connectivity, and affection

During our first interviews, the Diagne couple complained about the communication with Oumou's sisters in Senegal. Since the sisters had not yet started using apps for internet-based communication, they still relied on phone cards to stay in touch. Often a conflict would arise because they did not have the time to explain things properly or finish a discussion before the phone card was exhausted. At a later meeting, Oumou presented WhatsApp messages from one of her sisters who had sent her a video of how the sea had risen into their neighbourhood and destroyed houses. The video came with a voice message explaining the incident. Several changes co-occurred since Oumou's sisters started using WhatsApp: (a) thanks to its message storage capacity, they communicated with less time pressure, and fewer timing-related conflicts occurred; (b) their interaction became multimodal, as they now could send text and voice messages, share videos, and make phone and video calls; (c) this came along with an increase in multilingual interaction, as text messages were written in French and spoken exchanges came in Wolof. The sisters' use of diverse semiotic resources thus became more extended as the timeframe and semiotic modalities at their disposal expanded as well.

Sustaining, maintaining, and negotiating family relationships online is the topic of this chapter. As pointed out in Chapter 2, Section 2.2, current research in family multilingualism is more concerned with how families construct themselves through linguistic practices than with the question of whether languages are maintained or not; doing family is in focus, and language is considered as a resource for this (cf. King & Lanza 2019). Studies of transnational family communication from sociological and anthropological perspectives view the creation of mediated co-presence as crucial for 'doing family' (cf. Baldassar 2008, Nedelcu & Wyss 2016, Greschke 2021). Combining these two approaches, we analyse the construction of family through digital language practices, drawing on theories of family interaction (Ochs & Kremer-Sadlik 2007a, Tannen et al. 2007) and translocality in digital communication (Conradson & McKay 2007, Kytölä 2016). After a theoretical introduction to these frameworks (6.1), we examine how family members co-construct relationships with distant family members at different scales of (local, translocal, transnational)

DOI: 10.4324/9781003227311-6

connectivity (6.2). We then focus on a common feature across different types of interactions, namely the expression of emotions (6.3), and discuss how the diversity of the families' linguistic repertoires becomes a resource for expressing affection.

6.1 Language, power, morality, and solidarity in the family

Recent studies of family multilingualism investigate meaning-making and language-mediated experiences of families where several languages are in use (cf. Chapter 2, Section 2.2.3). These studies ask how families construct themselves through multilingual practices, and how language becomes a resource in family- and meaning-making (King & Lanza 2019). In understanding family-making in digital communication against this backdrop, we consider a number of points: how power and solidarity are negotiated in family talk (Tannen 1994, 2007); how morality is enacted and socialised (Ochs & Kremer-Sadlik 2007a, 2007b); how family ties are indexed, and how interactional routines are constructed (Gordon 2009). Of particular interest across these topics is the deployment of linguistic repertoires in 'doing family', against an understanding of family as practised, not as a given, biological entity (Morgan 1996).

Tannen's (1994, 2007) theory of the ambiguity and polysemy of power in conversational interaction suggests viewing power as intertwined with the negotiation of solidarity and intimacy. As introduced in Section 2.2.3, 'power manoeuvres' are carried out in family communication to negotiate status and hierarchy, while 'connection manoeuvres' modify the degrees of intimacy and solidarity. In conversational interaction, power and connection manoeuvres are often accomplished in the same exchange or even the very same utterance. In this line of thought, speakers' utterances are complex interplays of both power and connection manoeuvres, 'to reinforce and not undermine the intimate connections that constitute their involvement with each other as a family' (Tannen 2007: 46). Through these manoeuvres, they discursively negotiate their identities as members of a family. Our analysis of transnational mediated interaction shows a large portfolio of family member identities that does not stop at the core family –'mothers' and 'fathers', 'daughters' and 'sons' – but also includes extended relatives such as 'uncles', 'aunts', 'cousins', and 'grandmothers'.

The co-construction of family roles can be considered as kinship-oriented behaviour, that is, a practice through which kinship relations are performed and regulated by shared reference to cultural models (cf. Agha 2007: 344). Looking at the digital family practices through these lenses is fruitful. For example, we consider the use of vocatives and terms of address that index kinship in mediated interaction. The norms regarding the use or avoidance of kinship terms are embedded 'in locale-specific metasemiotic formulations of what to do and not to do to belong to the kinship community in question' (Agha 2015: 414). Violating these norms is socially perilous, and perhaps even more risky in relationships characterised by geographical distance, as migrated family members find themselves in places where kinship is directed by a different set of 'locale-specific metasemiotic formulations'. The lack of direct contact can lead to a greater emphasis on the few instances of kinship behaviour that are accomplished between spatially distant relatives. These encounters may also affect morality, as enacted and socialised through family interactions that are 'imbued with implicit and explicit messages about right and wrong, better and worse, rules, norms, obligations, duties, etiquette, moral reasoning, virtue, character, and other dimensions of how to lead a moral life' (Ochs & Kremer-Sadlik 2007a: 5). With digital connectivity, the space in which these interactions take place can be expanded, and even family members outside the household may take part in the family practices of morality.

Critical kinship studies are applied by Wright (2020, 2022) to study family multilingualism. Instead of starting from language, Wright's point of departure is kinship as action and discourse, as a process of exclusion and inclusion. This implies an analysis of how family members talk about family and use kinship terms, how they engage in family routines, and how they negotiate roles and relationships. The vocational and referential uses of kinterms in family interaction contribute to the establishment of kinship, the construction and contestation of normativities, and the shaping of interactions and discourse (Wright 2022: 16). All the above can facilitate an understanding of multilingual language use (Wright 2020: 3). For example, Wright studies the daily routine of mother and daughter walking together to school as a way of cultivating the use of Russian as a heritage language in the family. Such cultivation can be found in digital family interaction, too, for example in repeated patterns of greetings and interactional routines in messaging exchanges and transnational phone calls.

In a different approach, Gordon (2009) emphasises intertextual repetition as a means of binding families together as it directs a hearer or reader back into their memory, affirming interlocutors' shared history and membership of the same group. Building on frame theory (e.g. Goffman 1986), Gordon (2009: 13) suggests that intertextual repetition is a fundamental means of constructing and laminating interactional frames. It both creates shared meanings and contributes to constructing the family as a group and can be understood by the notion of 'familylect'. This concept was first introduced by Søndergaard (1991) in analogy to other -lect terms (e.g. idiolect, sociolect) in a study of code-switching in a Danish family. The term was taken up by Gordon (2009) and later by van Mensel (2018), who discusses a 'multilingual familylect' as characterised by specific linguistic features and code-switching practices or language choice patterns that are shared by family members. A familylect in this sense is an ongoing process under constant interactional negotiation. Hiratsuka and Pennycook (2020: 253) agree with van Mensel in that family multilingualism is characterised by 'a set of shared multilingual practices within the family that play a significant role in creating and maintaining family life', but choose a different epistemological approach. Instead of orienting to the structuralist underpinnings of a -lect paradigm, they advocate a practice perspective and prefer the notion of a translingual family repertoire. Focusing on how language regularities emerge from everyday social activities, Hiratsuka and Pennycook (2020: 253) seek to 'describe the particularity of the multilingual practices within the family, their importance in establishing family life, and their availability as a set of potential linguistic items that members of the family can use'. This approach also raises awareness of linguistic items that are *not* in use, even though they are available. Just as Gordon (2009) focuses on repetition and intertextuality in family interaction, Hiratsuka and Pennycook (2020) highlight the temporary stabilities afforded by language practices, focusing on the repeated use of specific linguistic items. As this chapter will show, a repeated use of specific linguistic items, in particular terms of endearment, is important in digital relationship building (cf. Section 6.3). Affection is closely related to children's moral development, in that morality entails both cognitive and affective competence (Ochs & Kremer-Sadlik 2007a: 7). We will therefore also look at morality in relation to the multilingual expressions of emotions online.

To sum up, language use in the family implies a negotiation and re-negotiation of power and solidarity (Tannen 2007), an affirmation of group coherence by means of intertextuality (Gordon 2009), explicit reference to the moral frame for specific interactions (Ochs & Kremer-Sadlik 2007a), and a use of the family repertoire as a resource (Hiratsuka & Pennycook 2020). Against this backdrop, we first examine how the Norwegian-Senegalese families make use of their linguistic repertoire to negotiate power and solidarity in family relationships characterised by different degrees of translocal presence (6.2), then turn to their use of terms of endearment in expressions of affection and morality practices in various family relationships (6.3).

6.2 Translocal connectivities

Territoriality and de-territoriality are reference points for communication, meaning-making, and identification (Leppänen et al. 2009). This comes to the fore in the families' digital interaction, which encompasses a wide range of translocal connectivities. The term 'translocal' is understood here with Kytölä (2016: 371) as 'a sense of *connectedness* between locales where both the local and the global are meaningful parameters for social and cultural activities' (original emphasis; cf. also Deumert 2014a). In our case, translocality in digital family communication stretches from household-internal interaction among the core family members in Norway to transnational exchange with relatives elsewhere in the world. At the same time, the frequency of interaction and degree of intimacy differ from one family relation to another. An additional parameter is the frequency of physical contact. Family members who live in the same area or former members of the household, e.g. children who have moved out, often meet regularly. Some migrants go frequently to Senegal or to other countries where relatives live, e.g. for summer holidays, while other families cross geographical distance to see friends and family more rarely. Patterns of translocal connectivity are therefore best thought of as a continuum that extends from very local contacts among cohabiting family members (6.2.1) to interaction within the Norwegian context (6.2.2), and finally communication across national borders (6.2.3). Across these sections we discuss the impact of translocality on language choice and heteroglossia, i.e. 'the coexistence, combination, alternation and juxtaposition of ways of using the communicative and expressive resources language/s offer us' (Leppänen et al. 2009).

6.2.1 Mediated interaction in the household: Coordinating family issues

Interaction within the household sits at the very local end of the translocality continuum. It differs from transnational interaction in terms of its topics, often related to everyday household matters such as grocery shopping, picking up children, inquiries about whereabouts, and micro-coordination. The families in our study often used SMS here, sometimes Facebook Messenger as well (cf. Chapter 5, Section 5.4). We start by looking at texting between parent and child. Excerpt 6.1 is an SMS exchange between father (Ousmane) and son (Momar) where household matters are discussed.

EXCERPT 6.1: MOMAR (SON) AND OUSMANE (FATHER) DIAGNE, SMS EXCHANGE[1]

1 Momar	Kommer dokker snart	
	Are you coming soon	
2 Ousmane	Hei! Hent [younger brother] kl 15.	
	Hi! Pick up [younger brother] at 15.00	
3 Momar	Ska møt mamma nå på obs	
	Will meet mum now at [store name]	
4 Ousmane	Henter han selv	
	Will pick him up myself	
5 Momar	Kommer hjem no snart	
	Will be home soon	

This excerpt is typical for mediated interaction between parents and children in all four families, including language choice, which is most often standard Norwegian (Bokmål) or a local dialect (cf. Chapter 3). The local dialect in the area of the Diagne family differs from Bokmål to the extent that text messages where dialect features appear are easy to distinguish.

Non-standard spelling representing Norwegian dialects is typically found among young texters (Strand 2019, Rotevatn 2014, see Chapter 3) and may explain why, even though both father and son used the local dialect when they spoke, only the son used it consistently in writing. In Excerpt 6.1, the words *dokker* ('you'), *ska* ('will'), *møt* ('meet'), and *no* ('now') are all specific to the local dialect. Similarly, in the first interview with the Coly family, Astou asked how her children wrote Norwegian, whether they used 'real words' or 'street words', and the son Ibou answered that he used 'Kebab-Norwegian on all of it', that is, based on spoken practices typical for urban, multilingual areas, as discussed in Chapter 3, Section 3.1.2.

As Excerpt 6.2 shows, Marième Diagne, the younger daughter, used Bokmål to write text messages to her parents, unlike her older brother. Marième is six years younger than her brother and her parents said in the interview that she did not use her mobile phone much. If she ever did, she probably wrote like them and as learnt in school. Excerpt 6.2 is also an example of 'morality practice' (Ochs & Kremer-Sadlik 2007a), as the mother seeks to promote specific routines in her daughter's behaviour.

EXCERPT 6.2: MARIÈME (DAUGHTER) AND OUMOU (MOTHER) DIAGNE, SMS EXCHANGE

1	Oumou	Hei! Hva gjør du etter skole? Du kan rydde rommet ditt for du koser deg. Klem mamma ☺
		Hi! What are you doing after school? You can tidy up your room before you play. Hug, mum ☺
2	Marième	Nei jeg kan ikke rydde rommet [unreadable] for de jeg skal til [friend]
		No, I can't tidy up [my?] room, because I'm going to [friend]
3	Oumou	Du må spørre for du går hjem til fokk. Jeg liker ikke det.
		You have to ask before you go home to people. I don't like that
4	Marième	Pappa sa jeg fikk lov
		Dad said I could

Mother opened this exchange with a power manoeuvre aimed at making her daughter tidy up her room and she ended the very same message with a connection manoeuvre, i.e. *Klem* ('hug'), a common way of closing a text message. At the closing she indexed their mother–daughter relationship, and the concluding smiling emoji contextualises the preceding assertion as a friendly reminder rather than an order. However, when the daughter refused, explaining she had made other arrangements with a friend, a power manoeuvre took over in Oumou's second message. Her previous choice of modal verb, *kan* ('can'), is now replaced by *må* ('have to'), and Oumou explicitly disprefers her daughter's response. In her own second message, Marième referred to another moral authority in the family, i.e. her father, and cited his permission to explain why she did not intend to do what her mother wanted her to do, thus claiming power over her mother's order. This strategy, reference to a different authority in the family in order to manage a power manoeuvre, was also used in other, non-local exchanges discussed below (cf. Excerpt 6.4). Examples like Excerpt 6.2 are documented for the other families as well. In an SMS exchange in the Bâ family, Sara urged her daughter to wash her hands and be thankful for the food she ate when while visiting a friend (cf. Excerpt 6.9). In the Sagna family, our data include a message sent by Felipe to his daughter, Rama, who was looking after her younger sister, reminding her to be responsible and answer him immediately. All these examples were in Norwegian and followed by connection manoeuvres.

We now look at an example of how language choice can be used for a connection manoeuvre. While Norwegian is the dominant language of parent–child texting in our data, there are some notable exceptions, such as Excerpt 6.3 between Astou Coly and her oldest daughter, Awa, who use French, English, and Arabic features in a span of two short messages each.

EXCERPT 6.3: ASTOU (MOTHER) AND AWA (DAUGHTER) COLY, SMS EXCHANGE

1 Astou   *Ok merci*
          Ok, thank you

2 Awa   *De rien*
          You're welcome

3 Astou   Nice
          Nice

4 Awa   *Alhamdulilah*
          Thank God

Astou showed us these messages as examples of their interaction not always being in Norwegian. She seemed very happy about it, and the few words exchanged here appear to signal a strong solidarity between the two. The mother's use of French and her daughter's follow-up, then the mother's use of *Nice*, which is used both in Norwegian and Senegalese everyday informal talk, and the daughter's subsequent closing in Arabic, appear as mutual connection manoeuvres. Amidst the stream of micro-coordination messages, these short expressions of thankfulness stood out in terms of a language choice that appears highly symbolic.

6.2.2 Translocal household interaction: Making decisions and sharing

The composition of a household is dynamic: people move in, people move out. When children grow up, they leave for studies or for work, to make their own households, and migrant families sometimes harbour newly arrived relatives or friends until they find their own place to live. Mobile phone communication sustains 'translocal family solidarity' (Lam 2013) between the household's former and current members. This was also the case in the Coly family, as Awa moved out to study, and the family created a chatgroup on Facebook Messenger in order to discuss household matters. Chatgroups afford multi-party coordination (Nag et al. 2016), and household members make up a manageable number of participants (Ling & Lai 2016). The Colys' chatgroup was called 'Weee Are Famiiily'. Ibou, the oldest son, originally created it to coordinate their summer holiday in Senegal, as they had to apply for visas and arrived on different flights. During the holiday, they used the chatgroup to share videos and pictures of events they found worth documenting, such as Senegalese children singing and dancing or a very young girl who could read parts of the Koran. After they had returned to Norway, the Colys revived their holiday memories through watching these videos and pictures again. The Colys thus used the affordances of a chatgroup to share 'significant moments' (cf. Androutsopoulos 2014a: 6), i.e. particular entextualisations of events that were important to the family itself. The audience for these shared moments is more limited in this case than in the social media contexts originally discussed by Androutsopoulos (2014a). While shared moments on a semi-public Facebook profile are interactively negotiated by an audience by means of likes, reactions, and user comments, the moments shared here in the Coly chatgroup were also discussed face-to-face, for example as the family members (re)watched and commented on these postings while sitting together in their living room, as they did during one of the interviews.

After the end of this holiday, the Coly family continued to use this chatgroup for more practical purposes. This coincided with important changes in family life. The oldest daughter, Awa, moved away from home to study and started using the chat to take part in family discussions. The remaining children still lived under their mother's roof but had now reached an age where they managed their activities on their own, and the time spent together was decreasing. These changing patterns of family life gave rise to new patterns of mediated connectivity. In particular, everyday micro-coordination was losing importance, while digital interaction started replacing physical discussions. This shift is well documented in the ways Awa made use of the chatgroup after leaving home. On one occasion, Awa sent a message to the group chat asking if mum was awake, instead of sending a message directly to her mother. On another, she sent a message to her mother without getting a reply, and then reached out to the rest of the household members to help her get in touch with her. On yet another occasion, Aida shared the picture of a cake she was selling to finance a school trip and asked if the mother could forward the offer to others.

In the following, we examine a chatgroup exchange where Astou, the mother, discusses a car purchase with her children. The exchange starts

114 'Doing family' online

with the mother's invitation to the children to take part in the decision-making (Excerpt 6.4).

EXCERPT 6.4: A COLY FAMILY GROUP CHAT ON FACEBOOK MESSENGER, FEATURING ASTOU (MOTHER), AWA (DAUGHTER), AIDA (DAUGHTER), ISSA (SON), AND IBOU (SON)

1 Astou	[Sends several pictures of a car]
2 Astou	Vil kjøpe den bilen Want to buy that car
3 Issa	👍
4 Issa	Nice
5 Aida	WOW
6 Issa	er det [uncle's] sin bil Is it [uncle's] car
7 Awa	spør [Ibou] Ask [Ibou]
8 Awa	Mamma spør [Ibou] hva han synes Mum, ask Ibou what he thinks
9 Awa	Mamma er bilen automat eller Manuel? Mum, is the car automatic or manual?
10 Astou	Det er ikke [uncle's] bil It's not [uncle's] car
11 Astou	Jeg sa d til han I told him
12 Ibou	Hmm… er det automat elr manuel Hmm… is it automatic or manual?
13 Ibou	Og kan du sende meg linken til annonsen? And can you send me the link to the advertisement?
14 Astou	D r ikke en annonce. Det er [uncle] som kjenner den som eier bilen It's not an advertisement. It's [uncle] who knows the person who owns the car
15 Ibou	Heftig Cool
16 Awa	@IBOU
17 Awa	Hva synes du What do you think
18 Awa	Skal mamma kjøpe den eller ikke? Should mum buy it or not?

19 Ibou	<u>Vel. Mamma sa at onkel likte den</u>
	Well. Mum said that uncle liked it
20 Ibou	<u>Onkel har prøvd den</u>
	Uncle has tested it
21 Ibou	<u>Så ja</u>
	So yes
22 Awa	<u>Ojaaaaaaaa</u>
	Oh yeeeeeaaaah

Astou, the mother, presented the issue, setting the frame of a family conversation and inviting everyone to take part in the decision-making. She sent several pictures of a car and then wrote that she intended to buy it (lines 1 and 2). Issa, the youngest son, was the first to react with a thumbs-up emoji (line 3) and a positive evaluation 'Nice' (line 4), an English word that is frequently used in Norwegian and in Senegalese multilingual discourse. The younger sister, Aida, was also positive, sending a text message with the word *wow*, a feature associated with multiple languages (line 5). Issa followed up, asking if it was their uncle's car (line 6), before the oldest, Awa, entered the discussion, telling her mother in a text message to ask her brother, Ibou (line 7), and repeating this in a more detailed follow-up message (line 8). Of course, Ibou was already part of the family chatgroup and therefore had access to his mother's question. Astou confirmed this ('I told him', line 11). Ibou then entered the discussion and repeated a question asked earlier by Awa (line 9) about the car's gear system (line 12), and asked about the advertisement (line 13). Astou added an explanation about who was selling the car (line 14), and Ibou replied positively (line 15). Awa did not seem happy about this answer and made use of the @ sign as an addressivity marker to put additional pressure on her brother to make up his mind about buying the car (line 16). Ibou finally did so, grounding his view on his uncle's authority: if his uncle likes the car (line 19) and has tested it (line 20), then his mother should buy it (line 21). Awa applauded this decision (line 22), positioning her brother's reasoning as relevant to the family's decision.

Astou's invitation to her children to take part in the choice of car was a connection manoeuvre where she initiated solidarity and framed the discussion as open for the sharing of opinions. Although she would pay for the car and make the transaction, she asked them what they thought about it. She did, however, not pose it as a question (e.g., 'Do you think I should buy this car?'), rather she said that she would like to buy it, signalling that the decision was not only up to the children. While the two youngest children reacted positively to their mother's suggested car purchase, Awa's stance was more ambiguous, and her turns can be considered as both power and connection manoeuvres. On the one hand, she empowered her brother by urging him to answer and eventually giving him the last word. When Awa concluded the episode with *Ojaaaaaaaa*, simulating a cry of enjoyment and happiness (line 22), she signalled that the family had come to a good decision, together, enacting solidarity. On the other hand, Awa was not really *giving* Ibou the role of family decision-maker on this question, she rather repeatedly urged him to make up his mind and state his views, and then framed his answer as the final answer to the discussion. She used her own role in the family to make her brother responsible for the choice and to signal this to the rest of the family. She was able to do this thanks to the chatgroup, even though she lived away at that point. Ibou, now the oldest child at home, refuted some of this responsibility and referred in his reasoning to the authority of an uncle who had previously stayed with the Coly family after migrating to Norway and now lived nearby.

At the level of language choice, Astou initiated this discussion in Norwegian, her children's preferred language of family interaction and at the same time the dominant language in their digital written interaction. Astou aligned here with her children's language preference, and they aligned with her own preferred style in Norwegian, leaving out features from the multiethnolectal style that they often used (as described in Chapter 3, Sections 3.1.2 and 3.3.7). The children knew that their mother did not like it when people wrote 'slang' in digital interaction: 'My brother who lives in the homeland now, he writes slang, I don't like it' (Interview data 3.6, Chapter 3). The fact that the entire discussion took place in Norwegian is not unexpected, since Norwegian was predominant in the family's written exchanges, although Arabic and French features did appear as well (Excerpt 6.3). Had the discussion taken place around the dinner table, it would probably have been carried out in a mixture of Wolof and Norwegian, perhaps also with some multiethnolectal features by the children (Astou often talked in Wolof and Norwegian, while the children answered in Norwegian). Language choice in the Coly family was less easily predictable with voice messages, as these afforded the use of Wolof. The choice of writing for some digital conversations led to Norwegian being used as a language of both connection and power across a wide range of topics.

The translocal connectivity illustrated by Excerpt 6.4 also applied to other members of the extended Coly family, such as their uncle who lived with the Colys when he arrived in Norway from Spain and now stayed in touch through physical meetings and messages in Norwegian, Wolof, and Spanish. Aida saw these exchanges as an opportunity to improve her own Spanish language skills and her uncle's Norwegian skills.

Translocal connectivity within Norway was important to the Diagne family as well, for example in maintaining contact to a close family friend from Senegal who now lived in the same city with his own family. Oumou Diagne and the other mother used Wolof while speaking on WhatsApp (observation data), and SMS exchanges between the two fathers were carried out in a mixture of Norwegian, Wolof, and French (interactional data). The fathers often opened these text messages by calling each other *jaambaar* ('brave person') in Wolof and then turned to Norwegian (including local dialect features) to make meeting plans, for instance to watch football. Ousmane Diagne preferred French, for instance to announce that a package he had bought from Senegal had arrived, and to instruct his friend how to watch football on Eurosport. Their language practices indexed their shared linguistic and cultural background as much as their shared country of residence, documenting once again the importance of Norwegian for Norwegian-Senegalese families.

6.2.3 Transnational family-making: Power, solidarity, and teasing

Transnational communication fulfils a wide range of purposes: keeping in touch with distant family members, discussing homeland news, exchanging festive greetings, sharing experiences. As Tsagarousianou (2016) shows for the case of European Muslims, experiences of remote others are woven into a narrative that constitutes frames through which to situate oneself. Even though Tsagourasianou focuses on mass media and a shared solidarity between Muslims living in Europe, the same dynamics can be observed in transnational family-making. Experiences are shared through interpersonal digital interaction and woven into the family narrative, which becomes a frame for situating oneself as a family member, as an immigrant, and so on.

Regarding the four families, their communication with extended family members extends beyond Senegal to several countries and continents. Figure 6.1 shows the parts of the world where members of

Figure 6.1 World map with locations of transnational interlocutors

118 *'Doing family' online*

the respective extended families were located. The Diagne family (red pins) interacted with relatives in China, Canada, France, Italy, Great Britain, Senegal, and Gabon; the Bâ family (blue pins) stayed in touch with family in Italy, France, and Senegal; the Sagna family (yellow pins) with family and friends in Spain, France, Italy, and Senegal, the Coly family (orange pins) with people in the USA, Germany, France, and Senegal.

Conradson and Mckay (2007) emphasise the emotional labour that comes with transnational migrants' feelings of fidelity and commitment towards family, friends, and community in particular locations (within nation-states) as a defining aspect of translocal subjectivity. The frequency of this contact varies greatly from relationship to relationship, and a balance must be sought between the desire to stay in touch on the one hand, and the material demands that may be expressed by relatives and friends in Senegal on the other. Conradson and Mckay (2007) argue that a 'migrant sense of self' is related to specific localities, but we also find it is related to specific relationships within the extended family. Being an uncle or aunt, a niece or a nephew brought with it specific obligations and rights for the Senegalese migrants, including an obligation to stay in touch and maintain a certain frequency of contact. We will now discuss examples of significant relationships, especially among siblings and between uncle and niece.

An important type of relationship in Senegal is that between a niece/ nephew and their maternal uncle, *nijaay* in Wolof, who is traditionally considered to have high moral authority towards his nephew, in particular (Diop 1985: 56). Ousmane Diagne communicated with several of his nieces and nephews, and together with his wife, Oumou, they even acted as mediators in the marriage-related conflicts of their nephews. In Excerpt 6.5 (from Facebook Messenger), Ousmane acts both as an authority and a support to his niece. The excerpt consists of two distinct interactional episodes. The first episode opened with a simple greeting, *salut*, by the niece (line 1). Ousmane Diagne immediately policed her language style, reminding her that she was addressing her uncle and therefore should use the vocative kin term *tonton* in the greeting, before he replied to the greeting, in the same turn (line 2). The niece would not accept his accusation of 'having a problem' saying '*tonton*', so she explained that she had sent this *salut* out to several contacts to check if Messenger worked. Then she returned to the polite greetings, asking about the uncle's wife and children (line 3). Ousmane expressed that he did not believe her explanation, and then continued the stream of greetings, mostly about the wellbeing of other family members (line 4). The niece insisted on her story (line 5), and the uncle closed the episode quite dryly: *ca marche, oui*, 'it works, yes' (line 6). We observe here a negotiation of power between uncle and niece. Both agreed on the premise that the niece should have used *tonton* if it had been a greeting addressed to the uncle only. However, when the uncle policed her, instead of inclining and excusing herself, she insisted on her explanation, that it wasn't a greeting only addressed to the uncle. The uncle insisted on his version of the story, i.e. that his niece forgot or did not bother addressing him properly. Their difference in language use accentuated the disagreement: Ousmane used only French, his niece both French and Wolof. Ousmane's exclusive use of French can be viewed as an attempt to emphasise his moral authority, an attempt resisted by his niece though.

EXCERPT 6.5: OUSMANE DIAGNE AND HIS NIECE, FACEBOOK MESSENGER

First episode:

1 Niece   *Salut*
          Hi

2 Ousmane *Qu est ce cela veut dire salut ? Tu parles a ton oncle meme si t a un probleme pr dire tonton. J esper q tt le monde va bien. A plus.*
          What do you mean by hi? You talk to your uncle even though you have a problem saying uncle. I hope everyone is well. Talk to you later.

3 Niece   *Je voudrais vérifier si le messenger marche c pourquoi j'ai envoyé beaucoup de salut a différent numéro pour voir si il yaura des réponses car je viens de linstalle* **naka.** [Your wife] *et les enfants j'espère que* **nieup ngissi diam**
          I wanted to check if Messenger works, that's why I sent many hi to different numbers to see if there were answers cause I just installed it. How is your wife and the children I hope all are well

4 Ousmane Ser ga, *depuis q le messenger existe tu viens de l installer.* [My wife] *va bien et les enfants aussi. Salut* [your husband] *et ta mere*
          (spelling error?) You installed Messenger at the time it came into being. [My wife] is fine and the children too. Greet [your husband] and your mother

5 Niece   *J'avais plus de portable pour me connecter je viens d'avoir un* téléphone **mo tax** hier **la si donne def** *applications* **mo tax ma donne** *vérifier est ce que ça marche*
          I didn't have a mobile phone to connect, I just got a phone that's why yesterday I downloaded apps that's why I checked if it works

6 Ousmane *Ca marche oui.*
          It works, yes

120 'Doing family' online

Second episode:

7 Niece		*Salut tonton et la famille j'espère que tout le monde va bien je salut* [your wife] *et je voudrais te dire que j'ai réussi à mon CAP écrit* **nianalma** *pratique* **yombe** Hi uncle and the family, I hope everyone is fine, I greet [your wife] and I wanted to tell you that I passed my written CAP (teaching exam) pray for me that the practical part will be easy
8 Ousmane		*Alhamdou* **sant yalla**. *N oublie pas q t a l enseignement ds le sang et ca ira in chaallah.* [My wife] *et* [my son] *te saluent. Salut ta mere, (ton mari) et les enfants* 👍 Thank God, I give prayers to God. Don't forget that you have teaching in your blood and it will be fine, by the will of God. [My wife] and [my son] greet you. Greet your mother, [your husband] and the children 👍
9 Niece		*Merci tonton* Thank you, uncle

In the second episode, the two interlocutors signal solidarity and support. Their tone and language choices are different. The niece opened with *salut tonton* (line 7), which, in the light of the preceding episode, can be seen as a connection manoeuvre. She went on to tell her uncle she made it through the theoretical exam and asked him to pray for her practical part to be easy. This part, *nianalma pratique yombe*, is mainly in Wolof, not French. Ousmane replied referring to their shared relatives, many of them teachers, and used Arabic, *Alhamdou*, as he would in a prayer, and the Wolof words *sant Yalla*, confirming he would pray as she asked him to. At the same time, he referred to the family supporting his niece, and even added a thumbs-up emoji (line 8). The niece again used *tonton* to thank him (line 9). Here, we observe connection manoeuvres with reference to family solidarity. Since Ousmane rarely used Wolof, we can interpret his choice here as an extra effort to support his niece, while the Wolof words refer to the moral dimension of family unity and thus underscore solidarity. Similar examples of co-construction of family solidarity between uncles/aunts and nephews/nieces were found across all families.

The importance of kinship words such as *tonton* in Excerpt 6.5 is also playfully evidenced in Rama Sagna's interaction with her uncle in Senegal. When Rama was in Senegal and met her uncle, she would refuse to call him *tonton*, and he would try to make her say it. Their Facebook Messenger interaction re-enacted this playful teasing.

EXCERPT 6.6: RAMA SAGNA AND HER UNCLE, FACEBOOK MESSENGER

1	Uncle	*Ma fille coma tu vas* My daughter, how are you doing
2	Rama	*Ça va bien toi ça fait longtemps* I am fine, you, it's been a while
3	Rama	[uncle's name] hahahahahahaha
4	Rama	😄 ☺
5	Uncle	*Oui tres lontan et a l'ecole* Yes, a long time and how is school
6	Rama	*Ça va un peu difficile* It's ok, a little difficult
7	Rama	☹ *mais je suis okay* ☺ ☹ but I am okay ☺
8	Uncle	*Et ton papa* And your father
9	Rama	*Il va bien* ☺ He's fine ☺
10	Uncle	*Dit lui k son grand le salut* Tell him that his older brother greets him
11	Rama	*Tu n'ait pas son grand* You're not his older brother
12	Rama	Hqhhqhq1
13	Uncle	*Si je suis son grand* Yes, I am the oldest
14	Rama	*Tu es le premier née?* Were you first born?
15	Uncle	*Oui* Yes
16	Rama	*Qoiiii* Whaaat?
17	Uncle	*Tu lui demande* Ask him
18	Uncle	*Je suis don [son] grand* I am older than him
19	Rama	*Dacord "tonton"* ☺ Okay, "tonton" ☺
20	Uncle	*Merci ma fille* Thank you, my daughter

122 *'Doing family' online*

The episode started when the uncle sent a text message asking Rama how she was, calling her his daughter (line 1). Rama first answered politely (line 2), then called her uncle by his name only, on purpose, followed by a laughter expression (line 3) and face with tears of joy and smiling face emoji (line 4). After some exchanges, in line 8, the uncle asked about Rama's father and then told her to greet him from his *grand* ('elder'). In her answer, she said that this was not true, again followed by laughter written out in text. But the uncle maintained that he was older than her father, indirectly signalling that she Rama should therefore call him *tonton*. When Rama finally did so, she placed the term in quotation marks (line 19). Uncle thanked her, calling her *ma fille* ('my daughter'), the kinship term he used earlier in opening this exchange in accordance with their relationship: an uncle on the father's side is also called *baay-bu-ndaw* ('little dad') in Wolof. The use of kinship terms is a connection manoeuvre here, even though Rama playfully downplayed her part in this ritual by using quotation marks. Kinship words are a kind of intertextual reference, indexing past situations of physical co-presence and signalling intimacy.

Not all family relationships allow for playfulness. According to Wolof tradition, relations between sisters and brothers should be close, but avoid joking (Diop 1985: 58). Our example here is the exchange between Ousmane Diagne and his younger sister who also had migrated to the North and lived in Canada. Their travels to Senegal were not coordinated, and the two of them did not meet often. However, Ousmane's daughter, Marième, was named after this sister, and with this honour came a responsibility for following up as the child grows up. The sister followed up on this duty mainly online and mostly via Ousmane, and often enquired about her *tuurandoo*, 'name sister', always making use of this kinship term, rather than the girl's own name, when asking for pictures of her and sending pictures of herself. She also sent gifts, and Marième expressed thanks for these through her father. In Excerpt 6.7, the sister expresses irritation that she has not yet heard from Ousmane after she texted him to announce she gave birth to a boy.

EXCERPT 6.7: OUSMANE DIAGNE AND HIS SISTER IN CANADA, FACEBOOK MESSENGER

1 Sister	*Allo tu dors*	
	Hello, do you sleep	
2 Sister	*J'espère que* **yagui ci diam** *car depuis* ma **accouché degoumala nouyoulma Sama tourodo**	
	I hope you are well cause since I gave birth I have not heard from you. Say hello to my 'name sister'	
3 Sister	Missed call	
4 Sister	Voice message (7 secs)	

5 Ousmane		*J etais meme au courant alors q t a mon telefon num. Un simple message gratuit par messenger ou viber et je suis au courant...* I was [not] even informed, even though you have my phone number. A simple, free message on Messenger or viber and I am informed...
6 Sister		Missed call (23.58)
7 Sister		*On a tout fait [my husband] ta envoyé un message alors que j'étais en salle d'accouchement* We did everything, my husband sent you a message while I was in the delivery room
8 Sister		*Moi aussi* **envoyela sms wola messenger mais dou dem khawma lou takh** And me too I sent you SMS or Messenger, but it didn't go out I don't know why
9 Ousmane		*En tt cas c est ma mere juste avant mon arrivee ici a ma grde surprise. Il faut pas oublier que je vis pas au Senegal. Felicitations a vous deux* ☺ ☺ In fact it was my mother (who told me) just before my arrival here to my surprise. You must not forget that I don't live in Senegal. Congratulations to both of you ☺ ☺
10 Sister		*Merci* **Yagui senegal gani** *tu es dejA en vacance* Thank you. You are in Senegal as a guest, you're already on holiday

Ousmane's sister sent two messages (lines 1 and 2), tried to call once (line 3) and sent a voice message (line 4) before she eventually heard back from her brother. In line 5, Ousmane answered quite harshly that he didn't know about the baby and accused his sister of not informing him properly, all in French. The sister tried to call him again (line 6) and then replied, also in French, explaining that her husband had sent Ousmane a text message (line 7). Then (line 8), she continued to explain in Wolof that she, too, had texted him. Ousmane answered, again in French, that their mother had informed him just before he came to Senegal for the summer holiday. He also pointed out that he did not live in Senegal and therefore did not know everything that happened (line 9). His wording here, *faut pas oublier* ('you must not forget'), can be interpreted as either an order or a friendly reminder, and the two smileys at the end of this message contextualise it as more of a connection than a power manoeuvre. Ousmane thus ended up by congratulating his sister and her husband, and she thanked back and remarked he was already in Senegal for his summer holiday (line 10).

Ousmane's sister wrote in a mix of French and Wolof, and Ousmane did not mirror her language use, but stuck to French (with only one exception in his 32 messages to his sister in our corpus). The difference in the way that they pattern their messages seems to create an asymmetry that signals distance between the two, a distance also indexed in the content of their messages. Norms of banter relate to degrees of intimacy in an almost schematic sense in Senegal, and the lack of Ousmane and his sister's adapting to each other's language use can be interpreted as adhering to the prescribed distance between an older brother and a younger sister in adulthood (Diop 1985). The siblings also address each other politely – later in the same exchange we find: *Bonjour petite soeur* ('Good morning little sister'), *Merci Grand Frere* ('Thank you, big brother') – instead of using informal nicknames like the ones we find in the exchange between Ousman Diagne and his cousin (cf. Excerpt 6.11). These are linguistic resources for negotiating the culturally expected degree of distance in this particular kin relationship, characterised by politeness and respect, as well as by the absence of banter.

In view of the status of French in Senegal, the use of French as related to authority and power in the relationship could be viewed as part of a power manoeuvre. However, Ousmane Diagne also used mainly French in his interaction with his younger and older brothers, where he was not supposed to be the authority. In Excerpts 6.5 and 6.7, we see that non-reciprocal language choices contribute to maintaining interpersonal distance. Ousmane did not adapt to his sister's or his niece's mixing French and Wolof, neither did they adapt to his nearly exclusive use of French. By contrast, symmetrical language choice characterised his interactions with his brothers, who also preferred French, and reciprocal bilingual choice of both Wolof and French was observed in Ousmane's exchange with a female cousin (see Section 6.3.3). We thus see how different choices from the shared pool of resources serve to maintain an interpersonal relationship in accordance with cultural norms for specific kinship patterns despite geographical distance.

6.3 Multilingual expressions of affection

An important aspect of the discussion so far is the expression of affection. One of the most significant effects of polymedia is the ability to manage how emotional stances are expressed in interpersonal communication (Madianou & Miller 2012a: 132). Expressing love, in particular, is closely related to the choice of a communication channel (Madianou & Miller 2012a: 91–121). In some parent–child relationships, for example, SMS messages were the only means used for declarations of love, whereas others preferred phone calls for the emotional depth gained through access to the voice channel. Email was considered too impersonal for this purpose, and webcam sessions were not as successful an environment for the expression of love, being felt as less private and more prone to distraction. Madianou and Miller (2012a) claim that:

> the very nature of each individual medium is radically changed by the wider environment of polymedia, since it now exists in a state

of contrast, but also synergy, with all the others (...) in a given context these contrasts become an idiom through which people express distinctions in the form and purpose of communication itself (...) we use polymedia to explore significant differences that are exploited to enact and control the expression of emotions themselves

(Madianou & Miller 2012a: 125)

Following this premise, we see here an opportunity to bring insights from polymedia research into the field of multilingualism and emotion. For a long time, research in this field took it for granted that L1 serves as 'language of intimacy' and L2 serves as 'language of distance'. However, questionnaire studies by Pavlenko (2005) and Dewaele (2004, 2010), nuanced the picture. These authors found a preference for L1 to express emotions even among individuals who were undergoing L1 attrition processes, especially in cases where a later-acquired language had become dominant (Pavlenko 2005: 133). However, they also found that the expression of emotions is related to the process of affective socialisation and may result in the development of distinct affective styles in the respective languages (Pavlenko 2005: 231). This insight fits well the Senegalese context, where French romantic vocabulary is considered very different from that of Wolof, and this difference is exploited by texters to distinguish various aspects of love through choice of language (cf. Lexander 2013). Joining insights from multilingualism and emotion research with our interests in mediated multilingualism and polymedia, we examine how affection is expressed in digital communication across the continuum of translocality laid out earlier in this chapter. We start with exchanges between husband and wife (6.3.1), then turn to parents and children (6.3.2), and finally to communication with the extended family (6.3.3).

6.3.1 Wife and husband

As already discussed (cf. Section 6.2.1), most SMS messages collected with the Diagne family related to household matters revolving around daily commitments, such as picking up kids and doing the groceries, and were cast in various registers of Norwegian. Ousmane, the father, claimed that the choice of Norwegian was intentional and aimed at improving the Norwegian skills of his wife. Indeed, he corrected both her and his daughter when they made spelling mistakes (cf. Lexander 2020a). However, this did not stop Oumou from using French words of endearment in these messages, and her husband followed her in this practice (Excerpt 6.8).

	EXCERPT 6.8: OUMOU AND OUSMANE DIAGNE,[2] SMS MESSAGES
1 Oumou	Hei! Kan du hente [youngest son] pappa *cheri* Hi! Can you pick up [youngest son] dear 'papa'
2 Ousmane	Ok *ma chere* kona Ok, my dear wife

3 Ousmane	Henter [youngest son] i dag	
	Am picking up [youngest son] today	
4 Oumou	Ok ☺ pappa *cheri*	
	Ok ☺ dear 'papa'	
5 Ousmane	*Chou* kan hente [youngest son]	
	Dear, I can pick up [youngest son]	

This pattern was iterated throughout their exchanges, and their reciprocity in the use of French words of endearment can be seen as a repeated connection manoeuvre that underscored solidarity in the couple's relationship. Oumou writes here, *pappa cheri*, and Ousmane replies, *ma chere kona*, making use of both Norwegian and French features. The use of *pappa* 'dad' is particularly interesting here. Its spelling follows Norwegian orthography, but the usage is Senegalese (Wolof: *pàppa*), based on a French borrowing (French: *papa*), to address the father of one's children. The husband, too, follows a similar pattern when writing 'dear' in French and 'wife' in Norwegian. Such fluid use of Norwegian and French was also found in other messages where Oumou expressed affection for her husband, such as: *Du er flink manen min. Je t aime for* ('You are good, my husband. I love you very much') or: *pappa cheri je t aime tu es mon plus for je t adore klem* ('dear papa, I love you, you are my strongest, I adore you, hug'). The Diagne parents drew on French to sustain their romantic relationship through everyday digital interaction, and this use of French is consonant with earlier findings about romantic texting in Senegal (Lexander 2013), thus alluding to their shared history as a couple in Senegal and through the time of separation when Ousmane lived in Norway and Oumou still lived in Senegal. Their texting practices, then, recreated 'couple-centred frames' (Kendall 2006: 424) which defined and maintained their relationship (Gordon 2009: 65). Strikingly, they had also agreed to write in Norwegian to improve Oumou's competence in the language. This resulted in a divergent, polycentric orientation (cf. Chapter 7) that is contingent to the couple's language socialisation and migration history.

There is a parallel between this story and the texting practices of the Bâ parents, Cheikh and Sara Bâ, who themselves brought up in the interview the topic of interpersonal language choice before and after the birth of their children. During their first time together they mostly spoke Wolof, and the very fact they could use this language together was part of their mutual affection. French entered the picture when they started discussing practical details, especially when becoming parents. Later, the need felt by Cheikh to learn Norwegian showed up in his wish to use the language in texting, while Sara often answered in French. They both used Norwegian with their children.

6.3.2 Parents and children

If French was associated with affection in the Diagne couple's interaction, parents in the Bâ and Sagna families expressed fondness for their children in Norwegian and English. In the following examples from the Bâ family (Excerpt 6.9), Cheikh uses Norwegian to express love to his daughter, Nabou, while Sara switches to English to do the same.

EXCERPT 6.9: CHEIKH/SARA AND NABOU BÂ, SMS MESSAGES

Cheikh and Nabou:

1 Cheikh   Hei! Hvordan går det med dagen! Gikk det bra med tanta i dag tidelig? Glade i deg elsker deg ♥ ☺
           Hi! How is your day? Did it go well with your aunt this morning? Love you, love you ♥ ☺

2 Nabou   Bra
           Good

Cheikh and Nabou:

1 Cheikh   Må sove nå. Elsker deg :) ♥♥♥♥
           Have to sleep now. Love you :) ♥♥♥♥

2 Nabou   OK
           OK

Sara to Nabou:

1 Sara   Kose deg hos [friend] jenta mi! ☺ ☺ ☺ Husk å vaske hender og si takk for måten og sånn ☺ ✱ Vet jo at du er flink og gjør det da 😁 ☺ 👍 📿 ♥
           Have fun at [friend's] my girl! ☺ ☺ ☺ Remember to wash your hands and say thanks for your meal and all that. ☺ ✱ I know for sure that you are good and will do it 😁 ☺ 👍 📿 ♥

2 Sara   Love u ☺

Cheikh's messages feature several declarations of love in Norwegian. Sara's SMS reminds her daughter of etiquette while visiting friends. Especially saying 'thank you' after a meal is an important norm for children in Norway. Sara's message shows that she knows Nabou is aware of this norm, thus indexing trust in her daughter. This is followed by a second message, a brief expression of love in English, which frames their mother–daughter relationship and the mother's guidance into moral life-worlds (Ochs & Kremer-Sadlik 2007a: 5) as characterised by love and trust. The intertwining of affection and morality is perhaps depicted by the emoji that follow up on Sara's admonition: a kissing face emoji and a glowing star emoji. It is remarkable that declarations of love in the parent–child relationship of these families draw on English and Norwegian but

128 'Doing family' online

make no use of French. This could be an outcome of the enregisterment of French as 'romantic language', which is valid in Norway as much as in Senegal (and elsewhere in the world), but the avoidance of French in parent–child interaction could also relate to the children's lack of competence in French. Even Rama's mother, who lived in Senegal and arranged for Rama a French-only day every week, switched from French to English to express affection to her daughter (Excerpt 6.10).

EXCERPT 6.10: RAMA SAGNA AND HER MOTHER (WHATSAPP) AND FATHER (MESSENGER)

Mother and daughter:

1 Mother	*Bonne nuit ma Cherie*
	Good night my dear
2 Mother	I love you my baby. Good night
3 Rama	Good night mom love u too ☺ ☺ ☺ ☺ and say good night to everyone
4 Mother	*Salut princesse*
	Hi princess
5 Rama	*Salut maman*
	Hi mum

Daughter and father:[3]

1 Rama	<u>papap eg ei på vei hjem nå</u>
	Dad, I'm on my way home now
2 Felipe	<u>ok:) sees snart</u> ☺
	Ok, see you soon ☺
3 Rama	so don't worrie
	So don't worry
4 Rama	worry
	Worry
5 Felipe	☺ ok, i happy that you let me know ☺
	Ok, I'm happy that you let me know ☺
6 Felipe	<u>Glad i deg</u> ☺, <u>vi sees snart</u>
	Love you ☺ see you soon

In the second part of Exerpt 6.10, Felipe switched from English to Norwegian to tell his daughter he loves her. In this exchange Rama presents herself as a daughter who cares about her father through caring about his feelings, and as a person of good morals. She let Felipe know about her whereabouts and even corrected her own spelling error in English (lines 3 and 4). Felipe in turn adopted her use of English in line 5 and positively sanctioned Rama's previous message before turning to

Norwegian to express affection. Again, we see how affection and morality are entangled in digital family practices.

Another notable feature of the messages between parents and children in Excerpts 6.9 and 6.10 is the use of emoji (pictorial signs) and emoticons (combinations of keyboard signs) to underline feelings that are also expressed lexically in the messages between parents and children, especially hearts and face emoji. Research suggests that both face emoji and object emoji convey affect (Riordan 2017), and that individuals attribute greater emotionality to a message when paired with an emoticon (Lo 2008). A relational function of emoji is to promote feelings of intimacy within a relationship (Kelly & Watts 2015). Dresner and Herring (2010) argue that emoticons can also indicate illocutionary force, for instance contextualise an utterance as a joke (e.g. with a winking eye) or mitigate a face threat. In Excerpts 6.9 and 6.10 above, emoji convey affect and intimacy. Both parents in the Bâ family and daughter and father in the Sagna family drew on smileys and sometimes on hearts and kissing face emoji to strengthen their directly preceding affective expressions. An example for emoji use that seems to mitigate a face threat is in Sara's message to Nabou (Excerpt 6.9), where a sequence of emoji, lexical expressions and more emoji signals Sara's trust in her daughter.

As mentioned at the beginning of this section, research on multilingualism and emotions highlights the role of L1 as a 'language of affection', but also shows that the picture is more complex. In the written digital exchanges of the four families in this study, first languages are actually not used for declarations of love. Recall that Pavlenko (2004) and Dewaele's (2010) findings about L1 as a preferred language for expressing emotions are limited to spoken interaction. However, as already posited by research on networked multilingualism (cf. Chapter 2, Section 2.3), modality of language is an important dimension of linguistic repertoires in mediated communication, inasmuch as spoken and written language skills do not always map together. This holds true in the Senegalese context, where none of the adult participants had learnt to read and write in Wolof, Joola, or Peul, their respective first languages. Their first written language, or language of written language socialisation, was French, replaced by Norwegian for their children. Although it is possible to text 'I love you' in Wolof, Senegalese texters use the 'linguistic means of affect performance' (Pavlenko 2004: 183) offered by Wolof less, especially in the context of romantic relations (Lexander 2013) and also directed to their children. Interestingly, the use of English 'I love you' was used in addressing daughters both by the mother in Senegal (Sagna) and the Norwegian born mother (Bâ). 'I love you' is a particularly popular choice among speakers of different languages (Pavlenko 2012: 461). As discussed in Deumert & Lexander (2013: 538), the concomitant possibility of multilingualism to establish meaningful linguistic contrasts can be used strategically to communicate different forms of attachment. Thus, a clichéd declaration of love in a text message can acquire gravity through the preceding text being in a different language (*ibid.*), like in Sara's 'Love u' to her daughter (Excerpt 6.9), which followed a message in Norwegian where she expressed trust in her daughter's good behaviour. Or, 'Love u' can be used exactly for the reason of being a clichéd coda, having less emotional impact on the daughter than the Norwegian equivalent, which may feel too intrusive in this case. The point is that language modality, and the extent to which different media afford language modalities, are crucially important for the expression of affection in digital communication.

6.3.3 Extended family and beyond

Finding the right balance between respect and playfulness is an important dimension of social relations in Senegal. As mentioned above (cf. Section 6.2.3), joking is viewed as not adequate for certain kinship relationships. But in others, teasing is part of what confirms the intimacy of the relationship, and this is especially the case for cross-cousins (Diop 1985: 61). In this regard, it is revealing to compare Ousmane Diagne's exchanges with his sister and niece, discussed earlier in this chapter (cf. Section 6.2.3) to his exchange with a female cousin who is also married to his brother (cf. Excerpt 6.11). Both of these kinship relationships, cross-cousins and sibling-in-law, are supposed to be close and playful by Senegalese custom.

EXCERPT 6.11: OUSMANE DIAGNE AND COUSIN/SISTER-IN-LAW, FACEBOOK MESSENGER

1	Cousin	*Slt* **TYSON naka wa keurgui mba lep diam** Hi TYSON, how is the family, I hope everyone is well
2	Ousmane	*Madama [Diagne]* **naga dėf?** *Ca va ici* **khana nam Senegal ak mbokyi.** *Et [your husband]? J espere* **migilay topoto bu bakh.** Mrs [Diagne] how are you? We are well, but miss Senegal and our relatives. How is [your husband]? I hope he takes good care of you.
3	Cousin	**Kokou fakman** *la et la petite famille* Hello runaway, how is your little family?
4	Ousmane	*Ca va bien, [Oumou] te salut. Et la mama et mon oncle ? J espere qu ils vt bien* We are well, [Oumou] says hi. And your mother and my uncle? I hope they are ok
5	Cousin	*Gros bisou a [Oumou]* **neko namnako pa ak mere** *ils vont bien dieu merci* Big kiss to [Oumou] tell her I miss her. Dad and mother are well, thank God

6 Ousmane	*Salut a tt le monde et soit plus exigeant avec [your husband], tu le merite et il est chanceux de t avoir comme epouse chere cousine*
	Greet everyone and be more demanding with [your husband], you deserve it and he is lucky to have you as wife dear cousin

Ousmane's cousin opened the episode, calling her brother-in-law by the name of a famous Senegalese wrestler, 'Tyson' (line 1). This is a game between the two, her calling him 'Tyson', him calling her by the nickname of another famous Senegalese wrestler, 'Yékini', or by other playful names such as *Madama* (line 2) followed their family name.[4] She then called him *fakman* (line 3), i.e. Wolof *fàqmaan* 'runaway', meant as a playful term. After exchanging family news for a couple of messages, they ended the conversation.

In our interviews, Ousmane reported his general preference for writing French, reserving Wolof just for specific purposes. These playful messages to his cousin are such a specific purpose, with the choice of Wolof underlining the intimate solidarity of their relationship and echoing the status of Wolof as language of playfulness in Senegalese texting (cf. Lexander 2011). However, the pragmatic effect of their language choices depends on the content of their messages as much as on lexical choice. Their connection manoeuvres are carried out both in Wolof and French, for instance when Ousmane calls his cross-cousin *chere cousine* or, in a later message, *chere cousine et epouse* ('dear cousin and wife'), 'wife' being a label that a man can use towards his (older) brother's wife in the levirate tradition (Diop 1985: 71). The available data for this dyad (39 text messages, two voice messages) consist of such bonding, as Ousmane sends compliments in French and Wolof ('I hope he takes good care of you', 'you should be more demanding with your husband', 'he is lucky to have you as his wife') and there is intertextual repetition through mutual labelling with the same or similar terms, in Wolof and French ('madame', 'runaway'). Exchange of important information is rare here, unlike Ousmane's messages with his sister (cf. 6.2.3). In our interview, Ousmane also underlined the special relationship with this cross-cousin when compared to other sisters-in-law and referred to the *kàll* tradition, according to which specific relationships, within or outside the family, should be characterised by playful teasing. For cross-cousins, teasing is even more systematic than in other relationships and a duty (Diop 1985: 60–61). The child of the maternal uncle (the cousin) has the status of *sang* ('master'), and the child of the paternal aunt (Ousmane) is called *jaam* ('slave') and the teasing plays on these roles (Diop 1985: 60). As a consequence of this, the cousin was allowed and expected to say even more impolite things to Ousmane than vice-versa, as Ousmane also explained in the interview. We can consider the asymmetry in the compliments as related to this. Through their interaction, they contributed to the social reproduction of their family (see Yount-André 2018 for a discussion of other aspects of transnational cross-cousin relations in the Senegalese context).

A similar pattern was found in Felipe Sagna's Facebook Messenger communication with a friend from childhood in Senegal. They opened each of their exchanges with a specific playful insult in Joola, i.e. *coucouli* ('your balls'), and then carried on their conversation in Wolof and French. Adopting a practice from spoken face-to-face interaction to transnational written communication, this *kukoli* game (Lexander & Watson 2022) signalled a strong emotional attachment through repetition at both the level of lexical choice and the sequential position of the ritual insult at the beginning of the interaction. Again, these mutual insults are an important connection manoeuvre playfully disguised as a power manoeuvre, and the use of Joola for this purpose was crucial.

These transnational multilingual expressions of affection went beyond the family. In a WhatsApp group where Astou Coly chatted with her old classmates (examples discussed in Chapter 7), kinship terms were used to co-construct solidarity and intimacy. In the interview, Astou explained that the participants in this chatgroup sent each other messages very often, and that she really enjoyed their conversations. Their community of schoolmates, another social formation of particular importance in Senegal, was revived through these message threads where they teased each other, discussed emotional matters, and called each other by various sorts of names. Some of these were playful names. Astou, for instance, was called 'Oslo', indexing her country of residence, and when she solved a mathematical puzzle posed by another group member, this member called her *La mathématicienne disciple de Mr [Name]*, probably referring to their former maths teacher. Other names referred to kinship. Astou herself addressed her schoolmates as 'sisters' and 'brothers', while other members talked about the group as *toute la Famille* ('the whole family'), and one took it all in: *Bonjour à vous toutes et tous mes chéries épouses, mes chéris époux, mes soeurs, mes frères, mes enfants nationaux et internationaux, Bonjour mes amis*. ('Greetings to all of you, all my dear wives, my dear husbands, my sisters, my brothers, my national and international children. Greetings my friends'). Kinship terms were used repeatedly to confirm the participants' close relations and other terms were used to index aspects of their life trajectories, such as their professions and locations of residence.

The discussion topics also underlined the solidarity of this group. For example, in a long episode that unfolded in 71 messages in the course of half a day, several group members started discussing whether the first love is eternal and ended up contemplating about how life does not always go as expected but is still worth living. Here we observe a process of transnational peer solidarity that resembles the family exchanges mainly discussed in this chapter in its intimacy and in indexing closeness through the use of kinship terms. Even though French is here, too, the main language of discussion, the frequent integration of Wolof expressions and proverbs contributes to the group's informal, playful, and sincere atmosphere. Interestingly, this conversation contains one of the rare examples of Astou writing in Wolof (cf. discussion of examples in Chapter 7). Just like Ousmane Diagne, Astou Coly seems to reserve written Wolof for particular settings and purposes, notably relations of intimacy.

Examples of Wolof for expressing affection through the spoken modality are also found in the data, even for romantic purposes. Awa Coly received a voice message where a young Senegalese performed a love song in Wolof dedicated to her, telling her *ku ma bëgge du dul yow* ('there's no one else I love but you') and *suma xol yow rekk yaa ci nekk* ('you're the only one in my heart'). It is also interesting how this personal message was shared with the siblings, who again shared it with the researcher, as they fetched a loudspeaker and put it on so that we could enjoy and discuss it together.

Overall, we observe a range of playful interaction patterns in transnational interaction with the extended family to express solidarity and affection. The participants use digital media affordances to create a space for multimodal and multilingual practices that sustain their relationships in accordance with culture-specific norms for kinship behaviour (Agha 2007, 2015).

6.4 Conclusions

This chapter examined how the family members carry out digital interaction to co-construct their relationships with family members near and far, with family members whom they meet regularly or rarely. The continuous accessibility afforded by mobile phones keeps family and peers more tightly connected, but may also feel overwhelming and imprisoning for this very reason (Baym 2010: 139). We aimed to assess how this situation, at times contradictory, is managed through language use. We also wanted to delve into shared elements across different types of translocal interaction, namely the expression of affection and morality on the one hand, and the management of the families' linguistic repertoires on the other. Our findings suggest that language choice is an important contextualisation cue in transnational family communication, and that many different degrees of translocal connectivity are afforded by digital media. Some of the examples we discussed are settings of temporary dispersion, children who move out but nonetheless stay in touch (e.g. the Coly family's Facebook group); others serve to maintain links to extended family and peers (e.g. Astou Coly's former classmates chatgroup). The interactional patterns in these exchanges are quite predictable in some cases, less so in others, and the same holds true for the balance between playfulness and distance. Playful nicknames and terms of endearment (e.g. *fakman, Tyson, Yékini, chere cousine et epouse, ma chere kona*) and teasing banter (e.g. *coucouli*) are repeated and to some extent ritualised, contributing to family and peer bonds (cf. Gordon 2009). To this aim, the written use of Senegalese languages, in particular Wolof and Joola, is crucial.

Doing family digitally is a thus a complex multimodal and multilingual process. Our analysis reconstructed a continuum from very 'local' digital exchanges within a household (see also Stæhr & Nørreby 2021) to transnational exchanges and revealed variation in the use of 'local' and 'global' linguistic resources. Norwegian is the main choice within written communication in the home, and other linguistic resources figure in extra-household and transnational interaction. We analysed several examples of kinship behaviour with and without the use of kinship terms, with reference to culture-specific norms of kinship behaviour in Senegal and in Norway. In these exchanges, terms of address and endearment are intertextually repeated and become transnationally shared symbols of a translingual family repertoire (Hiratsaku & Pennycook 2020). Emoji are part of morality practices (Ochs & Kremer-Sadlik 2007a) and connection manoeuvres (Tannen 2007), used in combination with various linguistic features. Our analysis has focused on written family practices, and on how modality affects language practices. This was particularly evident in the analysis of multilingual expressions of affection, in declarations of love as well as more indirect signs of emotion. Family members find a variety of ways of confirming their intimate relationships in online interaction, choosing from a variety of resources to do so. Understanding this digital 'doing' of family is essential if we want to fully comprehend the dynamic and situated nature of family relationships.

Notes

1 In all data extracts, Norwegian is underlined, **Wolof appears in bold**, *French in italics*, English in regular font, ***Arabic in bold italics***, **Peul in bold underlined**, ***Joola in bold italics underlined***. Proper names, anonymised throughout, come in small capitals. Text inserted by the analysts is marked with brackets. Transcripts include original typos.
2 Example from Lexander (2020a: 12).
3 Example from Lexander (2020a: 14).
4 As common in Senegal, this cousin has not taken her husband's family name. Married Senegalese women may however still be addressed with *madame* + husband's name.

7 Transnational families, diaspora practices, and digital polycentricity

The last two chapters of this book examined how family members deployed their repertoires of mediation to maintain and develop personal relationships within the opportunities afforded and constraints imposed by digital infrastructure. This chapter examines how family members engaged in diasporic communication. We follow an understanding of diaspora, digital media, and multilingualism as tightly intertwined. Digital media provide an essential backbone of diasporic connectivity, and language is a key resource in the construction of diasporic identities and relationships. Unlike the main focus of previous chapters on one-to-one communication, we cast here a wider view on how family members created and accessed mediated spaces of cultural participation, and on how these spaces were related to their multilingual repertoires. To this purpose we expand the range of data and turn to small-group discourse (notably in group chats) as well as to the digital publics afforded by social media. Theoretically, this chapter introduces two additional concepts – diaspora (Brubaker (2005) and polycentricity (Blommaert et al. 2005a) – and develops the notion of 'digital polycentricity' by which to identify in the data 'centres' of digital diasporic practice to which participants orient by digital literacy practices such as posting and sharing, commenting and chatting. After introducing these concepts in Sections 7.1 and 7.2, we examine how the participants' digital diaspora practices oriented to various sociolinguistic centres and how these centres constrained their selection of resources from their linguistic repertoires (7.3).

7.1 Diaspora and digital diaspora

Transnationalism (introduced in Chapter 2, Section 2.4) and diaspora are closely related, but not identical concepts. Both emphasise social mobility and translocal connectivity, but diaspora indexes a wider range of social contacts that share a common ancestry and may be dispersed worldwide. At the same time diaspora is a notoriously fuzzy concept that has been defined and debated in numerous waves. In an overview of such definitions, Brubaker (2005) identifies three core elements as constitutive of diaspora: (a) transnational dispersion, (b) a homeland orientation, and (c) boundary maintenance from the majority population. Ben-Rafael and Ben-Rafael (2019) define transnational diaspora mainly in terms of a tension between social integration and contact maintenance. They define transnational diaspora by the

> ability of contemporary immigrants to integrate into a new society without disengaging emotionally, culturally, even socially from their societies of origin. From the outset of their emigration, they are able to maintain direct contact with families, friends and relatives who remained in their homeland or settled elsewhere.
> (Ben-Rafael & Ben-Rafael 2019: 174)

Brubaker's discussion emphasises two points in recent diaspora research: the understanding of diaspora as a category of practice (rather than a bounded social group), and a shift from strict 'border maintenance' to hybridity and innovation. Brubaker rejects an essentialist use of the term 'diaspora' to refer to phenomena that are counted and quantified. Classifying people as belonging to 'a diaspora' only on the basis of their nationality or ethnic background, Brubaker argues, 'occludes the difference between the actively diasporan fraction and the majority who do not adopt a diasporic stance and are not committed to the diasporic project' (Brubaker 2005:13). Instead, Brubaker suggests thinking of diaspora as a category of practice, which can be evoked to make identity claims and articulate expectations and stances (2005: 12). To apply this to the four families in this study, the mere fact of their Senegalese nationality or background does not automatically turn them into a 'diasporic population'. Diaspora is not a given that derives automatically from a sociodemographic category, but a communicative achievement, the outcome of practices by which those who understand themselves as being and acting diasporic accomplish a 'homeland orientation'.

This understanding of diaspora as a practice ties in well with recent sociolinguistic research on language and diaspora (cf. Canagarajah & Silberstein 2012, Marquez Reiter & Martin Rojo 2015, Rosa & Trivedi 2017, Tseng & Hinrichs 2021). In line with diaspora studies in general, sociolinguists point out that diaspora identities and relationships are constructed through linguistic and semiotic practices (Canagarajah & Silberstein 2012), and develop a pluricentric view of diaspora groups and their linguistic practices. For example, Rosa and Trivedi (2017) suggest focusing not on diasporas, as apparently stable groups with fixed linguistic repertoires, but on the role of language in 'processes of diasporisation', such as narratives of ancestry and identity, actively maintained connections to people with common ancestry, engagement with discourses from 'homeland', and so on. Based on a non-essentialist understanding of diaspora as created in discursive practice, diaspora identities are viewed as tightly interconnected to other social identities and linked to a variety of social spaces. Diaspora practices may be intertwined with other social identities and life-projects that point away from diaspora, and they can grow or diminish in the course of time. New research on diaspora and language also turns to heritage language practices that rely on different proficiency skills and interact with multimodal semiotic resources (discussed in Chapter 8).

One aspect of diaspora communication that seems neglected from a sociolinguistic perspective is mediation. Ben-Rafael and Ben-Rafael (2019: 174) define transnational diaspora in terms of contact maintenance, and thus essentially mediated communication, when they say that transnational diaspora members 'create a space of exchange (…) where the retention of original linguistic elements and symbols remains pertinent'. Such spaces of exchange did not begin with the internet. If diaspora is conceived as a category of transnational practice, is must be understood as mediated in principle (Appadurai 1996, Ponzanesi 2020). Media in the widest sense, from private letters to cassette tapes and mobile messages, have always been indispensable in bridging the spatial distance from a country of residence to 'homeland'. But in a contemporary practice-based theorising of diaspora, digitally mediated communication moves centre stage. Processes of cultural consumption and exchange that have been formative for diaspora groups in modernity (Appadurai 1996), such as access to news, pop culture, and religious content from a homeland, are now carried over to, and replaced by, the web. 'All aspects of the migrant experience are now affected by the ubiquitous presence of digital technologies' (Marino 2015: 2).

The relevance of the internet for diasporic and transnational connectivity is well documented in interdisciplinary research (Canagarajah 2008, and see Chapter 2, Section 2.4), including sociolinguistics (Jacquemet 2005, Androutsopoulos 2006, Mc Laughlin 2014). In cultural anthropology, the insight that digital technologies constitute an affordable backbone of transnational connectivity created fertile soil for the idea of superdiversity, well received in the sociolinguistics of globalisation (cf. Blommaert & Rampton 2011 and Chapter 2, Section 2.1). In a seminal article on 'Cheap calls: the social glue of migrant transnationalism', Vertovec (2004) argues that 'nothing has facilitated global linkage more than the boom in ordinary, cheap international telephone calls', and points out that

> The personal, real-time contact provided by international telephone calls is transforming the everyday lives of innumerable migrants. [...] Whereas throughout the world non-migrant families commonly have discussions across a kitchen table (for example, can we buy a refrigerator? What do we do about the teenager's behaviour? Who should take care of grandmother?), now many families whose members are relocated through migration conduct the same everyday discussions in real time across oceans. Cheap telephone calls have largely facilitated this. It is now common for a single family to be

stretched across vast distances and between nation states, yet still retain its sense of collectivity.

(Vertovec 2004: 222)

We already discussed the resonance of these insights with scholarship on connected presence and polymedia (cf. Chapters 2, 5 and 6). In media studies, the notion of digital diaspora (Ponzanesi 2020) explores how diasporic connectivity is formed and transformed within the media logic of global digital networks and based on the affordances of communications media in the household of diaspora communities. Alonso and Oiarzabal (2010: 10) define digital diasporas as 'distinct online networks that diasporic people use to re-create identities, share opportunities, spread their culture, influence homeland and host-land policy, or create debate about common-interest issues by means of electronic devices'. This definition aptly illustrates the difference between digital diaspora and mere transnational contact maintenance. Diaspora engagement may entail political activism related to a homeland regime or an interest in and engagement with the cultural or religious experience of people imagined as 'one's own', as documented by Tsagarousianou (2016) in her research on global 'Muslim mediascapes'.

An understanding of diaspora in terms of practices rather than bounded social groups, then, must entail the crucial role of digital technologies in the reproduction of diasporic identities and relationships and examine how affordances and constraints of digital media shape language practices in post-migration multilingualism. This line of scholarship has only been pursued in a limited way in sociolinguistics, where only a few studies have examined self-expression, representation, and multilingual practices in digital diaspora (Jacquemet 2005, Androutsopoulos 2006, Mc Laughlin 2014, Kluge 2015, Theodoropoulou 2021). What is more, most of this research has not engaged with recent, individualised forms of mobile connectivity and social media in the 2010s. Early digital diasporic networks were hosted on web forums and portals (Androutsopoulos 2006, Diminescu 2008), which persisted into the 2000s and are documented e.g. for the Senegalese and Italian diaspora (Mc Laughlin 2014, Marino 2015). As social networking sites became popular in the early 2010s onwards, easily accessible group pages by and for diasporic and forced-migration populations came up. With the global spread of smartphones came messenger applications (e.g. WhatsApp, Viber, Telegram) that enable the formation of groups of various sizes and communication by text, voice, and video (Vincent 2015). This diversification of digital channels has consequences for diasporic networking, which is increasingly moving 'below' the level of the general public. As the findings presented in this chapter suggest, networks of interconnected sites and applications have emerged (e.g. chatgroups, Facebook pages, video channels), which diaspora groups traverse in pursuing engagement and interaction, thereby scale-shifting between degrees of publicness and privacy. In other words, the former idea of a virtual 'meeting place' for diasporic exchanges is giving way to smaller networks of digital sites that participants move across. We examine in this chapter repercussions of this shift in multilingual practices in diaspora contexts.

7.2 Digital diaspora and polycentricity

The diversification of digital tools and spaces for diaspora communication is fruitfully theorised with polymedia, a concept introduced in Chapter 2 and applied to our analysis of transnational family communication (Chapter 5). We already pointed out that transnational families develop repertoires of mediation that include coordinated choices of linguistic signs, pictorial signs, and media channels in order to carry out social interaction with relevant others. In these 'environment[s] of affordances' (Madianou 2014b: 670), language and media choices can become a more or less stable and expected part of transnational relationship maintenance. What the present chapter adds to the picture is an understanding of how polymedia environments enable not just family-level connectivity, but also other kinds of social interaction and discursive participation related to homeland society and culture. To explore this, we draw on the sociolinguistic notion of polycentricity and adapt it to the conditions of transnational digital communication.

Polycentricity is a theoretical metaphor based on the notion that communicative practices are spatially located and shaped by multiple sociolinguistic orientations (Blommaert 2010, Pietikäinen 2010, Koven & Simões Marques 2015, Stæhr 2016). In sociolinguistics the term has two related, but distinct readings. The first is concerned with the study of polycentric languages, i.e. languages that have standard language status in two or more nation states and develop nation-specific norms. Languages such as English, French, German, or Spanish, also termed pluricentric (Clyne 1992), develop distinct standard varieties by nation state (e.g. German in Germany, Austria, and Switzerland), which are differentiated by e.g. phonological or lexical features that constitute distinct norms for the respective national speech community. Relevant to our analysis is the second reading, where the spatial metaphor of 'centre' refers not to a nation state's imposition of a linguistic norm, but to a wide range of normative authorities, each coupled with (or instantiated in) a specific set of social spaces (Blommaert et al. 2005a). This second sense was originally developed in a sociolinguistic ethnography of Brugse Poort, an immigrant quarter in Ghent, Belgium, where the researchers identified centres such as the playground, the municipal school, the mosque, or the neighbourhood's cultural centre, each determining expectations of linguistic conduct for communication within this centre. This way, the multilingual repertoires of the residents of Brugse Poort are regimented not by a single normative force (say, the Belgian state), but by the various informal and institutional centres that are relevant to the residents' daily life.

Theoretically, polycentricity is closely related to the notion of orders of indexicality, i.e. hierarchies of sociolinguistic value pertaining to various registers of language within a linguistic repertoire. Blommaert (2005) defines orders of indexicality as 'systematically reproduced, stratified meanings often called "norms" or "rules" of language and always typically associated with particular shapes of language (i. e. the "standard", the prestige variety, the usual way of having conversation with my friends etc.)'. Polycentricity thus asserts that urban spaces are shaped by multiple and complex sociolinguistic orientations. A neighbourhood can be thought of as 'a patch-work of very different spaces, places and activities, often functioning as centres imposing or offering particular interactional regimes to their users' (Blommaert et al. 2005a: 213). The authors add:

> All neighbourhoods have multiple 'centres' which impose different orders of indexicality on their users – different codes and norms as to what is accepted as 'right', 'good', 'marked', 'unexpected', 'normal' and 'special' semiotic behaviour [...]. Understanding multilingualism in such neighbourhoods therefore requires an *understanding of the connections between different centres and their orders*. What counts as 'good' communicative behaviour in school may not qualify as such in the mosque and what is acquired successfully, and performed as 'successfully acquired', in one centre may be subsequently disqualified in another.
>
> (Blommaert et al. 2005a: 207, original emphasis)

Sociolinguistic centres may be constituted by authorities of various sorts, including influential individuals, collectives, or 'abstract entities or ideas' (Blommaert 2010: 39). Each centre within a polycentric system constitutes a language-ideological model, to which speakers orient in everyday practice. For example, the municipal school and the mosque encapsulate very different expectations of appropriate language use, including both language choice and embedded choices in the communicative process, e.g. regarding linguistic politeness, and these expectations are grounded in different social systems, i.e. the nation state vs. religion. As a result, polycentricity offers an understanding of speakers' versatile linguistic choices as they 'enter' (physically or communicatively) and engage within different sociolinguistic centres, and an understanding of how conflict between various centres may be indexed by heteroglossic discourse (manifested as code-switching or style shifting) For example, Stæhr (2016) shows how young people strategically deploy language style to orient towards various centres, such as schoolteachers, peer group members, or pop stars, thereby not always adopting the register expected within a centre. In addition, polycentricity entails that the status and value of a given register of language is specific to particular centres and may shift as speakers move from centre to centre. This is already evident in this study so far. Even though our analysis focused more or less exclusively on communication within the extended transnational families, the tension between Norwegian, French, and Wolof in the family members' everyday mediated exchanges has been noted. Using Norwegian as a base language of (mediated) interaction within the core family is a clear orientation to Norway as a sociolinguistic centre at the expense of Wolof and especially French, whose value to the families is an entirely new one post-migration.

Subsequent research on multilingualism, migration, and globalisation has taken polycentricity into two directions. The first focuses on polycentric languages, exploring their usage and status in different social arenas, often translocally distributed ones. For example, registers of Sámi in Finland take on different indexical values in education, tourism, the media, and rural environments, all of which constitute 'multiple, simultaneous, and sometimes conflicting points of navigation' for Sámi speakers (Pietikäinen 2010: 86). Portuguese is valued differently as a migrant language in France, as opposed to a national language in Portugal (Keating et al. 2015). In this reading, a centre ascribes different functions and values to (registers of) a given language. A second reading focuses on speakers' polycentric practices in various social spaces, charting out how individuals or groups orient to multiple centres of authority. For example, classroom and playground constitute distinct centres for elementary school children (Karrebæk 2016), likewise with school and online communication for young adults (Li & Juffermans 2015). Both lines of polycentricity analysis share an emphasis on the ideological stratification of linguistic repertoires; the spatial dimension of communicative events; and the link between polycentricity and superdiversity (Li & Juffermans 2015: 33). Some of this work examines digital communication as one among several centres (Li & Juffermans 2015), or as a discourse site where speakers' orientations to various centres may be displayed to audiences (Koven & Simões Marques 2015). Closest to our approach in this book is Stæhr's (2016) study of a social media network, Facebook, as polycentric in itself, in which participants draw on written-language variation to index a mainstream and youth-cultural orientation, respectively. This analysis, supported by our findings, offers evidence against the assumption that a social media platform would constitute a centre in its entirety (Blommaert 2013).

Adapting these ideas to the study of digital language and literacy practices in transnational diaspora, we coin the term 'digital polycentricity' (Androutsopoulos & Lexander 2021) to investigate how the diversity of digital language practices is organised across various digital spaces and audiences. We examine how family members orient to various centres as they traverse digital spaces, and how they mobilise features from their semiotic repertoires to engage with different discourses and practices, in diaspora and beyond. As will be seen below, a 'centre' is defined not by its technological infrastructure, but by the way diasporic connectivity is organised. In other words, a centre is not a particular social media platform (say, Facebook), but social media platforms and mobile communication apps are drawn together to provide infrastructure for e.g., a centre of religious discourse. One concern of this analysis will be how digital diasporic centres identified in the analysis relate to diasporic centres that can be expected to instantiate in physical spaces. Another concern, in line with the entire book, is to uncover relationships between digital activities and multilingual repertoires beyond family communication. We ask how members of Senegalese-Norwegian families mobilise resources from their linguistic repertoires to engage with diaspora discourses (e.g. politics, religion, family life in the homeland), and how their choices pattern together with selections at the level of digital spaces, content, genre, and semiotic means (e.g. emoji, memes, shared videos, etc.).

7.3 Polycentric participation: A kaleidoscope of practices

A note on the methodological and analytical specifics of this chapter seems appropriate at this point. The two previous chapters have almost exclusively focused on translocal and transnational exchanges in interpersonal dyads. By contrast, the interest in diasporic connectivity brings into relief group-level communication and public spheres enabled by social media platforms. This is a direct consequence of the idea that (digital) diaspora is not limited to relevant individuals but extends to participation and engagement in political, social, and cultural discourses relevant to a homeland. To uncover this layer of digital connectivity, we examine additional textual data shared by participants, including dyadic chats, chatgroup logfiles, and social media profiles (Table 7.1). Three participants offered excerpts from chatgroups (Cheikh Bâ, Felipe Sagna, and Astou Coly). Seven participants offered Facebook 'friend' status to the first author (on a dedicated researcher profile), enabling us to examine their personal profiles in terms of diaspora discourses and the semiotic resources associated with these. The decisive difference between the three types of data listed on Table 7.1 is not so much in the affordances of various platforms and applications (e.g. WhatsApp, Facebook Messenger, Viber, SMS), but in the audiences they constitute. While dyadic chats are by definition limited to one particular interlocutor, group chats are small groups whose members, while not always mutually acquainted, share a joint purpose, origin, or interest. Facebook profiles are open to larger audiences (in this data, a few hundred 'friends' per profile). They constitute a public arena for an array of topics and discourses, and are shaped by context collapse (Androutsopoulos 2014b), i.e. the presence of different social relationships in the audience (e.g. relatives from Senegal and work colleagues from Norway). Digital practices such as the choice of profile images, sharing media content, or consumption of online videos all underscore the importance for participants of a 'real or imagined "homeland" as an authoritative source of value, identity and loyalty' (Brubaker 2005: 5).

Table 7.1 Data for digital diaspora analysis by participant, platform, and audience

Participant	Dyadic chats	Group chats	Facebook profiles
Oumou Diagne	✓		✓
Ousmane Diagne	✓		✓
Momar Diagne	✓		✓
Cheikh Bâ		✓	
Felipe Sagna	✓	✓	✓
Astou Coly		✓	✓
Awa Coly	✓		✓
Aida Coly	✓		✓

To identify diaspora practices and their sociolinguistic centres in this data, qualitative analysis followed up on the idea that a centre could be identified as a distinct pattern, or homology, across these analytical levels. The first is discourse, operationalised in terms of thematic fields (e.g. family, politics, religion) with concomitant spatial orientations (Senegal, Norway, elsewhere). Second is the level of audience, drawing on the distinction introduced above between dyadic, group-level, and public social media communication. A third level comprises *mediational means*, i.e. the platforms and channels that form the backdrop for the production and reception of communicative acts within a given discourse. To give an example pre-empting the analysis below, media choices in the centre of religious discourse differ from those of diasporic sociality. The former include visiting YouTube channels that host religious sermons from Senegal, whereas the latter concentrate on messenger applications and interpersonal talk. The fourth level of analysis is that of the *resources* that participants draw on as they engage in digital diaspora practices. Language choices are the focus of attention here, but the analysis also orients to genres and other semiotic choices as afforded by each media channel.

These four levels of analysis were both the outcome and vehicle of iterative readings and viewings of the data, supported by interview-based ethnographic information, and followed by qualitative sociolinguistic microanalysis of selected data excerpts. Relevant media sites (especially the participants' social media profiles and other social media channels indexed by content in the profiles) were repeatedly revisited to identify the flow of digital messages and the choice of linguistic resources, taking into consideration the practices that the participants accomplished on each media site. Our analysis also focused on practice-based connections between different media sites and technologies (cf. Marino 2015: 8), for example by following links from profiles and messenger chats to YouTube videos and other web content, thereby focusing on shifts in the deployment of linguistic and pictorial resources.

7.3.1 Digital spaces of diasporic sociality

As described elsewhere in this study, all participants used media for informal transnational interaction with family members and friends from Senegal and elsewhere. These digital spaces of informal exchange also provided opportunities for diasporic engagement with issues as diverse as hometown support projects, homeland business projects, political discussions, or simply small talk. Individually and situationally diverse as they may have been, these exchanges shared a conversational character and an affinity to informal and vernacular registers of language, which for Senegalese people imply an interplay of French and Wolof (cf. Lexander 2011, Mc Laughlin 2014) with additional features from Senegal's other national languages and English, depending on speaker and interlocutor. The following examples illustrate three sites of diasporic sociality in the data: Astou Coly's chatgroup with former schoolmates (Excerpts 7.1 and 7.2), Felipe Sagna's diasporic chatgroup (Excerpt 7.3), and Ousmane Diagne's sharing and commenting hometown photos in social media (Excerpt 7.4).

Astou Coly is member of a group chat created by former classmates who attended school in Dakar (see also Chapter 6, Section 6.3.3). They mainly interact in French and Wolof, with French being more often than not the base language, and members (including Astou) drawing on Wolof to evaluate, qualify, or index irony. Excerpt 7.1 is part of a longer sequence, in which Astou and others discuss a range of topics in a jocular spirit. The sequence starts at 09.54 a.m. when Astou logs in with a 'Happy Friday' wish in a combination of French and Arabic lexis. A few minutes later at 10.15, another group member cracks a joke in French, and at 10.21 a third member comments on it with a Wolof utterance. Wolof comes in second position to evaluate the previous message rather than to cast a new topic.[1]

EXCERPT 7.1: ASTOU COLY'S CHAT GROUP WITH FORMER SCHOOLMATES

1 Astou   **Jummah Mubarak** les gars mes soeurs et free. Bon vendredi. Que Dieu nous benisse tous. Amin
Blessed Friday everyone my brothers and sisters. Happy Friday. May God bless you all. Amen

2 Adama   *MIRACLE DES MATHS*
La plus grande équation mathématique de tous les temps.
2017 est une année spéciale.
Essayez ceci
Age + Année de naissance = 2017
Partagez
Maths miracle | the biggest maths equation of all times. | 2017 is a special year. | Try this | * Age + year of birth = 2017 * | Share

3 Bouna   Adama **li doyna war de**
Adama you really want to show off

> **EXCERPT 7.2: ASTOU COLY'S CHAT GROUP WITH FORMER SCHOOLMATES**
>
> 1 Souleymane *Vrai ou Faux Oslo?*
> True or false, Oslo?
>
> 2 Astou **Souleymane daccorouma.** *Les premiers amours sont éternels.*
> Souleymane, I don't agree with you. First loves are eternal.
>
> 3 Souleymane *T libre j'en connais d'autres qui diront le contraire.*
> As you wish, I know others who'd say the contrary.
>
> 4 Astou *C'est sûr mais la règle veut que l'amour de l'adolescence reste pour toute la vie.... Même étant marié l'autre hante tes nuits de temps à autre* 😂😂😂😂 **Lolou dou dégn boy**
> Sure, but the rule is that adolescent love remains lifelong.... even if married, the other comes to haunt your nights now and then 😂😂😂😂 That cannot be taken away, mate

Excerpt 7.2 is another example from the same chatgroup. This exchange starts when a group member, 'Souleymane', posts a 'tile' with the following French-language text on red background: 'In your life, the person you'll love the most is not your first love, but the one who'll make you forget it [i.e. the first love]'. (Original: *Dans ta vie ce n'est pas ton premier amour que tu aimeras le plus mis bel et bien la personne qui te le fera oublier.*) Group members then discuss this claim. Souleymane asks Astou, dubbed 'Oslo' by her former classmates, about her opinion (line 1). Astou's following contributions draw on Wolof and French. In line 2, the Wolof part voices subjective disagreement, while French states her view of things. In line 4, Wolof provides the conclusive evaluation, or coda, to Astou's argument.

We now turn to Felipe Sagna who uses digital media to maintain both private and professional connections to his native town in the south of Senegal. For example, in a Facebook posting Felipe shared a photo of the town's youth football team that he was a trainer for before migrating to Norway. The caption of this photo read, 'Youth team of 1996, 1997, with trainer [Felipe's original name]'.[2] Felipe added to the sharing his own caption, starting with a formulaic phrase in English, continuing in French, and rounding up with a sequence of emoji that signify football, gratitude, and applause:

> **EXCERPT 7.3: FELIPE SAGNA'S POSTING CAPTION**
>
> still remember those days . Bravo a toute cette equipe, cette generation 😊
> ⚽🙏👏🙌

146 *Transnational families, diaspora practices, digital polycentricity*

Felipe Sagna is also member of a WhatsApp chatgroup for people from his hometown. Chatgroup members now live in several countries and also maintain an associated Facebook page with a repository of photographs and other documents. Excerpt 7.4 illustrates a recurrent interaction pattern in this group: a newcomer joins in, and a regular member offers to add them to the Facebook group.

EXCERPT 7.4: FELIPE SAGNA'S HOMETOWN CHAT GROUP

1 Abdou   *Bonsoir à tout le monde*
             Good evening everyone

2 Pape   **VOICE MESSAGE IN WOLOF**
             Abdou I don't know you, but welcome here

3 Pape   Abdou *faut donner ton facebook piur que l'on tajoute au groupe facebook*
             Abdou, you must give your Facebook [handle] to add you to the group

4) Abdou   Abdou *ex-mari d'Aminata Fall je vie à Toulouse*
             [I am] Abdou ex husband of Aminata Fall I live in Toulouse

5) Abdou   *Merci Pape*
             Thanks Pape

6) Pape   **Ah ok nln hamnala**
             Ah, ok I know you

7) Pape   **Boubah kay**
             Very much indeed

8) Abdou   **Bravo**

Completed within ten minutes, this exchange starts when a newcomer from France joins in and greets in French (line 1). Another member from France posts a voice message with welcome wishes in Wolof (line 2), then writes instructions for adding the newcomer to the Facebook group in French (line 3). One motivation for this mode-switch could be that the requested information must be given in written form. The newcomer gives information on himself (line 4), then signs off (line 5). In the following text messages, the regular member switches again to Wolof to address cordial greetings, followed by ratification by the newcomer. This is an overarching pattern in this group chat: the dual affordance of text and voice in WhatsApp patterns with language choice such that Wolof and Joola (the language of the group's home region) come mainly in voice messages, while text messages are mostly in French, but also English and Wolof. The affordance of voice messages favours the use of Wolof and Joola, which members may not be familiar or comfortable with writing.

The third example concerns posting and sharing hometown photos in social media, a practice that Ousmane Diagne, Felipe Sagna, and Astou Coly are fond of. Photography and video are powerful media of diasporic nostalgia (cf. Tsagarousianou 2016, Theodoropoulou 2021), sometimes leading to follow-up comments or collaborative narratives by members of the poster's networked audience. Ousmane Diagne made avid use of the visual affordances of Facebook to index diasporic nostalgia. During fieldwork, the background image of his Facebook profile featured a beach life scene with the headline 'Lions of Teranga', which is a popular name of the Senegal national football team. The first posting we encountered while browsing Ousmane's Facebook profile was a shared video from a Facebook group by the name of 'We love Saint-Louis City'. The video showed a historical river boat approaching the harbour of St Louis in Senegal, with its teaser reading *passage bateau bouyel*. The next content on Ousmane's profile showed a group of Senegalese children playing football on a dirt track, and the next one was a media story about a victory by the Senegal women's national handball team. All this shared content was in one way or another about Senegal, and Ousmane's (as well as Felipe's and Astou's) sharing practice came with little or no commentary of his own. On another occasion, Ousmane posted an aerial photo of his native city, St Louis. This elicited likes and comments, to which Ousmane responded as follows (Excerpt 7.5):

EXCERPT 7.5: COMMENTS ON HOMETOWN PHOTO POSTED ON FACEBOOK BY OUSMANE

1 Ousmane		*Merci mes amis; St louis c est dans mon coeur* Thank you my friends; St Louis is in my heart
2 Friend 1		**Wessou ratef, kharleen ba** *projets* **yeup takhaw,** **Visa rek** *pour les non* **ndar ndar. Mais Boy foo nek?** It will be even more beautiful, wait for all projects to come to an end, people from outside St Louis will need a visa. But mate, where are you?'
3 Ousmane		**Boy magi si al bu weet** Norway. *Ca fait tres tres longtemps! J espere q ca va.* Mate, I am alone in Norway. It's been a while, hope all is well.
4 Friend 2		*Naturellement belle ma saint Louis natale* Naturally beautiful, my native St Louis

---

Ousmane posts a 'thank you' message in French, his preferred literacy choice (as discussed in Chapter 3). Two days later, a comment comes in Wolof, interspersed with French-origin lexis: *projet, visa, les, non*. This commenter uses the city's name in Wolof, *Ndar*, and the informal term of address, *Boy*. Ousmane takes up this term of address and the interlocutor's selection of Wolof to answer his question, then switches back to his own preference, French. (Note *Norway* as part of the Wolof bit of his post.) Another comment references the photo, again with the city's French name.

From the viewpoint of multilingual practices, some lines of similarity are visible across these examples. When French is the base language of the exchange, the use of Wolof tends towards well-known participant- and discourse-related functions of code-switching (Androutsopoulos 2013), as in Excerpts 7.3 and 7.5. Following yet another well-established pattern of code-switching on- and offline, interlocutors index consent and conversational harmony by repetition of language choice and linguistic form across turns (Excerpt 7.4). Excerpt 7.4 exemplifies an overarching pattern of mode- and code-choice in the data: when a dual affordance of text and voice messaging is available (as in WhatsApp), Wolof and other national languages come mainly in voice messages, while text messages are mostly (though not exclusively) in French.

7.3.2 *The Senegalese public sphere*

Media consumption related to Senegal is important to all families, as reported in the interviews. For example, parents and children would watch Senegalese shows together on satellite TV or YouTube. We don't have adequate data to assess in detail the frequency of and participation in these activities, but it is evident that consuming media content from Senegal leads to exposure to a range of Senegalese speech styles depending on media genre (e.g. TV news as opposed to drama or comedy). However, the textual evidence for such practices in our data is limited to engagement with Senegalese news media, traces of which appear on the parents' Facebook profiles and in some messenger exchanges. These limitations aside, the Senegalese news media, and in particular media content on Senegalese politics and sports, can be seen as constituting a distinct sociolinguistic centre. From the participants' viewpoint, a characteristic of this second centre is that it relies on receptive literacy practices such as watching, reading, and sharing. Unlike many research findings on multilingual Facebook, our participants use their Facebook profiles not for sustained discussion, but rather as spaces for viewing and sharing, only occasionally commenting. In a sense, the position of Facebook profiles in the participants' digital media ecologies is similar to television.

Senegalese politics is popular with Ousmane Diagne, Felipe Sagna, and Astou Coly. During fieldwork, they followed the discourse on the forthcoming presidential elections and indexed their views on the candidates by sharing respective media stories and commentary. Astou Coly shared videos about the acting president, Macky Sall, and one of his opponents, Ousmane Sonko. Ousmane Diagne discussed politics in private messaging with a friend who lived in Italy. They shared screenshots and links on various topics, all written in French, and discussed them in French. One

Transnational families, diaspora practices, digital polycentricity 149

Image 7.1 Ma carte mon arme, 'My voting card, my gun' (data by Ousmane Diagne)

image they shared (Image 7.1) is a handgun with the words 'Republic of Senegal Voting Card' placed on the barrel, a ballot box on the handle, and the message: 'My [voting] card [is] my gun against Macky'.

All of the written media content from Senegal that flows through the participants' profiles comes entirely in French, the country's official language. Spoken Wolof, the national vernacular, is limited to genres such as political speeches or fictional dialogue, which are shared on social networking sites. Written Wolof is marginalised in Senegalese news media and rather exceptional even in participants' status updates of a private nature (for example, the only status update in Wolof we found in the participants' Facebook profiles was about the death of a relative), even though their Facebook contacts post status updates where Wolof figures and although it does come up in comments (see also Chapter 8 for a status update in Peul). Content from Senegal's media does not come up in English (except occasional English lexis in its Senegalese usage), nor Arabic (except if thematically connected to religion) or other national languages, and does not feature translanguaging. In sum, as participants orient to the Senegalese public sphere, they also recontextualise the country's official language regime, a dominance of French and institutional marginalisation of Wolof and other languages, in their timelines and messenger threads.

7.3.3 Religious discourse

A third discursive centre is constituted by digital literacy practices related to religion. Its ingredients are the religious content that flows across public and private channels of those participants who engage with either Christianity (Felipe Sagna) or Islam, notably Oumou Diagne, Cheikh Bâ, Astou Coly and her oldest daughter, Awa. We here focus on the latter. All Islam-related content that circulates in the data is multilingual and often vividly multimodal. A distinct resource is Arabic. Depending on genre and media channel, Arabic comes in spoken mode (e.g. in sermons and recitation), in the Roman script (e.g. in chain messages and captions in social media 'tiles' and video clips), and in Arabic script (sometimes as part of a multimodal, decorative layout). However, Arabic is never a stand-alone language choice in the data, but part of a multilingual (and multimodal) ensemble, thereby complemented by French and/or Wolof. By contrast, Senegal's other national languages, English or Norwegian, have no share in this centre, at least its digital instantiations examined here. To discuss the available data for religious digital discourse, we now carve out a few salient genre patterns, namely chain messages, shared video clips, religious chatgroups, and associated video channels.

Chain messages are a typical genre of religious discourse in the data. These messages focus thematically on major religious festivities (e.g. Ramadan) or religious plights and are typically fabricated to be recontextualisable, i.e. able to circulate across diverse and transnational Francophone Muslim audiences. This is indexed by the absence of individual identifiers (e.g. terms of address), the explicit request (as part of the content) to pass on the message to others, and the messages' language choices, which are mainly French with Arabic features for religious terminology, greetings/farewells, and excerpts from poetry or sermons. Chain messages are included in dyadic chats by Ousmane and Oumou Diagne as well as group chats by Cheikh Bâ and Felipe Sagna. They come mostly in writing (see examples below), occasionally in voice. In the data offered by Ousmane, we found various chain messages sent to him by his Senegalese friend from Italy, including but not limited to religious matters. For example, one chain message is about Chinese canned meat, another one is about fatherhood (*I just nominated you for the Loveliest and most Caring Dad's Award*), yet another one about broken friendships. Two religious chain messages from Ousmane's dataset are now examined in more detail, both received during Ramadan. The first concerns appropriate behaviour during Ramadan (Excerpt 7.6 and the second is a prayer (Excerpt 7.7). Since our focus is on multilingual usage rather than content, both messages are left untranslated and relevant content is explicated below as appropriate.

Transnational families, diaspora practices, digital polycentricity 151

EXCERPT 7.6: CHAIN MESSAGE ABOUT BEHAVIOUR DURING RAMADAN

Dated 14.06.17; data by Ousmane Diagne

Cheikh Maher (**imam** de Haram Makkah) *donne quelques conseils/ suggestions pratique ici.*
Quelques idées pour les 10 derniers jours du mois de Ramadan:

1. *Donne, par exemple, 5F en charité chaque nuit: si cela coincide avec* **laylatul qadr** *c'est comme si tu avais donné de la charité chaque nuit pendant 84 années*
2. *Prie 2* **rakka** *chaque nuit. Si une des nuits coincide avec* **laylatul qadr** *c'est comme si tu avais prié chaque nuit pendant 84 ans*
3. *Lis* **Sourah Ikhlaas (Qul Huwa Allahu Ahadun)** *trois fois chaque nuit de telle sorte que si une des nuit tombe sur* **laylatoul qadr** *c'est comme si tu avais récité tout le Coran chaque jour pendant 84 ans Passez ce message car vous trouverez cela dans votre compte de bonnes actions en ce mois béni de Ramadan.*

EXCERPT 7.7: KAABA CHAIN MESSAGE

Dated 02.06.17; data by Ousmane Diagne

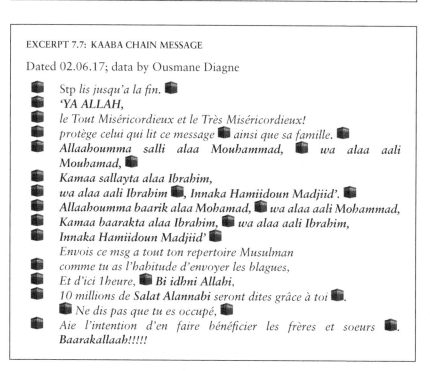

Stp *lis jusqu'a la fin.*
'YA ALLAH,
le Tout Miséricordieux et le Très Miséricordieux!
protège celui qui lit ce message ainsi que sa famille.
Allaahoumma salli alaa Mouhammad, wa alaa aali Mouhamad,
Kamaa sallayta alaa Ibrahim,
wa alaa aali Ibrahim , Innaka Hamiidoun Madjiid'.
Allaahoumma baarik alaa Mohamad, wa alaa aali Mohammad,
Kamaa baarakta alaa Ibrahim, wa alaa aali Ibrahim,
Innaka Hamiidoun Madjiid'
Envois ce msg a tout ton repertoire Musulman comme tu as l'habitude d'envoyer les blagues,
Et d'ici 1heure, **Bi idhni Allahi,**
10 millions de **Salat Alannabi** *seront dites grâce à toi .*
Ne dis pas que tu es occupé,
Aie l'intention d'en faire bénéficier les frères et soeurs .
Baarakallaah!!!!!

Both messages are bilingual in French and Romanised Arabic, but display two different bilingual patterns. In the chain message in Excerpt 7.6 – a list of 'best practice' suggestions related to prayer and donations during Ramadan – French is the base language throughout. Arabic comes in an insertional mode (cf. discussion in Chapter 2, Section 2.3) and is limited to proper names and religious terminology, with the term *laylatul qadr*[3] alone occurring three times. The message in Excerpt 7.7 displays a pattern of alternation that seems constrained by genre and speech act. It starts with a request to read, in French ('Please read through to the end.'). There follows an evocation of God, in Arabic and French. The main part is a chant in Romanised Arabic. The concluding request to share this message comes in French, interspersed with religious vows in Arabic, and the sign-off is again in Arabic, with expressive punctuation. All of the above is visually framed by the Kaaba emoji, repeated 28 times, which functions as a 'beat gesture' (Gawne & McCulloch 2019). Such decorative usage of emoji does not seem incompatible with religious messages in the data. For instance, in the hometown chatgroup that Felipe Sagna participates in we found a similar Ramadan message surrounded by a decorative line of black half-moon emoji.

Video clips are another genre of religious discourse that circulates in our data. Our example here is a video clip from Oumou Diagne's data. Oumou reported receiving this and other 'Friday messages' from her sister-in-law and her brother who both live in Senegal. This short (01:34) clip consists of a succession of still images and an audio track, the recited Quran surah 'Az' Zumar', which concerns the relationship between God and man. A large part of the clip's iconography consists of text in Arabic, on which we focus here. In a total of 36 still images 17 feature text in the Arabic script, and two stills contain text in Romanised Arabic and French, respectively (a few images are multilingual). A selection is shown in the four parts of Image 7.2.

Arabic characters appear on decorative cakes, hearts, plates, butterflies and pigeons, and only rarely in text blocks. The reception status of these signs, i.e. whether the viewers read or just gaze at them, is unclear. The clip itself clearly presupposes sufficient receptive proficiency to recognise Arabic as such and perhaps also selected signs such as < الله > 'Allah', which is repeated multiple times in various arrangements in this clip. However, whether the features in Arabic script are perceived on a symbolic (non-propositional) rather than informative level eventually depends on the proficiency individual viewers bring along. Oumou told us she does not understand what is written there, but just looks at the pictures, though she has sufficient receptive proficiency to recognise Arabic as such. When connected text is meant to be propositionally understood, a French translation is provided as well (see example 7.2b). This leads us to assume that much Arabic script in this and other similar clips is meant to be perceived on a symbolic rather than propositional level.

Despite their obvious differences in terms of media format and multimodal composition, chain messages and video clips in our data have some elements in common. They neither refer directly to Senegal nor are they produced in Senegal, as indexed by the absence of Wolof. Rather, they are fabricated for easy consumption and circulation across the (diasporic) Francophone Muslim world, including Senegalese Muslims.

Transnational families, diaspora practices, digital polycentricity 153

Image 7.2 Video-stills from 'Bon Vendredi' video (data by Oumou Diagne)

They are sent for specific occasions, like religious feasts, or Fridays, the day when Muslims gather to pray, so as to strengthen the solidarity at times of specific religious importance (see also Lexander 2010). The role of Arabic, in particular, in this content is perhaps best viewed from a translanguaging perspective (cf. Chapter 2, Sections 2.1 and 2.3). It is likely aimed at Muslim audiences who have knowledge of Arabic through Koranic school but do not forcibly speak or read Arabic regularly and fluently. However, the producers of chain messages and video clips seem to assume visual recognition and/or propositional and generic understanding of Arabic words, phrases, and verses. In addition, several religious terms such as *imam*, *rakka* and *Ramadan* must be seen as fully integrated in various varieties of French (cf. Ndiaye-Corréard et al. 2006). These Arabic features can thus be seen as constituting a transnational religious register for Muslim communities.

A strikingly different site of diasporic religious discourse in the data is a chatgroup for Mourides, a Sufi brotherhood that is specific to Senegal. The Mouride brotherhood has played a crucial role for Senegalese migration and transnational networks since the 1970s, when drought and economic crisis forced shopkeepers to leave their country. The solidarity of the network facilitates practical concerns like housing, supplies, and financial support (Bava 2002). The Mourides in one geographical space create their own places of worship (Bava 2002) while keeping close ties to Senegal, and in particular to the holy city of Touba, a central pole for transnational configurations (Riccio 2002). Cheikh Bâ, a Mouride himself, is the only participant who has access to this group and logs in daily, as reported in the interview. Hosted on WhatsApp and named after the city of Touba, this chatgroup is specific to the Mouride community in Norway and caters to it with religious messages and weblinks (on which more below). Comparing this chatgroup to the chain messages and videoclip discussed above reveals fine-grained differences within the religion centre postulated in our analysis, and offers additional insights regarding the polymedia connectivity in digital diasporic practices.

A first thing to point out is the distinctive writing style of messages in the Touba chatgroup. Unlike the chain messages discussed above, they feature mainly written Wolof in distinctive Wolof orthography, whereas French – either as base language or inserted lexis – is entirely absent. Two brief examples come in Excerpt 7.8. Some messages feature Wolof standard spelling that differentiates them from Wolof written in line with French spelling. In the examples below, there are double vowels (e.g. *bàalu*, *MAAM*), and <x> for [x], not <kh> as is common in spelling based on French (e.g. *xeweul*). The first message also features diacritics, more specifically ñ (*ñu*), whereas the second message presents the same phoneme by <ni>. In fact, the first message is written almost entirely in accordance with standard Wolof. There are, however, traces of French spelling there, as in *diégalu*, with <di> instead of standard Wolof <j>. In the second message, there is even more influence from French spelling (e.g. *yeuguoul* instead of *yëgul*). However, in both examples, the use of Wolof standard spelling is sufficient to appear as diverging from the French spelling found elsewhere in the corpus. This is emphasised by the insertion of Wolof lexis that is specific to Mourides (e.g. *ziar* or *siar* 'greetings' and *tawfex* 'peace'), proper names such as *MAAM SHEIX IBRA FAAL* (one of the main disciples of the founder of Mouridism), and Arabic formulaic expressions and religious terminology in variable spelling, e.g. *Assalamou' Haleykoum'* but also *ASSALAMU ALEYKUM*, and *Xassida* or *Xassaides* (variable spellings for *qasida*, i.e. religious poems). This specific Wolof usage, cast in Wolof orthography – with neologisms and lexical borrowings from Arabic, and intentionally, and to various degrees, kept free from French influence – indexes belonging to the Mouride community (Ngom 2002). On this ground, the Touba chatgroup can be seen as constituting a distinct niche within diasporic religious discourse.

Transnational families, diaspora practices, digital polycentricity 155

> EXCERPT 7.8: MESSAGES FROM 'TOUBA' GROUP CHAT (DATA BY CHEIKH BÂ)
>
> - Assalamou' Haleykoum' di siar ak diégalu di bàalu akh ñép ak dilén bal. di ñan sunu Borom djéggal ñu sunu bakkar yi nëbu ak yi feñ ta nangul ñu sunu kóor ci barkép Xassida yi.
>   'May peace be with you, I greet and forgive, may all be forgiven and may you forgive. I pray that our Lord forgive us for our hidden sins and our lies, and accept our fast in the blessing of the qasida.'
> - DEWENATI ASSALAMU ALEYKUM MAGUI ZIAR NIEUP DI BALU AKH SI LIMA YEUK AK LIMA YEUGUOUL BALNA NIEUP DI NIAN SUNIOU BOROM DEFAL NIOU JAAM TAWFEX MOUTHIE AK XEWEUL BARKE MAAM SHEIX IBRA FAAL
>   'Happy New (Muslim) Year, may you be in peace, I pay homage to all of you. May you forgive me if I offended you or not. I have forgiven everyone and pray that God give us peace, divine protection, safety, and prosperity, with the blessing of Maam Cheikh Ibrah Fall'

Another specific of the Touba chatgroup is its integration in a cross-platform circuit of digital literacy practices related to the Mouride community. Many messages to this chatgroup are plain weblinks to YouTube channels by names such as *Diwaanu Xassaides TV*, *Touba TV*, or *Al Mouridiyyah TV* ('Mourides' TV'). These channels cater for the transnational Mouride brotherhood with extensive collections of video recordings of prayers, sermons, and festivities. Most of these recordings originate in Touba, Senegal, and are in a Mouride-specific register of spoken Wolof.[4] This indexes a digital literacy practice by which group members visit the group, then follow these links to the respective YouTube channels, where they can watch, make comments, and share sermons and other content from Touba. The web banner of one of these channels is shown in Image 7.3.

In the multimodal and multilingual arrangement of this banner, the channel's name comes in Romanised Arabic, but commercial information about video-recording services for community events comes in French. Most of the banner space is covered by excerpts from poems (*xassaides*) written in Arabic language by Cheikh Amadou Bamba, the founder of Mouridism, who is depicted to the right. The communicative status of these calligraphic excerpts, i.e. whether they are in fact read by site visitors or just gazed at, is again ambiguous, as discussed above. However, important information

Image 7.3 Banner of YouTube channel *Diwaanu Xassaides TV*

about the channel's commercial services is given in French. So overall, the marketing framing of this video channel (commercial information cast in French, visual design drawing in Arabic) is quite different to the actual content (sermons and prayers in Wolof) and in fact again more similar to the chain messages and videoclips discussed above, addressing a much larger group of imagined recipients in Mouride diaspora.

7.3.4 Beyond diaspora: Traces of Norway and global pop culture

Informal transnational sociality, consumption of media content from Senegal, and participation in religious discourse, these are the main axes of diasporic engagement in the data. The preceding analysis attempts to reconstruct them as elements of a polycentric arrangement and to bring out fine-graded differences within each centre. However, the traces of these digital diaspora practices coexist with traces of other centres. On Facebook, in particular, diasporic content is adjacent to, and interspersed with, messages that point away from diaspora. The decision to include these in the analysis is grounded in the theoretical insight that diaspora practices coexist with practices beyond diaspora in people's everyday lives (hybrid character of diasporic identity formation) and in the empirical coexistence of messages and interactions that index multiple orientations.

An important non-diasporic centre is, of course, Norway, with its national language. As outlined in Chapter 3, our four families fit well into a view of diaspora as diverse and culturally hybrid. We know that all participants use spoken Norwegian for interaction at home and the workplace, and Norwegian surfaces in their digital exchanges too, as evidenced in various examples so far (e.g. Chapter 6). Remarkably, Norwegian cultural and political content is largely absent from the families' elicited digital practices. This lends support to Brubaker's (2005) third diaspora element discussed above, i.e. boundary maintenance towards the majority society. However, it also implies that Norwegian public discourse may reach these families by other media channels, whereas their digital media usage is geared towards diasporic interests. But even though the fieldwork did not aim to elicit participants' mediated interaction with Norway-based interlocutors beyond family and close friends, traces of living and interacting in Norway sometimes show up in the data, e.g. wishes on festive occasions or photos from joint workplace undertakings.

This is particularly visible for the Diagne family. For example, Ousmane and Oumou Diagne posted on their Facebook profile several photos of the family in the famous Vigeland park in Oslo. Ousmane's profile also features an English-language BBC video about Norway being named 'the happiest place on earth'. On one occasion, Oumou Diagne went out for dinner with work colleagues, and photos of the event were posted and discussed on Facebook. Their older son, Momar, was greeted by schoolmates on his birthday, in Norwegian, and responded in the same language. Ousmane used to post birthday wishes to his three

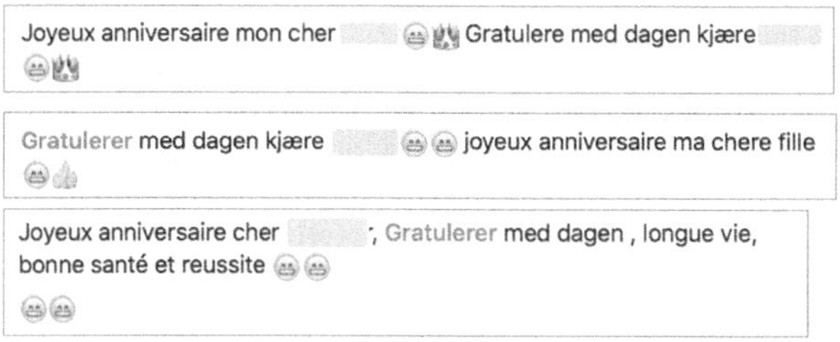

Transnational families, diaspora practices, digital polycentricity 157

> Joyeux anniversaire mon cher   😂 🎉 Gratulere med dagen kjære
> 😂 🎉
>
> Gratulerer med dagen kjære   😂 😂 joyeux anniversaire ma chere fille
> 😂 👍
>
> Joyeux anniversaire cher   ; Gratulerer med dagen , longue vie,
> bonne santé et reussite 😂 😂
> 😂 😂

Image 7.4 'Happy birthday' postings by Ousmane Diagne to his three children

children on his Facebook page, in Norwegian and French (cf. Image 7.4). These posts, in the comment section, elicit wishes in different languages, some by residents of the Norwegian city where the family lives. Ousmane uses no Wolof here. French effectively works as a heritage language next to Norwegian, the predominant language in the children's everyday life.

As discussed in Chapter 6, Oumou and Ousmane Diagne have decided to text each other in Norwegian, so that Oumou, being more recent in the country, would practise her Norwegian writing skills. In an example discussed in Chapter 6, we saw how the two of them (especially Oumou) spice up their exchanges with French, which indexes their romantic connection that dates back to Senegal. In the following example (cf. Excerpt 7.9 from the same set of text messages, we see how Ousmane corrects Oumou's Norwegian.

	EXCERPT 7.9: OUMOU AND OUSMANE DIAGNE, SMS
1 Ousmane	Er det svømming i dag? Håper ikke det.
	Will there be swimming today? I hope not.
2 Oumou	Nei ☺ det er ikke svømming i dag. Bare kjapp av 😄
	No, there is no swimming today, just relax
3 Ousmane	Slapp av ikke kjapp av. Jeg kjører bil i dag og kan gå i butikken.
	Slapp av not *kjapp av*. I am going by car today and can go to the store. _

Features of Norwegian also surfaced in interactions between family members and other Senegalese diasporans who were living in Norway during our fieldwork or had lived there in the past. One such interaction was that between Ousmane and a Senegalese friend of his who was living in Italy during our fieldwork but had lived in Norway before. Norwegian pops up several times in their digital exchanges, as a reminder of their shared transnational trajectories and a reference to Norway itself. On one occasion, this Senegalese friend posted a 'happy birthday' message in Norwegian to Ousmane's Facebook profile. On another, he code-switched in a voice message from Wolof to Norwegian to express how *koselig* ('cosy') it was to discover that he had access to a Norwegian TV channel from Italy, thereby using a Norwegian phrase to index his good feelings about Norway (original: *nei, men det er veldig koselig, se på TV2 igjen*, 'no, but it is very cosy to watch TV2 again'). In yet another message exchange between the two, Ousmane code-switched from French to Norwegian to explain his daughter's schedule for that day. *Vi snakkes*, the friend replied in Norwegian, 'we'll talk'.

A second important orientation that coexists with digital diaspora practices is global pop culture. On Facebook profiles in particular, participants shared and displayed snapshots from globally circulating discourses that were neither 'Senegalese' nor 'Muslim' nor ethnically 'Norwegian', but concerned a wide range of other issues, such as Black justice, gender equality, yoga, Buddhism, environmental protection, or dance music. Even though the content, origin, and circulation of these messages varied by individual, we view them as constituting yet another 'centre' of digital diasporic practice whose distinctiveness is precisely the absence of either homeland or residence orientation. A typical digital genre in this centre is the 'tile', a prefabricated multimodal text unit that is formatted as an image file and can be easily posted and shared online. Tiles in the data often come with a three-zone vertical layout that is reminiscent of internet memes, with lines of text in the top and bottom zone and an image in the middle. Family members engaged with social media tiles as viewers and sharers rather than producers, at least this was the case in the Facebook profiles we had access to. Linguistically, Wolof and Arabic did not have a part in these messages and the frequency of French was diminished, while different English(es) come to the foreground.

Examples from four participants illustrate the diversity of topics and characters in this centre. Astou Coly often shared on her Facebook profile tiles with English and French messages about life, love, female courage, and gender equality. These often came in various typography stylings and with no image. One example is a card with a winter landscape image in the background and a superimposed text in a philosophical mood: 'The thing with life is that nobody will understand you until the moment they'll find themselves in the very same situation.' (Original: *Le truc dans la vie, c'est que personne ne va te comprendre jusqu'au moment où ils serons dans la meme situation.*) Another tile, generated by a Facebook app called 'Nametests', features in the middle a photo of Astou, which she herself uploaded while compiling a quiz. The top tier reads: *What Is The Summary Of Your Life?* The bottom tier starts thus: *[Astou] loves to laugh. She always has a smile for her friends and a kind word.* Felipe Sagna's social media tiles were quite different. Felipe was raised in the Christian faith and his shared images and videos index his interest in spirituality, meditation, yoga, and environmental protection. These are all cast in English, and the video files could be played while browsing Felipe's

Transnational families, diaspora practices, digital polycentricity

profile. Examples are 'Jane Goodall's message about creating a more peaceful world', a message on 'How to deal with anger?' and a moving video about being compassionate to other humans, regardless of how dire their situation might be. Just like Astou, Felipe shares these images and videos now and again, though without introducing or commenting on them in his own words.

The interests indexed by some of the adolescents were different. Momar, the Diagne's oldest child, was 16 years old and was keenly interested in cultural politics and social justice at the time when we were conducting fieldwork. He shared a lot of US American content. One tile is about *Michelle Obama destroys Trump*, another on an Afro-American family who fell victim to police brutality, again without commenting any of these himself. Aida, Astou Coly's second daughter, followed a Facebook channel called *N.W.E.* that broadcasts 'Afro Dance' videos recorded in various countries. Boosting more than one million followers during fieldwork, this channel presents itself in English (*#1 Afro Media Afro Dance Afro Urban Music & Entertainment*) but is managed by a French-language Web TV channel by the name of *BET, LA CHAÎNE CULTURE NOIRE-AMERICAINE* ('the Black American culture channel'). There is a confluence here between French and English, and the digital content shared by Aida features both languages, too. Images 7.5a and 7.5b show two examples for the text area below the posted videos. From top to bottom, they feature the number of viewings, channel name, date of posting, a 'like' button to the right, and a caption for each video. All French displayed here is algorithmically produced, prompted by the researcher profile's language settings. Compositions of this kind (Androutsopoulos 2006, 2010) exemplify how Artificial Intelligence had become an agent in the display of multilingualism online. The English caption is the only part composed by a human, and emoji are deployed here as signifiers of origin (flags, in part following a country name) or evaluations (the fire icon can be read as signifying 'hot').

Image 7.5a and 7.5b Text area of 'NWE' dance videos (data by Aida Coly)

7.4 Conclusions

This chapter adds to our understanding of family multilingualism and digital communication by casting a wider view on how members of these transnational families used digital media to engage in a wide range of diaspora practices related to their multiple identities as Senegalese, religious practitioners, and popular culture followers. They used media to follow homeland discourses of politics, religion, and entertainment, and to do conversational exchange and informal heritage language learning with relatives and close friends, in each case mobilising different resources from their linguistic and media repertoires. The findings offer evidence for a key claim in language and diaspora research, i.e., the fine-grained, context-sensitive patterning of linguistic resources in diaspora communities. Features from participants' rich multilingual repertoires were selected in many different ways, depending on audience, speaker preference, and communicative purpose. Wrapping it all up as 'French/Wolof bilingualism' would be too simplistic, not only because Arabic, English, other national languages, and Norwegian also played a part, but also because Wolof and French came together in many contextually shifting patterns. A 'homeland orientation' certainly constitutes a bottom line for various digital practices, but does not lead to homogenous linguistic choices. Rather, different portions of participants' linguistic repertoires were woven together as they engaged with different homeland discourses. At the same time, the 'hybrid' practices and identities of diaspora populations, emphasised in diaspora scholarship, are evident in the data.

Table 7.2 Digital polycentricity: Overview

Centre	Linguistic resources	Media choices	Family members
Spaces of diasporic sociality	French/Wolof; English/Wolof; (limited) Peul/Joola, English	Group chats, dyadic chats, SMS texting	Parents and children
Senegal's public sphere	French, (limited) Wolof	Social media timelines	Parents
Religion	French, Wolof (Mouride register), Arabic (in Arabic and Romanised script)	Social media timelines; chatgroups	Mainly parents
Norway	Norwegian	Social media timelines, dyadic chats, SMS texting	Parents and children
Global pop culture	English; French	Social media timelines	Parents and children

The participants' language practices were organised in centres, defined by discourses and audiences to which participants oriented and whose established indexical conventions they adhered to. Orienting to a centre has consequences for the linguistic choices activated by participants. We summarise the findings at this point (see also Table 7.2 above). A first centre comprises group-level spaces of diasporic interaction, which participants set up and join by means of messenger applications and associated social media profiles. Language practices in this centre were similar to those described elsewhere in this study. Participants resemiotised well attested patterns of Senegalese multilingualism, alternating between French, (Urban) Wolof, regional languages, and sometimes English. Second, adult participants oriented to Senegal's public discourse, especially on politics and sport, by viewing and sharing content in their social media timelines and messenger threads. Their largely receptive engagement with Senegal's public sphere was found to reproduce the indexical order of Senegal's diglossic stratification between French and Wolof, especially so in professional media writing. Admittedly, however, our textual data perhaps overemphasised the predominance of French in this centre. Had we documented the TV series and movies from Senegal that our participants also consumed, spoken Wolof would probably seize a larger part (see Chapter 3 for further discussion). Third, some family members engaged with religious discourses online, for example by participating in chatgroups, sharing chain messages, or watching social media content. These practices entailed distinct configurations of linguistic and multimodal resources, which centre on a polymorphic Arabic (in native and Romanised script), with the choice of French and/or Wolof depending on the production and intended circulation of messages. Fourth, participants also oriented to discourses, genres, images, and language styles 'beyond diaspora' (Norway, global pop culture). The decision to model these as additional 'centres' is grounded both in the theoretical insight that diaspora identities are multiple and layered and the empirical observation that these messages are contextually and sequentially adjacent to diasporic ones. Digital engagement with pop culture, in particular, was shaped by largely receptive literacy practices and a specific indexical stratification of languages. Neither Wolof nor Arabic played a role here, and French was less prominent than English, a shift motivated by US American cultural hegemony and perhaps also by the fact that participants might not have had access to French-language digital content on issues they were interested in beyond diaspora.

Turning to the media infrastructure for digital polycentricity, our analysis suggests that a 'centre' is not a media platform or technology in itself. For example, Facebook and WhatsApp do not constitute centres in themselves, nor do smartphones and laptops. Quite the contrary; it seems safe to say that global social media technologies are inherently polycentric, i.e. designed to allow for a multitude of discourses and normative orientations to flow across user networks. We think of a digital centre as a communicative space established by participants as they orient to particular discourses by exploiting the affordances of particular channels and platforms. Centres are by necessity built on digital infrastructures, but may extend across several. Digital infrastructures constrain the range of semiotic affordances that participants have at their disposal when orienting to, and engaging with, a centre. But the selection of which resources from a semiotic repertoire to mobilise is not determined by platforms, but rather shaped by conventions (Blommaert et al. 2005a speak of 'norms') that are specific to each centre.

This modelling of digital polycentricity does suggest a degree of analogy to polycentricity in physical co-presence as originally conceived by Blommaert et al. (2005a, 2005b) for migrant communities in Ghent. To a certain measure, digital centres serve as extensions of physical centres (e.g. the neighbourhood café, the mosque) and/or earlier technologies of transnational mediation. Indeed, some of today's digital content is a direct successor of older diasporic media. For example, video recordings of religious sermons that are viewed on YouTube can be considered remediated versions of tape-recorded sermons that circulated in the 1990s from Pakistan to Chicago, as described by Appadurai (1996). Had the fieldwork for this research focused on the families' life offline, some of these parallels – informal interaction among diasporics, religious ceremonies, reading, and watching the news – would be quite likely. However, if that is the case, what is then particular to *digital* polycentricity and multilingualism?

Answers to this question must be sought in the resources and opportunities that make digital communication distinct from, and not reducible to a substitute of, embodied co-present semiotic action (Androutsopoulos 2015). Three concluding points will be made. First, social media spaces afford a unique simultaneity in the display and observation of orientations both towards and away from diaspora. The most striking evidence for this are participants' social media timelines, where shared content and comments that index different discourses and centres are intermingled. Second, our modelling of digital polycentricity presupposes an approach to participation that is not limited to spoken language and interaction. The analysis shows that participation in a digital centre is achieved through an interplay of writing (posting, commenting), reading, watching, sharing, liking, and so on. Sharing, in particular, is widely understood as implying identification with the shared item, unless otherwise commented on (cf. Androutsopoulos 2014a). Even in the absence of active writing, the orientation to a centre promotes exposure to and engagement with the languages associated with this centre. For example, those reading and sharing religious messages maintain exposure to Arabic script and Arabic lexis, presumably leading to an increase in their recognition and understanding (cf. discussion of receptive skills and recognitional competence in Canagarajah 2012 and Blommaert & Backus 2013). Likewise, reading media news from Senegal transposes indexical orders from the home country to the diasporic context, while orientations beyond diaspora bring to the foreground English, a choice that is not so common in informal talk, but frequently displayed in prefabricated shared content. The point is: not just participants' active language use, but their receptive practices, too, afford their linguistic repertoires opportunities of maintenance and elaboration.

Finally, the data offers vivid evidence of the interface between interpersonal mediated interaction and mediatised messages from or about the homeland, and their importance for self-presentation and identity construction (Agha 2011, Androutsopoulos 2017). Mass-media messages designed for unspecified recipients are taken up and integrated into interpersonal mediated activities directed towards individual interlocutors or personal audiences, as for example with soap opera bits, political videos, popular imagery, or memes that travel from Senegal and other places to the participants' threads and profile pages. Such practices of identification through the uptake and recontextualisation of mediatised messages are neither specific to the Norwegian-Senegalese families nor a genuine innovation of the digital era (cf. Shankar 2004), but rather echo more widely documented patterns of global semiotic circulation in relation to the construction of social identities (cf. Jonsson & Muhonen 2014, Schreiber 2015). The same holds true for the high degree of individual differentiation afforded by digital media practices. For example, Norway-born children do not show interest in Senegalese politics, and those who practise Islam engage with different literacies from those interested in environmental protection or Afro Dance. These family members differ in the centres they orient to and in the kinds of messages they post and share, thereby performing generational, gendered, religious, and lifestyle identities.

Notes

1 In all data excerpts, Norwegian is underlined, **Wolof appears in bold**, *French in italics*, English in regular font, ***Arabic in bold italics***. Text inserted by the analysts is marked with square brackets.
2 Original: *L'équipe cadette* [town name] *des année 1996 1997. Avec comme entreneur* [Felipe].
3 This is *Laylat al-Qadr* in standard French spelling, or 'Qadr Night' in English, a particularly important night during Ramadan.
4 There is also an instance of Wolofal in one of the videos linked in the chat, that is Wolof in Arabic script.

8 Heritage language repertoires

The previous chapters examined how the families deploy their linguistic resources to 'do family' in digital interaction and to engage in more public communication in social media. In this chapter, we focus on one part of their linguistic repertoire, namely resources associated with linguistic heritage. We provide evidence that digital communication provides opportunities to engage in heritage language interaction and examine the extent to which the children, in particular, were interested in these opportunities and motivated or encouraged to seize them. In order to study the children's practices, we also need to take into account their parents' language ideologies, experiences, and emotions with respect to heritage language maintenance. The interplay between parents' hopes and wishes about their children's language learning and digital heritage language practices is illustrated by Image 8.1, a Facebook post by Sara Bâ.

Baba, medoyidima 'Dad, we love you'

Image 8.1 Sara Bâ, Facebook post (screenshot)

DOI: 10.4324/9781003227311-8

> PAPPA
> 'Dad'
>
> *Baba medoyidima*
> 'Dad, we love you'

Here, Norwegian-born Sara Bâ uses her husband Cheikh's first language, Peul, to present a drawing of him by their 5-year-old son. While the Norwegian text on the drawing means 'Dad' (see discussion of *Pappa* in Chapter 6), Sara's status line, visible at the top right of Image 8.1, reads *Baba medoyidima*, 'Dad, we love you', in Peul. Cheikh does not have a Facebook profile, so publishing this drawing was not really meant for him, but rather for Sara's in-laws who were the only Peul speakers among her Facebook contacts. The post was presented as a collective achievement. The drawing presented the son's own writing, and Sara ventriloquised her children's voices with the Peul kinship term *Baba* and the inclusive indexical, *we*. Confirming that this post was a result of careful composition, Sara explained in a text message to Kristin her motivation for this minimal, but meaningful use of Peul:

> INTERVIEW DATA 8.1: SARA BÂ, TEXT MESSAGE
>
> Sara   *Det var viktig for meg å skrive på peul, fremfor wolof, fransk og norsk, som vi veksler mellom i det daglige, først og fremst fordi det er [Cheikh]s morsmål og en stor del av hans identitet, så selv om vi, hans nærmeste ikke snakker hans språk fullt ut, kan vi allikevel uttrykke det vi mener er det viktigste og største for oss å fortelle ham. At vi elsker ham ☺ På hans språk, det aller første han lærte. I tillegg, men ikke en avgjørende grunn, er det hyggelig at hans familie kan se at vi ønsker å uttrykke dette på peul.*
> It was important for me to write in Peul, instead of Wolof, French, and Norwegian, the languages we alternate daily, first and foremost because it is [Cheikh]'s mother tongue and a big part of his identity, so even though we, his closest, do not fully speak his language, we may still express what we think is the most important and biggest [thing] for us to tell him. That we love him ☺ In his language, the very first he learnt. In addition, but not a decisive reason, it is nice that his family can see that we want to express this in Peul.

Following Androutsopoulos (2014a), this semiotic practice can be viewed as an instance of sharing by which Sara Bâ recontextualises a family moment for her networked audience. She actively demonstrates that her family is Norwegian- and Peul-speaking, thus 'displaying the family' (Finch 2007) as multilingual in social media. For most of Sara's Facebook contacts, who do not speak Peul, the post's meaning may stop there, as simply a display of the family's multilingualism. But as Sara is indirectly voicing her commitment to Peul and her aspiration for her children to learn it, this post can moreover be considered an attempt to reinforce solidarity with extended family members among her Facebook contacts (cf. Shannon 2019, Share et al. 2018). This she states in her message to Kristin too. However, as Sara also indicates in her text message to Kristin, even though Peul is the language of Cheikh's ethnic group, it was not necessarily his preferred choice of intergenerational language transmission. For the Bâ family, the value of Peul was of a more symbolic kind (for similar findings among West African migrants in France see Leconte 1997). These complex and sometimes contradictory family discourses about language and identity are examined in this chapter.

In FLP research, the relationship between language and identity has often been studied as a dichotomy between a heritage language on the one hand and a dominant language on the other (e.g. Guardado 2018). However, our analysis suggests that the Norwegian-Senegalese families' language practices can more usefully be analysed with the notion of a heritage language repertoire, i.e. a repertoire of linguistic resources that are relevant both for communication with relatives in Senegal and for symbolising belonging and identity (cf. Cho et al. 1997). As discussed in Chapter 2, Section 2.1, the concept of repertoire enhances our understanding of languages as sets of resources rather than bounded entities. In a sociolinguistic repertoire approach, languages are understood in relation to one another, in distinction from one another, and as functionally as well as emotionally differentiated in themselves (Busch 2012: 520). Repertoires are formed through various learning processes which can lead to diversity and fluidity in language practices. Therefore, instead of studying linguistic heritage as consisting of one or more distinct heritage languages, we examine which linguistic resources are central for transnational interaction with relatives and for symbolic aspects of identity construction related to a speaker's or group's ethnolinguistic background. In this sense, a heritage language repertoire is a spatial repertoire inasmuch as it links 'the repertoires formed through individual life trajectories to the available linguistic resources in particular places' (Pennycook & Otsuji 2014: 166). In our case, these places are not only material environments, such as a family home in Norway and Senegal, but are created through interpersonal mediated communication.

Language ideologies weave together social and interactional practices with historical and political knowledge and personal, biographical experience (Busch 2017). In this book, we therefore seek to understand how family members conceive of their linguistic heritage and how heritage language features and practices surface in their digital communication. We first examine how parents value different linguistic resources and negotiate linguistic heritage (8.1). We then focus on repertoire in a biographical perspective (Busch 2012), investigating participants' reflections on past, present, and future uses of heritage languages (8.2). Third, we adopt a language socialisation lens and examine excerpts of transnational interaction where family children draw on their heritage repertoire (8.3). In this process, we also look closely at the heritage language resources in relation to mediagrams (8.3.1), diverse heritage language registers that are available to the family children in digital interaction (8.3.2), and their heritage language learning activities online (8.3.3). In concluding, we summarise how the practices examined in this chapter affect language use in the family and revisit the advantages of a repertoire approach to heritage language (8.4).

8.1 Parents' ideologies of linguistic heritage

As discussed in Chapter 2, Section 2.2, FLP research investigates how ideologies of language and learning affect a family's interactional practices. To discuss the relationship between the two, we start with how the four families value linguistic resources in terms of their own conceptions of identity. Many studies of heritage language and family multilingualism examine bilingual situations where there is a clear distinction between a heritage language, on the one side, and a majority language on the other, as in the case of Tamil or Italian families in the USA (Canagarajah 2019, De Fina 2012) or Spanish speakers in Canada (Guardado 2018). However, this is not so straightforward with families of Senegalese background in Norway. As discussed in Chapter 3, different languages are associated with different social domains, identities, and values in Senegal, and while the use of these languages is often fluid, the language-ideological boundaries between them are quite clear-cut, a fact that is also reflected in their use in stylisation (Lexander 2018). In the process of (post-)migration, the rich linguistic repertoires of Senegalese speakers are reconfigured. The new social environments favour the use of certain languages and disfavour others, and new resources and practices are incorporated into the repertoire. But if Senegalese immigrants associate Senegality with multilingualism (cf. Smith 2019 and Chapter 3), how can we assume a single and specific 'heritage language'? Rather, there seem to exist several heritage language candidates in a migration and diaspora context such as Norway: Wolof, 'the national language', various other Senegalese languages such as Joola and Peul, and also French, Senegal's official and formal literacy language. Arabic, too, is part of language practices associated with the cultural background of three of the families. How do all these options play out when parents who have migrated decide what languages to pass on to their children? An important aspect of this issue is also the extent to which parents' and children's understanding of heritage languages differ. As Blackledge et al. (2008: 537) suggest, 'it cannot be assumed that the preservation and transmission of "heritage" is straightforward. Simply the process of "passing on" resources will alter them.'

The Bâ family presents an interesting illustration of this. In one of our first interviews, the two parents talked about language as interrelated with identity. As presented in Chapter 3, Sara and Cheikh Bâ named several different languages in their repertoire, related to their multilingual childhoods, their mobility in adulthood, their work life, and religion. Cheikh Bâ grew up speaking Peul, Joola, and Wolof from birth, then acquired French, English, Arabic, Spanish, and Italian through schooling. He claimed that he thought in Wolof and spoke this language with other Senegalese. With his family in Senegal and France, he used Peul. Joola was a third language he learnt in childhood, but rarely spoke (see Interview data 3.2). Norwegian-born Sara also spoke Wolof. During data collection, the two of them mostly used Norwegian and French and Cheikh expressed a desire to improve his Norwegian skills. He used Peul with his daughter when she was a toddler, but Norwegian later took over. Sara wanted their children to learn Peul, but as Interview data 8.2 below shows, the parents did not fully agree on what languages to prioritise for the children.

INTERVIEW DATA 8.2: SARA AND CHEIKH BÂ

Sara   Men jeg tror det er der vi har vært litt uenige, fordi, jeg som har to kulturer selv, ehm, jeg mener, det er jo ikke ofte jeg har villet kunne brukt [språk], men det ville vært så viktig for min identitet, og min kultur, og min, ja mest min identitet, å kunne snakke det, fordi det er så mye kultur i et språk, ikke sant, at da kunne jeg forstå meg selv bedre, hvis jeg hadde det språket og det er derfor jeg har tenkt at det er viktig at barna får [Cheikh] sitt språk, selv om det ikke er så mange som snakker det, så der har vi kanskje tenkt litt forskjellig
But I think that we have disagreed on that, because, I have two cultures myself, erm, I mean, it is not so often that I have had the opportunity to speak [my father's language], but it would be so important for my identity, and my culture, and my, yeah, mostly my identity, to be able to speak it, because there is so much culture in a language, right, and then I could understand myself better, if I had that language, and that is why I have thought that it is important that the children get [Cheikh]'s language, even if there are not so many who speak it, so there, we've maybe reflected differently on it
(...)

Cheikh   Ja. Jeg synes på en måte også, jeg tenker, ok, det er viktig at hun [datteren] snakker peul, men først, den identiteten, hvis hun vil finne identitet, hvis hun noen ganger føler seg Senegalese, er det ikke best å finne seg et språk som hun skal snakke med alle?
Yes. I also find that, I think, okay, it is important that she [Nabou] speaks Peul, but first, that identity, if she wants to find identity, if she ever feels Senegalese, isn't it better to find a language that she can speak to everybody?

This excerpt illustrates the ambiguities of the association between identity and language. Both parents refer to identity, but define it differently, and their disagreement seems to be congruent with their language socialisation experiences, their *Spracherleben* (Busch 2017). Sara, who grew up in Norway with a Norwegian mother and a father from a different country, explained how her own experience of missing the opportunity to use her father's first language, the language of her 'second culture', affected her wishes for her children. She justified this by raising the importance of language to emotional and self-realising aspects of identity ('I could understand myself better, if I had that language') and by the ways in which language and culture are intertwined ('there is so much culture in a language'), adding that her husband's family were very attached to their Peul identity.

Cheikh agreed on this. He, too, viewed language as important for identity, but instead of emphasising the link of language to emotions and cultural belonging, he argued for his daughter learning French for communicative purposes ('a language that she can speak to everybody'). He viewed identity as primarily related to nation rather than ethnic origin, and thus prioritised French as a heritage identity marker for his children ('if she wants to find identity, if she ever feels Senegalese…'). Cheikh's statement can further be considered in relation to his current use of Peul, which he only spoke with closest family members back in the homeland. His choice of French rather than Wolof as a heritage language for his daughter is interesting, given that Wolof is the language he himself claimed to think in and use with Senegalese people outside his family. If he were to take a purely pragmatic stance and choose the language with the highest number of speakers in Senegal, he should have picked Wolof. However, Wolof does not have the same formal status as French. As explained in Chapter 3, Section 3.3, many non-Wolof Senegalese, including Peul speakers, express concern about the 'Wolofisation' of Senegalese society, whereby an increasing number of people adopt Wolof as their first language. In Cheikh's statements, the ideological link of French to cultural and economic capital seems to come into play. Furthermore, French may appear as more neutral, not entangled in interethnic competition among other ethnolinguistic communities in Senegal. And finally, in the Norwegian context, learning and practising French appears as more feasible than acquiring Wolof.

Sara, too, referred to language-ideological aspects, but linked French to colonialism and arrogance. Sara claimed: *Jeg vil ikke at de skal komme til Senegal og bare snakke fransk. Det blir så toubab, liksom* ('I don't want them to come to Senegal and speak French only. That's so "white people", kind of' (interview data)). The word *toubab* (Wolof for 'white people'), is a slightly pejorative term for a white person or an African considered to be westernised (N'Diaye Corréard et al. 2006: 540). It thus indexes a Eurocentric attitude that disregards Senegalese languages. By rejecting a *toubab* viewpoint, Sara adopts a Senegalese perspective vis-à-vis her children. Sara herself did not 'speak French only' either, as was evident for example in her Instagram exchanges with her Senegalese sister-in-law where Sara emblematically used Peul words like *a jaaraama* ('thank you') along with French. Sara's narrative becomes meaningful in the light of her own experience with using Wolof in Senegal to facilitate inclusion and interaction. She said she wanted to learn Peul, but her husband was not 'that eager' to help, and Cheikh's response on this was that he never learnt Peul formally himself and therefore would not be good at teaching it. In fact, Cheikh used the pronoun 'we' to index an assumed (indeed, imagined) broader lack of Peul teaching competence among Peul speakers. Cheikh's wishes for his daughter to learn French may also be seen along these lines. Having himself learnt French in school, he might find it easier to teach it. To this end, he was also supported by the Norwegian school system, while this was not the case for Peul and Wolof.

Other studies of families with ideologically stratified linguistic repertoires present similar findings in terms of how heritage languages are defined. For example, Li & Zhu (2019a) discuss the case of a mother who encouraged her children to learn Mandarin, not the parents' first languages Hakka and Cantonese, because it would be useful to them if they went to China to work and study. A family taking part in Little's (2020a) study, where both parents spoke Malay, reported passing on Chinese, which only the mother spoke, to the son. Across these examples, the importance of a language for the children's future possibilities, as currently imagined by the parents, gains priority in their decisions concerning intergenerational transmission.

We find a comparable situation in the Coly family. Astou, the mother, grew up with Joola-speaking parents in Wolof-speaking Dakar, using Wolof with her siblings and later also with her own children. Her oldest, Awa, included both Joola and Seereer (spoken by her father's ethnic group) in her language portrait. She said that she felt she should know these languages since her parents knew them, thus referring more to a moral obligation, responsibility, and emotions than to the languages' practical usefulness. Astou also expressed positive emotions toward the Mandinka language, which was spoken by her parents and relatives in the Gambia: 'it's a very nice language, I like Mandingue' (original: *det er et veldig fint språk, jeg liker mandingue* (interview data)), though her appreciation of Mandinka did not extend to using it with the children. For the Coly family, Wolof was a heritage language in practice, while other named languages appeared more as emotionally linked to identity.

In the Sagna family, Felipe and Rama presented their linguistic heritage as including Joola, Wolof, and French. Rama said in the interview: 'Joola is kind of my mother tongue' (original: *joola er liksom det morsmålet-språket mitt*), and added that her mother did not want her to speak too much Wolof, because of many 'bad words' in this language. Rama reported she did use Wolof with her friends and her sister, but the spoken interaction that Kristin observed during her visits to the Sagna family was in Wolof and Norwegian. This may of course be related to Kristin's competence in these two languages, but Rama also explained that she wrote to her mother in Wolof and French, adding that she kept forgetting Joola, because she did not use it with her father that much (cf. Chapter 3, Section 3.3.2). Rama defined French as 'a little mother tongue in a way', and Felipe added that he wanted his daughter to improve her skills in French. Felipe, too, viewed Joola as 'mother tongue' (*morsmål*) and Wolof as 'the national language' (*nasjonalspråket*) and suggested they needed to use both languages more actively in their daily life in Norway, because 'they are our languages and are needed when you go down there', i.e. to Senegal (original: *det er våres språk og det trengs når man går ned der* (interview data)). So languages with different metalinguistic designations – 'mother tongue' and 'national language' – were considered to be part of an integrated repertoire.

A concern about relatives' negative reactions was also expressed by the Diagne parents who belonged to the Wolof ethnic group, came from a dominantly Wolof-speaking city, did not count any other Senegalese languages in their repertoire, and consequently talked about Wolof as their 'mother tongue'. Even though many relatives tried to talk to the children in French when they met them face-to-face or online, it was Wolof that the parents wanted their children to learn. They claimed that while their relatives expected their children to master French, they also criticised them if they did not speak Wolof. The two languages seemed to represent different types of identity, one 'emigrated' and one 'Senegalese', and the parents prioritised the latter.

We see, then, that there is not one single heritage language in any of these families; their linguistic heritage is multilingual. Even the Diagnes considered French important as a written heritage language. While the families' linguistic heritage was diverse, particular linguistic resources carried different values in the families, related to the status they had in Senegalese society and to the language ideologies of different family members. Although not explicitly mentioned by the families, the Norwegian context probably also affected the families' discourses on language. For example, the concept of 'mother tongue' is frequently used in public (educational) discourse and was taken up by the Sagna and Diagne families, even though it does not fit well with the linguistic repertoire of many multilingual Norwegian families, including those with Senegalese background. The families' perspectives on French, English, and Arabic, too, were influenced by the values assigned to these languages in Norwegian society, especially in schools and the mass media.

Overall, all four families expressed two main motivations for investing in their heritage language repertoire, one related to symbolic value, the other to communicative status. On the one hand they referred to their identity and socio-emotional well-being as individuals and as a family. On the other they also expressed more peripheral communication needs (cf. Little 2020a) with regard to people in Senegal. In the Bâ parents' discourse, the ideology surrounding Senegal's languages and the parents' desired identities for their children appeared as particularly important. For Cheikh, the French language would lead to an anticipated 'Senegalese' identity, associated with the educated elite; his perception of language as capital trumped the association of language to local identity. For Sara, French language skills represented as such a European or Eurocentric identity. It is only by looking at ideology, capital, and identity together that we can explain the parents' investment in heritage language for their children (cf. Norton 2013).

8.2 Heritage language repertoires in time and space

We now delve into the participants' conceptualisations of repertoires in a temporal and biographical perspective, comparing the metalinguistic reflections by Ousmane Diagne and his oldest son, Momar. We examine the meanings they attribute to named languages and language practices in light of their life trajectories, past experiences, and hopes for the future (cf. Busch 2012). As discussed in our polycentricity analysis (Chapter 7), speakers participate in various spaces of communication, each with its own language ideologies and pragmatic expectations. Following up on the importance of space in sociolinguistic analysis, Pennycook and Otsuji (2014: 167) emphasise the relationships between language-biographical trajectories, communicative activities, and spatial organisation, focusing on how spatial and individual repertoires are entangled as speakers bring linguistic resources into particular places, and places afford linguistic resources for speakers to take up. In a similar vein, we examine our participants' perspectives on heritage repertoires linked to past, present, and future practices and located in offline and online spaces of communication.

As explained in Chapter 4, we used language portraits to gain insight into our participants' emotional experience of language (cf. Busch 2012). Comparing the language portraits and corresponding interview data by Ousmane and Momar Diagne, we ask about the chronotopes (Bakhtin 1981) they evoke and how these are linked to heritage language repertoires. Ousmane Diagne's language portrait features a man with a big heart inside and tears streaming from his eyes (Image 8.2).

Ousmane relates his linguistic repertoire to statements in three languages, which appear in three bubbles placed around the silhouette's head. The top bubble says *boulma fate!* ('don't forget me') with *Wolof* written on top, the bubble to the right reads *Hei! Se på meg NORSK* ('Hi! Look at me Norwegian'), and the one to the left has French text, *j'arrive!* ('I'm coming'), and *Fransk* ('French') written on top. The three bubbles represent the three main languages Ousmane and his family used. The Wolof caption, *boulma fate!* relates to his wish of maintaining Wolof and his concern about his children not learning it, while Norwegian *Hei! Se på meg* and French *j'arrive!* indicate his wish for attention, Ousmane explained.

Heritage language repertoires 173

Image 8.2 Language portrait of Ousmane Diagne

INTERVIEW DATA 8.3: OUSMANE DIAGNE

Ousmane   *Jeg har tegna en stor og sterk mann som e veldig trygg, men som egentlig ikke er det, for at han er bekymra for det språkutviklinga sitt*
I have drawn a big and strong man who is very secure, but who isn't actually, because he is worried about his language development

Kristin   *Ja, akkurat*
Yeah, right

Ousmane   *På grunn av at han vil ta vare på wolof som som e morsmål, som vi må ha med videre i livet så ser jeg at det går ikke riktig vei for noen av dem. [yngste sønn], for eksempel, han forstår ingenting på wolof og [datter] har lite ord på wolof så det bekymrer meg veldig. Samtidig så ser jeg at det kan gå bra, de har en storebror som er interessert i wolof, så de ser ham som et eksempel, et forbilde, det kan kanskje hjelpe de, en dag vil de være interessert i morsmålet. Som e en del av dem. Som e veldig viktig med tanke på å reise til Senegal*

> Because he wants to conserve Wolof, which is mother tongue, that we need to bring with us in life, I see that it doesn't go right for any of them. [Abdou] for instance, he doesn't understand any Wolof, and [Marième] has only a few words in Wolof, so that worries me a lot. At the same time, I see that it may turn out alright; they have a brother who is interested in Wolof, so they see him as an example, an ideal; this might help them. One day they will be interested in their mother tongue, which is part of them, which is very important when you go to Senegal.

Ousmane Diagne was particularly concerned about his two youngest children's lack of competence in Wolof, and his concerns related to both identity ('we need to bring it with us in life') and practical communication needs linked to a distant place and time ('very important when you go to Senegal'). His daughter, Marième, confirmed this observation when commenting on her own language portrait: the parents spoke Wolof to her, but she answered in Norwegian. His youngest, Abdou, called Wolof *Senegal-språk* 'Senegal language' and added it was not used in kindergarten; there they only spoke *ordentlig språk* 'real language'. Oumou shared the same concerns as her husband, and therefore, as she pointed out in the interview, aimed to speak only Wolof to the children at home. However, she admitted that Abdou asked her to speak 'real language' when spoken to in Wolof. An interesting turn took place during the language portrait interview with Abdou, who was then 5 years old. The interview was conducted in Norwegian, but suddenly Abdou started speaking Wolof. Both the parents and the researcher thought he was giving an example of Wolof language use. However, as Abdou repeated over and over the same phrase, it became evident that he was thirsty and uttered a request in Wolof to get something to drink. It is likely that Abdou considered Wolof the most powerful linguistic resource in that specific situation in order to make his parents and the interviewer stop talking and help him out instead. We instantly interpreted his use of Wolof along this line, i.e. as an intentional display of his Wolof skills. Abdou not only contested his parents' concerns, but also demonstrated that his apparent negative stance towards Wolof did not restrain him from using it purposefully in a setting where Norwegian would also be an acceptable option. This incident supported Ousmane's optimism, expressed in the interview: 'One day they will be interested in their mother tongue'. In this respect, Ousmane held his oldest son, Momar, as a model speaker (cf. Little 2020a on older children as heritage language speakers for the younger siblings). Moreover, Ousmane had noticed a change in his daughter's attitude after a presentation on Senegal that she gave in school. The parents encouraged Marième to do a presentation about her country of heritage, and its success apparently had important consequences for her view of Wolof:

> **INTERVIEW DATA 8.4: OUSMANE DIAGNE**
>
> Ousmane: *Det var så populært at ho måtte ta det på nytt igjen (...) Læreren var liksom, oj... Og så sa ho. Og da var ho veldig stolt. Da kom ho tilbake og så sa ho, Pappa, vet du hva, jeg, dem trodde jeg bodde i sånn, he, he, he, ha, ha*
> It was so popular that she had to repeat it. (...) The teacher was like oh! And then she said. And she was so proud. She came back and then she said, Dad, you know what, they thought that I lived in like, he, he, he, ha, ha
>
> Kristin: *Ja*
> Yeah
>
> Ousmane: *Ja, ho viste bilder av [home city], masse bilder av fine, da var dem sånn, elevene var sjokkert, dem, for dem trodde ikke at [daughter] kom fra et land hvor det var, eh.. som var sånn, da. Da kom hun hjem og så sa hun Pappa, vet du hva, jeg... siden det så har jeg sett at hun har begynt å bli interessert i Senegal. I [home city] og hvor hun kommer fra og sånne ting, for det at det vekker litt noen ting når dem merker at andre, hva andre synes om dem (...) Siden det så har ho begynt å bli veldig opptatt av språket sitt, da. Av å lære. Det synes jeg er veldig bra. Det blir bare mer og mer.*
> She showed pictures of [home city], lots of pictures of beautiful, they were like, the classmates were shocked, they didn't think that [Marième] came from a country that was ehrm... like that. When she came home, then she said, Dad, you know what, I... since then I have seen that she has become interested in Senegal. In [home city] and where she comes from and such, because it wakes up something in them when they notice that others, what others think about them. (...) since then she has become very interested in her language, to learn. I think that is very good. It's just more and more.

This way, school became a place where Marième's geographical, cultural, and linguistic background was valued. Her family's life trajectory was linked to the school context as a valuable resource for schoolwork, raising positive attention to the language of the country she presented to the group. This way, the spatial repertoire of the school was extended to include Wolof, if only in a symbolic way. This story illustrates how feelings of pride and support, or at least acceptance, affect the motivation to develop skills, making the identity associated with specific linguistic resources more attractive (Norton 2013). In fact, Marième's Wolof skills continued to grow during the project. At the last data collection meeting with the family in 2020, Marième said that she used her mobile phone for contact with her cousin in Senegal, without her parents as mediators. This was in line with the wishes her parents expressed for future contact between their children and their relatives in Senegal.

176 *Heritage language repertoires*

Image 8.3 Language portrait of Momar Diagne

Momar Diagne was already communicating with relatives online at the beginning of the project. During the language portrait session, he expressed the wish to maintain Wolof, just like his father. Since he had lived in Senegal until he turned six, Wolof was his main language before coming to Norway. Momar's portrait (Image 8.3), like his father's, has lines going from the head to bubbles with various language labels: *Wolof*, *Fransk* ('French'), *Sleng* ('slang'), *Engelsk* ('English'), *Norsk bokmål/ nynorsk* ('Norwegian Bokmål' and 'New Norwegian', Norway's two official written languages).

When commenting on his drawing, Momar expressed a similar perspective on Wolof to his father:

INTERVIEW DATA 8.5: MOMAR DIAGNE

Momar   *Ja, jeg har laga en tegning av en mann som er litt forvirra for at en har liksom, skal kunne så mange, så mye språk, så han kan blande litt, da*
I have drawn a guy who is a little confused, because he has kind of, he is supposed to know so many languages, so he may mix (...)

Kristin	*Ja* Yes
Momar	*Det er alle språkene han kan litt av og han kan litt av alle språkene og han skal prøve å lære seg litt mer norsk og wolof og huske wolof. Det er liksom litt slik jeg har det nå, fordi at jeg må jo prøve å huske litt på wolof og så må jeg fortsette med å lære norsk og, jeg kan jo norsk, men det er jo fortsatt ting som jeg fortsatt må lære meg, engelsk også må jeg lære meg og fransk og litt slangspråk og litt sånn.* Those are all the languages he knows a little, and he knows a little of all the languages and he is trying to learn more Norwegian and Wolof, and remember Wolof. It is kind of the way it is for me now, because I do have to remember Wolof a little, and I have to continue learning Norwegian too, and I do know Norwegian, but there are still things that I have to learn. English I also have to learn and French and a little slang language and so on

Here Momar justified his wish to maintain Wolof in both symbolic and communicative terms. First, by the fact that he is from Senegal and therefore needs to know his 'mother tongue', which is 'part of' him, thus referring to identity in a way that mirrored his father's statements. Second, by his wish to communicate with his cousins whose first language is Wolof, again taking up a point made by Ousmane. Momar thus reflected on both the ethnic-cultural aspect of identity upheld by Sara Bâ *and* the communicative benefits of language that Cheikh Bâ focused on (cf. Section 8.1). Both Ousmane and Momar mentioned an 'unconscious' use of French in the home, in interaction, and on TV. Momar also identified French-Wolof fluidity when he said 'there is much French in Wolof', thereby articulating a translanguaging perspective on heritage language practices. Even though Wolof was identified as their main heritage language, French was also viewed as part of heritage language practices. Anxiousness related to Wolof was expressed by both participants.

Several factors related to the promotion of the heritage language repertoire were mentioned by the Diagne parents, and three spaces in particular were invoked as essential for the development of their children's linguistic repertoire: home, school, and digital space. First, they indicated that they made an effort to engage in domestic use of Wolof in interactions between parents and children, but apparently with varying levels of success. This commitment to the use of Wolof was particularly salient for them, as large parts of their communicative repertoire were not in everyday use outside the family. Wolof literacy was not mentioned; even though they sometimes used it in digital interaction, their focus was on spoken language. When they texted each other in the family, they used mainly Norwegian. Within the family, Momar was considered a 'good' Wolof-speaking model for his younger siblings. This was not a role that Momar himself directly addressed, but through his reflections around his linguistic repertoire, he showed that he represented attitudes and practices that could inspire his siblings, even though this is not necessarily the case, as we know from other research (see King 2013).

Second, the school: as pointed out above, Abdou, the family's youngest, linked the distinction between 'real language' and 'Senegal language' to the distinction between pre-school space, where Norwegian predominated, and home, where Wolof was also present. On the other hand, Marième's school presentation and the positive feedback it received led to an increased interest in her linguistic heritage. The school appears to be a space that can support heritage language symbolically, even though it puts Norwegian in a superior position.

Third, the digital space was mentioned as offering motivation and occasions for using Wolof. The parents observed how relatives in Senegal were eager to communicate with their children on Facebook Messenger or Skype, but that the latter's Wolof competence was a challenge. However, our focus group data (cf. Interview data 8.6 below) shows that through dealing with the gap between relatives' expectations and children's heritage language skills, parents and children could reflect on their own sociocultural identity and strengthen their family ties, sharing ideas, thoughts, and feelings.

During this focus group discussion with all the parents, children's language learning was also among the topics discussed. All parents agreed that digital communication affected their heritage language repertoire in a positive manner, and Astou Coly shared some examples of how she acted as a broker between her children and their relatives, both linguistically and socio-culturally. When her children asked her to explain words in messages they had received, she took the occasion to explain Senegalese cultural practices. Sometimes, it was not the meaning of the word, but the meaning of culturally specific language behaviour that the children wanted to have explained:

INTERVIEW DATA 8.6: FOCUS GROUP (ADULTS)

Astou Coly	*Ja, og jeg synes også, selv om de snakker, de som er her, de skal snakke med de som er der nede, jeg synes av og til de opplever en kulturkræsj*
	Yeah, and I also think, even if they talk, those who are here, they are going to talk to those who are down there [i.e. in Senegal], I think that sometimes they experience a culture shock
Sara Bâ	*Mhm*
	Mhm
Astou Coly	*Fordi du vet barna her, de er oppvokst her, de er oppvokst der av og til barna mine kommer til meg og sier, men det er*

| | så rart!? hvorfor tenker de sånn, hvorfor sier han sånn? jeg sier, vet du hva de mener ikke det, de bare sier det, men det er ikke det som de mener fordi vi i hjemlandet vi pleier å si ting til hverandre, barna her kan se det som det er stygt
Because, you know the children here, they grew up here, they grew up there, sometimes my children come to me and say: But it is so strange!? Why do they think like that, why does he say that? I say, you know what, they don't mean it, they just say it, but it is not what they mean, because we, in the home country we usually say things to each other, the children may consider it as bad |
|---|---|
| Sara Bâ | Mhm
Mhm |
| Astou Coly | Det er ikke respekt
It is not respect |
| Sara Bâ | Mhm
Mhm |
| Astou Coly | Men vi gjør ikke det, for vi er vant til det, vi er vokst opp sånn
But we don't do that, because we are used to it, we grew up like that |

Astou Coly thus contrasted the spaces of 'here' and 'there' when reflecting on how her children were socialised into specific interactional norms in Norway ('they grew up here', past tense), then experienced that these were broken by their Senegalese interlocutors ('those who are down there', present tense). Through their conversations about digital transnational communication, cultural differences and specific expressions like *déwénati* (Wolof greeting for the Muslim New Year), Astou and her children could reflect together on these different spaces and their own positions with regard to them, i.e. their identity as multilingual individuals and family. Similar findings are reported by Al-Salmi and Smith (2015) and Szecsi and Szilagyi (2012): children actively turn to their parents as 'teachers' when they interact digitally in heritage languages.

8.3 Children's transnational heritage language practices

Against this backdrop, we now turn to digital opportunities for the family children to practise their linguistic heritage. As discussed in Chapter 2, Section 2.2.2, we adopt a language socialisation approach to examine heritage language learning. Language socialisation is 'socialisation through the use of language and socialisation to use language' (Schieffelin & Ochs 1986: 163). As an analytical tool, it provides 'important insights into the ways in which language ideologies, practices, and management in the family connect with societal language, maintenance and shift,

180 *Heritage language repertoires*

children's educational experiences, and the construction of identity and belonging' (Fogle & King 2017: 14).

For the younger participants in this study, interpersonal digitally mediated communication as well as participation in social media were important potential spaces for language socialisation, including socialisation into culturally specific heritage practices. The role of digital communication was all the more pertinent to these families, as there are so few Senegalese speakers in Norway (cf. Chapter 3) and as a consequence, opportunities for minority language socialisation in the neighbourhood or at social events were few and far between. The family children rarely met Senegalese outside the household, nor did they have an opportunity to study Wolof, Joola, or Peul in a community school. Digital media content (e.g. watching TV programs and videos where Wolof is used) and digitally mediated interaction thus came to the foreground as enablers of language learning activities, providing an environment with potentially less focus on standards than a school setting. In particular, the lack of normative control in most settings of interpersonal written interaction online makes it less risky to write a language that the writer is not literate in and offers freedom to draw on all available linguistic resources, making it easier to practise a language that the writer does not master in full (cf. Deumert 2014a, Lee 2006, Lee 2017, Reershemius 2017 and Chapter 2, Section 2.3).

To investigate how the family children made use of digital spaces for heritage language socialisation, we first analyse mediagrams to find out whom they used heritage languages (especially Wolof) with, in which language modalities, and on which media (cf. 8.3.1) Then we examine selected interactional sequences from their transnational communication with extended family members to find out *how* elements of their linguistic heritage came into play, according to interlocutor and language modality (8.3.2). In a third step we look at some instances of explicit language learning (8.3.3).

8.3.1 Heritage language repertoires by interlocutors

The oldest children in the Diagne and Coly families were considered the most prolific Wolof speakers among their siblings and were the most eager users of Wolof in digital interaction as well. Awa Coly thought her Wolof competence was 'ok', Momar Diagne found his competence to be 'fluent', and both thought that they spoke Wolof better than they wrote it. We now look at Awa and Momar's transnational digital interaction with extended family members, reviewing their mediagrams to identify interlocutors they used Wolof with.

Awa's mediagram, presented in Chapter 4 (Figure 8.1) and discussed in Chapter 5, Section 5.2, shows that Awa is an avid transnational communicator who maintains contact with aunts, uncles, and a range of peers, young men of her own age that were known to the rest of the Diagne household as well. One of them lived in Germany (labelled 'Friend Germany' on her mediagram), the rest in Senegal ('Friend 1/2/3 Senegal').

Heritage language repertoires 181

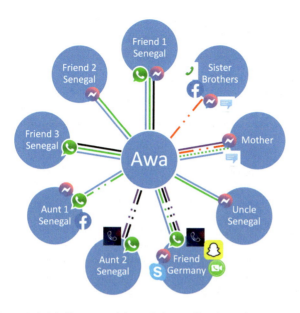

Figure 8.1 Mediagram of Awa Coly (replication of Figure 4.4)

The distribution of Wolof across these contacts was uneven. Awa claimed to use only Norwegian with her siblings and mainly Norwegian, but also some Wolof, with her mother; interactional data show that she occasionally inserted French and Arabic features in text messages to her mother (cf. Excerpt 6.3, Chapter 6). With the rest of her interlocutors (except from 'Aunt 2'), Awa used Wolof and French, and in some cases English and Arabic features as well. Awa's communication with family friends in Senegal was only written, including Wolof. We do not have digital data from these, but other available evidence (notably, Awa's exchanges with her peer in Germany, discussed below in 8.3.3, and excerpts from her brother Ibou and a young man in Senegal, cf. 8.3.2) suggests that language practices in these exchanges with Senegalese peers index youth by drawing on French, English, and Wolof. To sum up, Awa used both written and spoken Wolof and French with almost all her transnational contacts, but never used Wolof in writing with her mother and siblings. Her Wolof literacy practices were exclusively reserved for her extended family, including friends of her own age group.

Momar's mediagram (see Figure 8.2) illustrates a different pattern with respect to language and modality choice. First, Momar claimed he used Wolof to all of his interlocutors, though only in speech. In writing he switched to French or English. His mode-switching seemed to trigger code-switching (cf. Sindoni 2013 and Chapter 2, Section 2.3). Second, Momar used Wolof as one out of several resources with most of his transnational interlocutors, save his grandparents, whom he only addressed in spoken

182 *Heritage language repertoires*

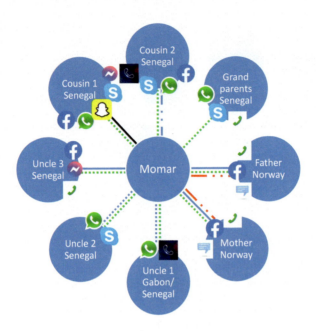

Figure 8.2 Mediagram of Momar Diagne

Wolof. This mirrored Rama's mediagram (cf. Chapter 5, Section 5.2) who only used spoken Joola to her grandmothers. Momar communicated with three uncles too, often by chiming in during his parents' conversations. He spoke both French and Wolof with two of them and spoke Wolof and wrote French with the third one. Available data (cf. Section 8.3.2) show that the French Momar used with this third uncle was rather formal and limited to polite greetings. Within his own generation Momar interacted mainly with two cousins who lived with him in the extended family home before Momar moved to Norway. One of them ('Cousin 1') studied English, and their interactive written discourse came mainly in English, while voice messages came mainly in Wolof. Momar also spoke Wolof and French with his second cousin ('Cousin 2') and their text messages were written mainly in French.

When comparing Momar's practices to Awa's, we see that language modality is an important difference. As described in Chapter 3, Wolof is more used in spoken than in written communication in Senegal. Digital interaction consolidated Wolof practices that Momar engaged with in his family household, and French practices he also encountered at his school classes. Unlike Momar, Awa used Wolof for both written and spoken communication. While she did speak Wolof with her mother, and wrote and spoke French in school, she also wrote Wolof, a practice she did not engage in offline. It was through digital interaction that she extended her Wolof practices to include writing, and it was thus digital communication with relatives outside the household that made up a potential space for practising the heritage language repertoire in writing.

8.3.2 Heritage language registers

Through communicating with transnational relatives of different generations, our younger participants interacted with different heritage language registers. While mediagrams provide information about a speaker's language, modality, and media choices towards named (groups of) interlocutors, they are not sufficient to investigate the stylistic differentiation the participants experience and/or deploy when interacting with different types of interlocutors in a heritage language. We now turn to interview and interactional data to this purpose. Recall that we theorise a heritage language register along the lines of enregisterment theory, i.e. as a cultural model that links together aspects of linguistic and social conduct in the Senegalese context (cf. Agha 2007: 145 and discussion in Chapter 2, Section 2.1.3). A register models culturally entrenched expectations of specific language practices in specific social relationships, such as the link between playfulness and specific kinship or friendship relationships illustrated in Chapter 6. In the Norwegian context, Senegalese registers are transformed into heritage language registers that are not readily observed in daily life, but are nonetheless associated with the families' cultural background (cf. Cho et al. 1997) and therefore provide important resources for engaging in social interaction with transnational family members. However, children and adolescents in diaspora do not necessarily have access to the entire range of registers of a distant society (in this case, the Senegalese). Therefore, language socialisation with respect to heritage language registers ultimately depends on the particular family interactions and relationships that younger participants have access to. We now exemplify this by comparing transnational exchanges of Momar Diagne and Ibou Coly with family members of different ages. These exchanges acted as sites of socialisation into different Senegalese registers, such as *ordentlig Wolof* ('real Wolof') or 'more modern' Wolof 'with a little French (cf. Interview data 8.7) (similar to 'Dakar Wolof'or 'Urban Wolof').

Momar Diagne interacted on the phone and via Facebook Messenger with family members of three generations: grandparents, uncles, and cousins. As for communication with grandparents, Momar described his language use with them in the interview:

INTERVIEW DATA 8.7: MOMAR DIAGNE

Momar   *Da er det bare wolof, da, for dem kan ikke noe anna, da det er sånn ordentlig wolof, for dem kan ikke fransk heller, så*
Then it's Wolof only, since they don't speak anything else. Then it's this real Wolof, because they don't speak French either, so

> Kristin   Da er det bare ren wolof?
> Then it's just pure Wolof?
>
> Momar   Ja, da er det ikke alltid at jeg forstår ting, for at dem ganske gammeldags wolof, da, for wolof har jo blitt litt mer moderne med litt fransk og sånn, da, men dem bruker skikkelige ord som jeg ikke har hørt og sånn, så kan det hende at Pappa må hjelpe meg litt
> Yes, then I don't always understand stuff, since they speak quite old-fashioned Wolof, yeah, Wolof has become a little more modern with a little French and so on, but they use real words that I haven't heard and stuff, so it may happen that Dad has to help me a little

This excerpt shows Momar's attention to his grandparents' register, which he qualifies as 'real' and 'old-fashioned'. He distinguished this from 'more modern' Wolof, which may come 'with a little French'. Since he sometimes had trouble understanding his grandparents, his father served as a language broker. This could be an occasion to learn new expressions (cf. Section 8.3.3), expressions that were not necessarily in use in other transnational family interactions in which he took part. French may have been absent in these dialogues with grandparents, but not so with his maternal uncle ('Uncle 3'). Momar wrote him short text messages with polite greetings, mainly in French (Excerpt 8.1).

> EXCERPT 8.1: MOMAR DIAGNE AND UNCLE, FACEBOOK MESSENGER
>
> Uncle   SALUT [MOMAR]
> Hi [MOMAR]
>
> Momar   Salut ☺
> Hi ☺
>
> Uncle   COMEN VAS TU ET LES ETUDES
> How are you, and the studies
>
> Momar   Ca va bien oncle. Salut ma tante et les enfants
> I am fine, uncle. Greet my aunt and the children
>
> Uncle   OK SALUT MOI TOUTE LA FAMILLE
> Ok, greet the entire family for me
>
> Uncle   **MAIS NAMENALA**
> But I miss you
>
> Momar   Moi aussi. Je vais a l école maintenant. A bientot
> Me too. I am going to school now. See you later.

Here Momar used French in a way that echoed how French is taught in school. When the uncle wrote *Namenala* 'I miss you' in Wolof, Momar answered *Moi aussi* 'me too' in French instead of the idiomatic Wolof response (such as *maa la raw* 'I exceed you', i.e. 'I miss you more'). But the uncle did not show any sign of disapproval. The predominance of French in their exchange could be motivated by the fact that they communicate in writing. From interview data with Momar, we know that he preferred speaking to writing French, but in these short messages he did write French in line with the style of French used by his uncle.

This link between distinct language and modality choices to different addressees becomes even clearer when we turn to Momar's WhatsApp exchanges with 'Cousin 1', one of his closest transnational interlocutors (in terms of contact frequency) during the data collection phase of our study. 'Cousin 1' was slightly older and studied English at the University, and the two of them lived together before Momar migrated. As Momar's mediagram shows (cf. Figure 8.2), they used a range of media, including WhatsApp, Messenger, Snapchat, and Facebook. Their spoken exchanges, including voice messages, phone, and video calls came mainly in urban Wolof, while all written exchanges came in English. Excerpt 8.2 presents transcripts of some of their voice messages.

EXCERPT 8.2: MOMAR DIAGNE AND COUSIN, WHATSAPP VOICE MESSAGES

1 Cousin   Booy sama néeg, bayyi nga ma dé
           Mate, I'm in my room, you've left me!

2 Momar   Waay nekku ma ci dara, na jàng rek, dama komanse jàng, loolu
           There's not much going on, I only do my schoolwork, I started school, that's why

3 Momar   Su'a na la woo Skype ñu waxtaan
           Tomorrow, I will call you on Skype, so that we can talk

4 Cousin   *Afin* nga share-al, nga share-al, nga *parta*... nga share -al, sama ki, sama video Facebook dégg na, nga *partage* ko
           Well, can you share, you share, you share, you share, my thing, my Facebook video, you understand, you share it

5 Momar   Waaw okey, (uh) ba suba
           Yes, okay, see you tomorrow

This episode opens with the cousin indirectly asking why he had not heard from Momar. 'You've left me' (line 1) is a typical Senegalese greeting when time has passed since the last contact. Momar gave a school-related reason (line 2) and proposed to arrange a video meeting the following day (line 3). The cousin then asked Momar to share a video of his on Facebook (line 4), Momar agreed to do so and brought their conversation to a close with reference to their video meeting the next day (line 5). In these messages, as with all other voice messages collected between them, there is spoken Wolof with French lexis, characteristic of urban Wolof, and features indexing youth such as English words and expressions (e.g. *share-al* in message 5, a grammatically integrated token of English 'share' with the Wolof imperative suffix, '–al'). However, whenever Momar and the cousin mode-switched into writing they also code-switched into English. This holds true for a large part of the entire conversation Momar shared with us (consisting of 101 messages). Momar reported that his exchange with his other cousin ('Cousin 2') followed a similar pattern, but that they used French instead of English when they exchanged written messages. This co-occurrence of code- and mode-switching – writing French or English and speaking in an urban Wolof style indexing youth – shaped Momar's transnational peer interaction. Comparing this to Momar's exchanges with his uncle and his report about communication with his grandparents, clear differences in register appear. Through these digital encounters, then, Momar developed his sociolinguistic competence, his sensitivity to Senegalese norms of interactional patterns. Even though he sometimes pronounced Wolof in a way that diverged from his cousin', his cousin never commented on that, nor did he, or the uncle, correct terms that were not idiomatic in nature.

In the corpus that we collected, Wolof was favoured in the spoken mode, but not exclusively used for spoken communication. Awa's mediagram suggests that she wrote in Wolof, too, and this was also the case for her sibling, Ibou, who interacted with uncles of different ages in online spaces. The Facebook Messenger exchange in Excerpt 8.3 took place between Ibou and a man of about his own age that the siblings called 'uncle'. Typical features of young people's texting are found here, such as English expressions, unconventional abbreviations of French words, and translanguaging.

Heritage language repertoires 187

EXCERPT 8.3: IBOU COLY WITH 'UNCLE' (IMAGE 8.4), FACEBOOK MESSENGER

Uncle: '*Hi* [Ibou], I miss you. Are you fine? If you have WhatsApp, *send* me your call number *so that* I can send you my new music *so that* you can send it to [Awa] for me. She can dance it with the *group* and send me a *video* of it.'

Ibou: 'I think I understood everything you wrote... I am fine, thanks to God. How are things in Dakar? No, I don't have WhatsApp.'

Uncle: '*Well* okay, all is well in Dakar. Is there no way I can send you music?'

Image 8.4 Ibou Coly with 'Uncle', Facebook Messenger

188 *Heritage language repertoires*

In 'Uncle's first message, there is use of Wolof with some English, in line with everyday informal discourse (spoken and in texting) among urban youth in Senegal. In particular, the expressions *new sound* and *numbr call* were more likely to be used by young than older Senegalese. Ibou opened in English, acknowledging understanding of what his interlocutor wrote in Wolof; using English not as single carefully selected words, but in the entire sentence. Then he turned to Wolof for casual greetings and to answer the uncle's question about WhatsApp. Ibou used English to convey something that he was not able to communicate in Wolof, at the same time signalling a lack of Wolof skills. However, he then switched to Wolof in a way that fit his own skills, drawing on linguistic resources similar to those of 'Uncle', but in a different way.

As with Momar, Ibou's language practices towards Senegalese peers can be contrasted with those towards Senegalese of his parents' generation, more specifically with his *bàjjen*, i.e. paternal aunt. *Bàjjen* is a female representative of the paternal line with important responsibilities for her young nephews and nieces (Diop 1985). All four Coly children maintained contact with their *bàjjen* (see Lexander 2021a), and called her by the Wolof term. Ibou in particular exchanged regular voice messages with her. Excerpt 8.4 shows a voice message from Ibou's *bàjjen* who, at that point, knew that Ibou was away from home playing football. She first asked him how the match went, then prayed for her nephew to become a successful and rich football player.

EXCERPT 8.4: IBOU COLY AND HIS BÀJJEN, WHATSAPP VOICE MESSAGES

Bàjjen Match bi leegi naka la démé? Yéna dóoro walla dan leen dóor? Insàllaa dinga toog tey bay féyè ko si *milliard* yi ci *foot*, dëgge bu neexe yalla Insàllaa rabbi dina am dé. Toog bañ lay tudde *comme* niñiy tuddè gaa yi ci télé yi, waaw-waaw, dina am dé. Ñu lay tudde di la feey ay *milliard*, insàllaa rabbi dina am. Yalna yalla japp, yalla lafal la cat, yalla lafal la cat rék, insàllaa lëpaay am. Baax na [last name], jërëjëf.

How did the match go? Did you win or did they beat you? By the grace of God, someday you'll be earning billions while playing football, indeed, by God's will, by the grace of God, that will happen. Someday your name will be all over just like the others on TV. Oh yes, it will happen. Not only will your name be famous but on top of that you'll be paid billions, by the grace of God that will come to pass. May God help, may God protect you against evil, may only God protect you from evil. By the grace of God, all will come to pass. Everything is fine, [last name], thank you.

> Ibou Waa *bàjjen* amiin, amiin *merci beaucoup*. Waay nu beenen yuul, su ma deme ba am xaalis bu bëri ma yobbula, ma yobbula Makka dengna, insàllaa, amiin, insàllaa
> Yes, aunt, amen, amen, thank you very much. By God's grace, another time, if I get a lot of money I will take you, I will take you to Mecca, do you hear me, by the grace of God, amen, by the grace of God.

As the excerpt shows, Ibou recorded another voice message in response to this, in a frame of Wolof including Arabic expressions regularly used by Muslims in Senegal and elsewhere in the world, and some French words inserted. First, as would be customary in this kind of blessing, he answered her prayer with *amen*, then he thanked her. He furthermore responded to the blessing with a promise, that if he made a lot of money, he would take her on a pilgrimage to Mecca, repeating *insàllaa* ('by the grace of God') like his aunt did. Here, Ibou designed both the form and content of his message to fit that of *bàjjen*, thereby drawing on a register of ritualised language that framed their relationship, demonstrating cultural and genre knowledge. In this example, the register is connected to kinship behaviour. Just as Momar addressed his uncle as *oncle* (Excerpt 8.1), Ibou addressed his aunt as *bajjen*, thus explicitly engaging in kinship behaviour (Chapter 6, Section 6.1). Ibou's language style in this exchange is quite different to that of Excerpt 8.3, not least in terms of making more extended use of Wolof, and a different register of Wolof, for that matter. In Ibou's Facebook Messenger conversations with uncles, a similar pattern could be observed: voice messages came in Wolof, written messages in Wolof, French, and English.

While Ibou, Awa, and Momar found it more comfortable to speak than write Wolof, the opposite was true for Aida, the youngest Coly sibling. Aida found voice messages embarrassing and preferred to answer her *bàjjen* in writing, using Wolof together with Norwegian and French features, while *bàjjen* kept on answering in voice (cf. Lexander 2021a). For Aida, it seemed like the freedom to make modality choices divergent from those of her interlocutor (i.e. to send her text rather than voice messages) facilitated her use of Wolof.

By accomplishing digitally mediated interaction with relatives of different generations, our younger participants thus interacted with heritage language registers, which featured different genres and levels of formality. Both generational and modality differences were important in this process. By alternating between speaking and writing, the participants also alternated between different linguistic resources, showing both agency and accommodation to the interlocutor. In line with other evidence in this study, spoken messages favoured the choice of Wolof. In sum, the interactional environments described in this section seemed to promote reception and/or production of heritage language registers, socialisation into culture-specific models of conduct, and the linguistic expressions of these.

8.3.3 Learning Wolof through online interaction

Several young participants discussed online activities that helped them to learn language in digital family interaction. Aida Coly claimed that she had improved her Wolof writing through taking part in a Facebook group where this language was dominant. Rama Sagna explained that she had made a deal with her cousin in France that they should correct each other: he would correct her when she made mistakes in French, and she would correct him when he made errors in English. Similarly, Momar Diagne's cousin was able to practise English, the language that he was studying in university, in digital interaction with Momar. In this final section, we analyse how heritage language learning takes place in one specific interaction, that of Awa Coly with her Senegalese peer in Germany. In this transnational peer interaction, the boundaries of learning are fluid and various resources are shared.

Awa Coly's family friend in Germany grew up in Senegal and migrated to Germany to study. He therefore used Wolof and French more confidently than her, whereas Awa's English was better than his. We see this in the 309 Facebook Messenger and 45 WhatsApp messages we have from this dyad. Playful metalinguistic discourse was central in their conversation, with the friend taking on an expert role in Wolof, and Awa acting as an eager novice. However, these roles were not stable, but constantly negotiated and contested in their interactions. In fact, this friend wanted Awa to use Wolof and repeatedly encouraged her to improve it, directly and indirectly, through text messages like **Degouma** *anglais* ('I don't understand English') and *Cest triste que tu continues a me repondre en anglais* ('It's sad that you continue to answer me in English'). He referred to both Wolof and French as preferred languages of interaction in these messages, while Awa tended to prefer English, sometimes with Wolof, Arabic, and French words and expressions. However, she did express a positive stance toward Wolof. When her friend wrote *Cest triste le fait que tu comprenais pas mes souhaits* ('It's a sad fact that you did not understand my wishes'), she replied: 'but it sounded beautiful', in English. Despite these efforts of the family friend, and his disapproval of Awa's use of English, this language seemed to be given more space in their written communication as years went by. This is illustrated in the two following excerpts: Excerpt 8.5 is from the earlier stages, prior to data collection, while Excerpt 8.6 is from a later stage, during data collection. In both excerpts, Awa's Wolof language skills are part of the conversation.

Excerpt 8.5 shows a language-learning exchange. The episode started with some opening greetings (lines 1–7), among them an expression that is new to Awa, *Louy deal bi* (line 8). Awa first asked for an explanation

Heritage language repertoires 191

(lines 9 and 10), which the friend offered (lines 15 and 17), and then Awa tried to use the expression herself in a slightly modified way (line 20). The friend corrected her and repeated the correct version (line 21).

EXCERPT 8.5: AWA COLY AND HER SENEGALESE FRIEND IN GERMANY, FACEBOOK MESSENGER

1 Friend	**Mangui doga yeksi** I just came home
2 Awa	Well daaaaaaam
3 Friend	Yep
4 Friend	**Nakala** How is it?
5 Awa	Just chilling
6 Awa	**Nakamouuu** What's up?'
7 Friend	**Sant** *fils* I thank the son', [i.e. I'm fine]
8 Friend	**Louy deal bi** What's the plan
9 Awa	Huh
10 Awa	Deal?
11 Awa	You can speak english now 😊
12 Awa	Sant in norwegian means true
13 Awa	Sant = tru
14 Awa	True*
15 Friend	**Louy deal bi** means like what is the plan
16 Awa	Ooooo
17 Friend	Or what is the deal
18 Awa	The plan is to get off the bed soon
19 Awa	Then getting ready to school
20 Awa	**Lan moy** *ca* **deal bi tay?**
21 Friend	**Louy deal bi tay***

Awa positioned herself as a novice, an eager learner of Wolof as she asked for an explanation of the new expression (likely a current popular expression) and then tried it out. In a second language acquisition perspective, the expert's reaction in message 21 may be considered a reformulation. With the purpose of clarifying and promoting the speaker's communicative purpose, the recipient presented an alternative rendering of the speaker's utterance (cf. He 2016: 669–670). Awa's friend thus positioned himself as an expert, an understanding teacher. In lines 8–21, this conversation followed the stages of 'learner-initiated negotiation routines' described by Tudini (2007: 583). It started with a 'trigger' that launched a 'linguistic, interpretive or intercultural element', by the expert, i.e. *louy deal bi* (line 8). It continued with an 'indicator', whereby Awa requested clarification ('Deal?', line 10) and expressed non-understanding ('Huh' line 9), led on to a 'response' where the expert explained (lines 15 and 17), and ended with a 'reaction to the response', here Awa testing out the new expression (line 20). However, this last response served as a 'trigger' for another round of negotiation, this time expert-initiated, leading to an 'indicator', where the expert corrected her (line 21).

This exchange features more than an expert–novice exchange around Wolof, though. Immediately after having asked the friend about the meaning of *louy deal bi*, thus positioning herself as a learner, Awa took on the expert role when, in line 11, she noted 'you can speak english now'. This continued in the next lines, as she explained that *sant*, 'thank' in Wolof, means 'true' in Norwegian. She thus reversed their usual roles of expert and novice, as well as the novice role she just accepted when she asked for an explanation. Her friend did not provide an answer to her 'expert' utterances, but rather to her novice question as he explained the meaning of the expression he introduced (line 15). Awa replied with a reception token: *Ooooo*, and the friend went on to paraphrase his explanation (line 16). Then Awa answered the Wolof question in English, in lines 18–19, thus rupturing the learning frame with a small talk frame, before she returned to the expert–novice learning frame in line 20, where she tested out the expression. This frameshifting from a small-talk frame (lines 1–8) to a learning frame (lines 8–17) and then again to a small-talk frame (lines 18–20) and back to learning (line 21) is thus interrelated with Awa's role-shifting from novice to expert to novice. She not only took on the role as the learner of Wolof, but also the role of expert in English and Norwegian. Apart from the last turn (line 21), it was Awa who directed these shifts, positioning herself and her interlocutor in various roles. Her friend mainly responded to the frames defined by Awa, but did not accept the novice role that she initiated for him in lines 11–14. However, he seized the expert role in line 21.

We see this interaction as an instance of translanguaging at the level of both practice and ideology (Chapter 2, Section 2.1.1, Chapter 3, Section 3.2.3). Both Awa and her friend drew in fluid ways on linguistic resources shared on a transnational scale. Not only did they make use of resources connected to their Senegalese background, they also drew on (global) English and (global) Arabic, and even inserted Norwegian and German words referring to their own respective local contexts. Although the latter were resources they did not have equal access to, they included them seamlessly in their conversations. In the interview, Awa referred to this as unproblematic for comprehension, since many words are similar in Norwegian and German in her view. And even though her friend did not respond to Awa's comment about the homonym, *sant*, he did express interest in and insight into the Norwegian language, sending Awa a video (of a football match from Norway) with the text: 'i am not sure but i think that's what i hear you speak norwegian right' (English in original). In addition to drawing on their entire repertoires to communicate, they also acknowledged each other's linguistic resources as valuable for acquiring new ones. The playful metalinguistic talk upon which their relationship was being constructed, built on these premises of translanguaging (Chapter 2, Section 2.1.1). As the two interlocutors played with linguistic resources and expert–novice roles throughout their year-long interaction, they created favourable conditions for heritage language practices while building a close relationship.

The insistence on language ideologies of 'good language' persisted throughout their conversations, over the years. As mentioned above, there seemed to be more English in the later conversations, that is, in the written interaction. In Excerpt 8.6, which took place approximately two years after 8.5, Wolof is reserved for voice messages while English is used in text messages.

EXCERPT 8.6: AWA COLY AND FRIEND IN GERMANY, WHATSAPP VOICE AND TEXT MESSAGES

1 Friend	Heacache [sic] each time i hear u speaking wolof
2 Friend	😷
3 Awa	😂😂😂😂
4 Friend	👤
5 Awa	👊 👊 👊 👊
6 Awa	At least i tried 🙂
7 Friend	Did u notice the way you EVERY TIME say **mais** !? [bold in original]
8 Friend	It seems you take a pause
9 Friend	And boooooom
10 Friend	Punch the poor word.
11 Awa	😂😂😂 👊 👊 👊
12 Friend	[Voice] *mais...* ha, ha, ha, ha
13 Awa	😂😂😂😂
14 Awa	Whatever!

194 *Heritage language repertoires*

15	Friend	😂😂
16	Awa	Practice makes perfect 😊
17	Awa	👊👊👊
18	Friend	Nah! It wouldn be funny if you speak well
19	Friend	So keep being like this
20	Friend	Me to have fun
21	Awa	Haha nooooo, poor my future kids
22	Friend	Yeah poor them
23	Awa	They can't speak broken Wolof
24	Friend	But dont worry SUPER COOL uncle [Friend] will force them to speak wolof
25	Friend	A good wolof
26	Awa	good idea! 😊

The episode started when Awa sent a voice message in Wolof to her friend, and he answered with written messages, first mocking her pronunciation (lines 1, 2, 4, 7, 8, 9, 10), then imitating it in a voice message (line 12). Interestingly, the friend used the French loanword *mais*, frequently used in everyday Wolof interaction, as an example when he wanted to mock her pronunciation of Wolof, thus underlining the fluidity of boundaries between these languages. When Awa responded to her friend's mocking, she did not appear as hurt or upset. She played along as the novice, bringing in her good intentions: 'At least i tried' (message 6), and a series of emoji-only messages (lines 3, 5, 11, 13). The 'face with tears of joy' emoji seem to signal that she interpreted her friend's mocking as playful teasing, while the 'oncoming fist' emoji can signal several meanings. In line 5, they can be interpreted as a way of congratulating her friend's punch line, or cheering up in view of the facepalm emoji, in both cases playful responses. In line 11, they can be interpreted as a direct response to the friend's claim that it sounds as if Awa punches the word, showing alignment with the friend's discourse on her pronunciation. Awa also responded to the voice message mocking her pronunciation with the 'face with tears of joy' emoji (line 13). Then, she stated 'Whatever!' (line 14), marking a turn, perhaps signalling that the mocking had been going on for long enough. In the following message (line 15), the friend responded with the same emoji as Awa used in line 13, as if indicating alignment with her, and confirming that he was only teasing her, not criticising. In line 16, Awa added a 'smiling face with sunglasses' emoji, signalling again that she was not upset about the friend's mocking. In this message (line 16), Awa pointed to the need for practice to learn, defending her imperfect pronunciation: 'Practice makes perfect'.

In this excerpt, Awa positioned herself first as a heritage language learner, like in Excerpt 8.5 above, but then also as a transmitter of Wolof, as she talked about 'my future kids' (line 21). The quality of the input for these 'future kids' thus came up as a topic, as the two interlocutors distinguished 'good' and 'broken' Wolof (lines 23 and 25). Finally, her friend brought up the importance of extended family members, when he suggested that he could be the 'SUPER COOL uncle' who 'forces' Awa's children to speak Wolof (message 24). It is not clear if Awa found this to be a 'good idea', as she wrote in message 26, since she added a face screaming in fear emoji, but it could perhaps also signal that she was frightened by the task of transmitting Wolof to her own children. Kinship terms were used to talk about the future family life, presenting Awa as a responsible mother, transmitting linguistic heritage to children, and then engaging her German friend, who positioned himself as an 'uncle' to support her in this task. Even though the two interlocutors practised languages in fluid ways, Awa discussed the transmission of Wolof in terms of not wanting to pass on a 'broken' language in the conventional terms of a mother passing on a heritage language to the children, and her friend also talked about 'forcing' children to speak 'good' Wolof.

When Awa talked about her future as a mother, she presented it as given that she would use Wolof with her children, but she also presented doubts and fear – in a playful way, as signalled by emoji. This excerpt resonates with Sara Bâ's Facebook post presented at the beginning of this chapter as it expresses the wish that the children speak a language related to their Senegalese background. Here, however, it is the children's generation reflecting on future family language policy, on the significance of their own learning of heritage language and their responsibility towards the coming generations. If this playful interaction revealed some of Awa's actual ideas about her language use with her future children, it indicated that she, too, intended to strive towards the use of Wolof, as part of a broad repertoire.

The examples analysed in this section displayed how the children's generation executed agency for learning purposes in digital transnational peer communication. Their strategies for doing so included playfulness, meta talk, and translanguaging. Several studies look at computer games and online videos as spaces for learning heritage languages (Little 2019, Said 2021). However, for languages like Wolof, let alone Peul and Joola, such pedagogical resources do not exist. Furthermore, learning in transnational interpersonal interaction has advantages that computer games cannot provide, like up-to-date knowledge of the most appropriate expressions in specific interactions. As such, the heritage language competence acquired here aligns with the practice-based approaches by Canagarajah (2019) and De Fina (2012). This competence is also developed in situations in which the parents want their children to be able to draw on such competence, in encounters with their transnational family members. Awa's interaction with her friend in Germany illustrates several aspects of language socialisation. First, it exposes the negotiation of roles of 'expert' and 'novice' in learning language and the negotiation of language norms. Related to this, it shows how the novice executes agency, sometimes to reverse the roles, and how the language socialisation in itself is closely related to the forming of relationships.

8.4 Conclusions: Heritage languages and mediational repertoires

Our investigation of the families' heritage language repertoires shows the importance of metalinguistic labels in the discourse about linguistic heritage, with different languages being pointed out as having stratified symbolic values with regard to identity. It also demonstrates fluidity, as diverse linguistic resources are drawn upon to interact with relatives in Senegal, and as these resources are considered to be part of the same heritage language repertoire. The wishes expressed by both parents and children to engage with heritage resources can be realised in digital interaction. In dialogues with their relatives, they may test out words and expressions, and communicate with diverging accents and non-normative language use. Detailed analysis of interactional data reveals children's engagement with different heritage registers, as communication varies with interlocutors and modality. As discussed above, language socialisation is both learning through language and learning to use language (Schieffelin and Ochs 1986). It implies the internalisation of norms and expectations in specific cultural contexts (He 2008). These contexts may be created online, and the learning, or the incorporation of new practices into the repertoire, can take place as mediated by the screen (Zhao & Flewitt 2020), or around the screen in intergenerational interaction (Kenner et al. 2008, He 2016, Parven 2016). Through digital interaction, the younger members of the Norwegian-Senegalese families take part in language socialisation into the Senegalese family community. As the examples suggest, they show agency as active actors in these encounters, which become part of their lived experience of language (Busch 2012, 2017). We also observe that the heritage language repertoire is part of the participants' larger mediational repertoire, where language, modality, and media choice interrelate. This chapter once again demonstrates that digital media affordances influence (but do not determine) language practices. Not only does the affordance of speech favour the use of Wolof, but the mere affordance of both language modalities can impact on mediated interaction, as the exchanges between Aida and her *bàjjen* shows. The heritage language repertoire thus makes up one of several resources that interlocutors draw on in mediated interaction. For migrated parents who want their children to learn heritage languages, transnational interaction with extended family members definitely seems to support this aim. However, adolescents in these families also create their own private spaces for exchange with transnational interlocutors, in which to try out their multilingual heritage. In sum, digital communication enables the Senegalese-background families to carve out occasions to engage with their linguistic heritage in ways that are not part of their local everyday life in Norway. We can thus conclude that transnational digital communication is a key site for the enactment of family language policy in its broadest sense.

9 Conclusions

In this book we have explored how the linguistic repertoires of four Norwegian-Senegalese families are constantly negotiated in digital spaces, informed by patterns of language use in Senegal and Norway as well as by global linguistic flows. At the core of this process lie practices of mediated interaction, whereby family members draw on multimodal resources to manage their interpersonal networks, express affection, and engage in diaspora practices and multilingual language socialisation. We presented evidence of how digital interactions encompass maintenance and development of both family relationships and heritage languages, providing an analysis that is not only valid for the specific case of Norwegian-Senegalese families, but also for the transformation of family multilingualism in a digital age. Our work also points to more general issues of language and migration, more precisely regarding how the maintenance of transnational social relations through digital connectivity creates spaces where specific language practices are developed.

The research presented in this book focuses on multilingual families through the lens of digitally mediated communication. Our theoretical approach pulls together practice and repertoire approaches to family multilingualism and online communication (Chapter 2). We also draw on language socialisation approaches to family multilingualism and on media anthropological research with transnational families, in particular polymedia theory. Key to our analysis of families' linguistic repertoires is an understanding of how language practices are contextualised in settings with multiple, sometimes contradictory sociolinguistic norms. Chapter 3 spelled out the sociolinguistic dynamics that are relevant to the four families we followed in fieldwork. We coined the concept of mediational repertoires and developed mediagrams as a method to chart the interrelation between the linguistic and media resources deployed by the family members to engage with translocal interlocutors (Chapter 4). We then analysed mediagrams of seven participants, exploring their media and language choices, and showing how they framed their communication with specific interlocutors (Chapter 5). Against this backdrop, we explored three main topics by means of fine-grained analysis of interactional data: families as translocal discursive

DOI: 10.4324/9781003227311-9

spaces (Chapter 6), digital diaspora practices (Chapter 7), and heritage language repertoires (Chapter 8). Overall, our findings show that digital communication is a key enabler of transnational sociability, with the family as the point of departure, and language is a key indicator of the ways in which practices in the societies of origin retain significance for family identities.

In the remainder of this conclusion, we discuss the implications of our methodological framework for studying linguistic aspects of digital connections (9.1). We then discuss how the findings of this book extend our understanding of the relationship between digital transnational communication and family multilingualism (9.2), and conclude on how we contribute to the field of family multilingualism with our perspective on the digital heritage language repertoire (9.3).

9.1 Multi-sited ethnography: Studying mediational repertoires

The aim of our framework was to bridge current gaps in family multilingualism and media studies of transnational families. Simply put, family multilingualism research largely lacks a digital dimension, while media studies with transnational families lack a sociolinguistic dimension. However, we argue that the integration of the two is crucial in building an understanding of the specifics of digital language practices in transnational families and, thereby, gaining broader insight into family multilingualism, given the role played by digital interaction in contemporary family life. We coined the concept of mediational repertoire to explore the integrated set of language and media resources that interlocutors mobilise in interaction and developed mediagrams as a visualisation technique in order to represent this repertoire with reference to the family relationships that our participants mediated. As argued in Chapter 2, it seems important to go beyond collecting data from single domains or origin and in particular public social media platforms that shape much previous CMC research. Justified as this focus may be in other respects, it bears the risk of making practices of mediated interaction by groups and individuals invisible, including the practices of members of transnational families. We also saw it as important to go beyond the focus of much CMC research on online-only data. Our study responds by developing a blended approach, combining interview data and digital interactional data in online centred discourse analysis, taking relationships between off- and online communication into consideration. Taking inspiration from polymedia research, our approach has not been limited to linguistic aspects of media choice, but rather zooms in on how participants' media choices relate to relational and emotional aspects of mediated interaction. In framing our research this way, we avoid looking at heritage language in isolation from other linguistic resources, and by emphasising the dense imbrication of language and media practices, we capture how they are part of broader practices of doing family.

Mediagrams enable the visualisation, analysis, and collaborative interpretation of patterns of media, language, and modality choices in relation to named (groups of) interlocutors. Mediagram analysis casts a bird's eye view of how media channels, linguistic resources, modalities, and interlocutors of individual family members pattern together. By taking into consideration participants' reflections on their own mediagrams, we learn about their practices, routines, and strategies; their perceived challenges of transnational connectivity; and their response to others' expectations of staying in touch. Mediagrams open a dimension of analysis that we consider crucial, namely participants' active collaboration with and ownership of the research process. Working with mediagrams is a process of going back and forth between participants' and researchers' perspectives, with both parties being actively engaged with the research.

A crucial dimension of our approach is that it extends the biographical understanding of multilingualism (Busch 2012, Léglise 2019). We combine language portraits with mediagrams to connect offline and online language experiences, and the revisiting of participant-selected interactions is then carried out against the backdrop of these overall reflections. We thus investigate participants' digitally lived experience of language, in a manner similar to the development of techno-linguistic biographies (Barton & Lee 2013), but with additional visual support. In several ways, records of digital practices give detailed insight into the individual and collective language experiences of family members. On the one hand, we can observe how language practices in a specific dyad develop along with the relationship between the interlocutors, as in the case of Awa and her friend in Germany (cf. Chapter 8, Section 8.3.3). On the other hand, when participants discuss specific digital practices in the research process, they narrate their language experience. This brings up memories and emotions that are constitutive of the families' life and migration trajectories. Considering the choices that the participants make, or feel obliged to make, in their digital practices allows us to tap into agency in their language biography. Our work shows that, to gain full insight into family repertoires and individual repertoires, it is essential to take account of digital practices. This is actually a prerequisite for addressing transnational family ties.

9.2 Transnational connectivity and family multilingualism

Our findings show that the family constitutes an institutional point of departure for transnational social relationships, and that family multilingualism plays a crucial role in negotiating these relationships. Interactional identities in digitally mediated communication are intertwined with family bonds, and as linguistic and cultural resources circulate in the family space, they retain their value as symbolic and cultural capital. We therefore place the family centre stage in understanding multilingualism online and examine diaspora practices, too, from a family perspective.

We analyse the processes of creating translocal solidarity as a practice of transnational family-making and identify how it relates to families' linguistic and media repertoires.

In these digital spaces, family relationships are negotiated through a wide range of linguistic resources, including language choice; choice of kinship terms (Wright 2020); culturally typified kinship behaviour, e.g. teasing (or lack thereof) and concomitant language style; power and connection manoeuvres (Tannen et al. 2007); and morality practices (Ochs & Kremer-Sadlik 2015). The choice of media channel and language modality for communication with specific interlocutors affects the interaction itself, the linguistic resources that are drawn upon, and the cultural norms and practices referred to. Some digital family practices are collective: for instance, some are carried out through group chats, through sharing and liking content, while others are more individual, taking place in dyadic interactions. In these processes, the family members differ in the kinds of messages they post and share, thereby performing generational, gender, religious, and lifestyle identities. Participation in a digital centre is achieved through an interplay of activities online, including writing (posting, commenting), reading, watching, sharing, and liking.

Our findings intersect with anthropological studies of migrants in West African contexts, which show how family norms, marital unions, and upbringing of children are negotiated transnationally (Mbodj-Pouye & Le Courant 2017, Vives & Silva 2017, Yount-André 2018). We add here the role of linguistic resources in the negotiation of family relations and show how they are drawn upon to stay in touch. Some recent research has shown that the transnational negotiation of marital unions is part of a wider discussion about the common future of a diasporic group being constructed (Mbodj-Pouye & Le Courant 2017: 112); the negotiation of family relationships through digital linguistic practice is part of a process where future transnational connections are in the making. On the one hand, interaction by members of both older and younger generations contributes to the continuity of the bonds to the homeland and to relatives in other parts of the world. On the other hand, the language practices that develop in these interactions strengthen the multilingualism of the families. These linguistic resources are important resources for maintaining transnational bonds in the future, and they are a means to construct new relationships too. Awa's friendship with the Senegalese student in Germany (Chapter 8, section 8.3) is an example of how new transnational relationships are generated through the family and become central to social and linguistic connections with Senegal.

These transnational connections can be important for resilience in a migrant context. In his essay on *The African diaspora in Norway* (2020), Samba Diop discusses the double set of prejudice that most Senegalese in Norway, as people of colour with Muslim faith, must deal with. Racism against people of colour and negative attitudes towards Islam in Norway are well documented (cf. e.g. Ali 2018, Joof 2018). The digital space can thus be an arena for resilience (Mainsah 2014), for instance to negotiate belonging to an African or Senegalese diaspora or to a more tightly knit religious community (cf. Chapter 7). Resilience and identity construction in young people's online practices have been studied in Norway and elsewhere (e.g. Cutler & Røyneland 2018, Røyneland 2018), but the issue has not received much attention in a family context. The family deserves such attention, however, as online spaces and social media have become sites of engagement for the entire range of family members (cf. 'Grannies on the net', Ivan & Hebblethwaite 2016), giving rise to a variety of language practices to construct interactional identities.

Examples from the families in this study show that relationships and family identities are indeed closely related to multilingual practices, for instance in displaying family relationships as intertwined with specific linguistic features. Comparing Ousmane Diagne's interaction with his sister, his niece, and his cousin/sister-in-law exemplifies the process of positioning family members through the use or non-use of Wolof. Linguistic resources are not just symbolic elements in the interactional environment but mobilised by the interlocutors to manage these specific relationships online. This is most evident in dyadic interactions, where we can observe in detail how participants' alignments go beyond language choice and extend to the observation and imposition of interactional norms that index kinship relations. For instance, metapragmatic comments in Ousmane's conversation with his sister centre around what information should be transmitted and by whom and how in relation to the sister's childbirth (Excerpt 6.7), and in Ousmane's conversation with his niece, his emphasis on her using the kin term *tonton* is part of how they negotiate their relationship (Excerpt 6.5). Communicative norms may even be the object of playful teasing, as found in Rama's interaction with her *tonton* (Excerpt 6.6).

Bringing family practices into the study of multilingualism online enhances our understanding of the fine-tuning that interlocutors undertake to build complex relationships while relating to sociolinguistic norms. It also allows us to tap into sociolinguistic dynamics as appropriated by the participants. These dynamics are part of the complexities regarding how identity is constructed and conceived, how relationships, in particular family relations, are constantly negotiated and evolving, and how questions of what constitutes linguistic heritage are given different answers by different actors.

9.3 A digital perspective on heritage language repertoires

A digital perspective on heritage language repertoires contributes to a shift from 'language' as a bounded entity towards 'repertoire' in family multilingualism research. By pulling together digitally mediated interaction and family multilingualism, we turn the gaze away from a binary perspective on intergenerational language transmission towards new questions: what heritage language resources are circulating, how are they circulating, what are they mobilised for in a family setting? Furthermore, in the analysis of the language practices investigated in this book, we have uncovered how they are shaped by the choice of media and modality and the relationship they mediate. We thus contribute to the recent interest in multimodality and semiotic resources in FLP research (De Meulder, Kusters & Napier 2021, Kozminska & Zhu 2021), confirming that language cannot be considered in isolation from the other resources drawn upon in family communication. Our study therefore resonates with Palvianen's (2020a) call for the inclusion of digital practices into the family language policy definition. Our work furthermore takes up the task formulated by Purkarthofer (2021) to highlight family members' agency and differing meanings attached to various linguistic resources.

FLP research and other work on family multilingualism have indeed centred around the question of heritage language transmission and maintenance, and this still is an essential concern. On the one hand, a heritage language constitutes a symbolic link to the (parents') country of origin, and on the other, it often constitutes a (necessary) means to engage in conversations with transnational family members. However, as our analysis shows, neither symbolic value nor practical usefulness are necessarily straightforward concepts; instead they are subject to ongoing evaluation. As in the case of the Norwegian-Senegalese families, there is not just one linguistic resource that makes up this link (cf. Chapter 8). Instead, there is a multilingual repertoire of resources and registers, and heritage language use is part of translanguaging practices with different linguistic and multimodal features. In our data, these range from Wolof, Peul, Joola, and French to Arabic, mediated through speech, writing, videos, images of various kinds, emoji, and other visuals. For a minority language group who do not have many speakers in the immediate environment, digital spaces become crucial in offering opportunities to practise these different registers, and translanguaging attitudes make it possible to do so with whatever resources are available. As we have shown in this book, various linguistic resources are mobilised by the interlocutors to practise family (Morgan 1996) and display family practice (Finch 2007).

Practising heritage language with family members online is not readily comparable to learning heritage language in a community school. First, the educational context represents one sociolinguistic norm, based on standard language. In the digital family interaction context, however, several centres of sociolinguistic norms are constructed, so that it becomes a polycentric space (Chapter 7). Different family practices imply orientation to different sociolinguistic centres, e.g., a phone call to the grandparents involves language practices that are significantly different from those involved in texting with peers. Second, positioning and family relations are part of the process of heritage language socialisation (Chapter 8). Transnational connections facilitate contact with a variety of 'experts' in interaction, relatives who wish to assist the 'novices' to acquire values, ideologies, identities, stances, and practices associated with their cultural and linguistic background (cf. Duff 2012: 566). As He (2012: 594) notes, heritage language learning is enhanced by the learner's desire to communicate successfully in a moment-by-moment fashion, a purpose that digital communication affords. Third, various types of co-presence imply different sets of heritage language practices. In practices of ritual co-presence (Nedelcu & Wyss 2016), participants draw heavily on formulaic language, which implies norms and expectations for socio-culturally appropriate ways to participate in interaction (Burdelski & Cook 2012: 182). This is observed for instance for children with their uncles and aunts (Excerpts 8.1 and 8.4). Ritual co-presence also brings into play other expressions, formulations, and signs of politeness which are different from those involved in 'omnipresent co-presence', such as that practised by Awa Coly with her friend in Germany and by Momar Diagne with his cousin (Excerpts 8.2, 8.5, 8.6). In the multimodal and multilingual digital environment where this socialisation takes place, participants alternate roles of 'novices' and 'experts' as they also take on other positions in their conversations. This way, some family members appear as central socialisation agents, others as more peripheral, and they bring different sociolinguistic norms to the online family space. Brought into institutional learning, this range of family communication can complement formal heritage language teaching. Apart from phone and video calls, digitally mediated interaction can be conserved and then discussed for pedagogical purposes, as in the case of Astou Coly's discussions with her children (Chapter 8, Interview data 8.6). Vice versa, the language socialisation taking place in digital family interaction will benefit from school-based learning, as the 'novices' can bring meta-level understanding to their encounters with 'experts' in the family.

It is our hope that the theoretical framework, methods, and findings presented in this book can inspire students and researchers to cast new light on family communication in a digital age. We also hope they can stimulate development of further innovation in research approaches. In a rapidly changing digital age our research framework provides the opportunity to learn more about people's multilingual transnational lives, how 'doing family' is part of this, and how it is grounded in linguistic and social practice.

References

Ag, A. & J. N. Jørgensen. 2013. Ideologies, norms, and practices in youth polylanguaging. *The International Journal of Blingualism: Cross-Disciplinary, Cross-Linguistic Studies of Language Behavior* 17 (4): 525–539.

Agence Nationale de la Statistique et de la Démographie. 2020. *La population du Sénégal en 2020*. www.ansd.sn/index.php?option=com_ansd&view=titrepublication&id=30

Agha, A. 2003. The social life of cultural value. *Language & Communication* 23 (3–4), 231–273.

Agha, A. 2007. *Language and social relations*. Cambridge, Cambridge University Press.

Agha, A. 2011. Meet mediatization. *Language & Communication* 31: 163–170.

Agha, A. 2015. Chronotopic formulations and kinship behavior in social history. *Anthropological Quarterly* 88 (2): 401–415.

Agha, A. & Frog (eds). 2015. *Registers of communication*. Vantaa: Hansaprint Oy.

Ahlin, T. 2020. Frequent callers: "Good care" with ICTs in Indian transnational families. *Medical Anthropology* 39 (1): 69–82.

Ali, S. J. 2018. *Ikkje ver redd sånne som meg ['Don't be afraid of people like me']*. Oslo, Samlaget.

Alonso, A. & P. J. Oiarzabal. 2010. The immigrant worlds' digital harbors: an introduction. In *Diasporas in the new media age: identity, politics, and community*, edited by A. Alonso & P. J. Oiarzabal, 1–15. Reno, University of Nevada Press.

Al-Salmi, L. Z. & P. H. Smith. 2015. The digital biliteracies of Arab immigrant women. *Literacy Research: Theory, Method and Practice* 64 (1): 193–209.

Androutsopoulos, J. 2006. Multilingualism, diaspora, and the internet: Codes and identities on German-based diaspora websites. *Journal of Sociolinguistics* 70: 520–547.

Androutsopoulos, J. 2007. Language choice and code-switching in German-based diasporic web forums. In *The multilingual internet*, edited by B. Danet & S. C. Herring, 340–361. New York, Oxford University Press.

Androutsopoulos, J. 2008. Potentials and limitations of discourse-centred online ethnography. *Language@Internet* 5 (08). www.languageatinternet.org/articles/2008/1610

Androutsopoulos, J. 2010. Localising the global on the participatory web. In *Handbook of language and globalization*, edited by N. Coupland, 203–231. Oxford, Blackwell.

References

Androutsopoulos, J. 2011. From variation to heteroglossia in the study of computer-mediated discourse. In *Digital discourse: Language in the new media*, edited by C. Thurlow & K. Mroczek, 277–298. Oxford/New York, Oxford University Press.

Androutsopoulos, J. 2013. Code-switching in computer-mediated communication. In *Pragmatics of Computer-mediated Communication*, edited by S. C. Herring, D. Stein, & T. Virtanen, 667–694. Berlin, de Gruyter.

Androutsopoulos, J. 2014a. Moments of sharing: Entextualization and linguistic repertoires in social networking. *Journal of Pragmatics* 73: 4–18.

Androutsopoulos, J. 2014b. Languaging when contexts collapse: Audience design in social networking. *Discourse, Context & Media* 4/5: 62–73.

Androutsopoulos, J. 2015. Networked multilingualism. Some practices on Facebook. *International Journal of Bilingualism* 19 (2): 185–205.

Androutsopoulos, J. 2017. Media and language change: Expanding the framework. In *The Routledge handbook of language and media*, edited by C. Cotter & D. Perrin, 403–421. New York, Routledge.

Androutsopoulos, J. 2020. Trans-scripting as a multilingual practice: The case of Hellenized English. *International Journal of Multilingualism* 17 (3): 286–308. https://doi.org/10.1080/14790718.2020.1766053

Androutsopoulos, J. (ed.) 2021a. Polymedia in interaction. *Special Issue. Pragmatics and Society* 12 (5).

Androutsopoulos, J. 2021b. Polymedia in interaction. Introduction. *Pragmatics and Society* 12 (5): 707–724.

Androutsopoulos, J. & F. Busch. 2021. Digital punctuation as an interactional resource: The message-final period among German adolescents. *Linguistics & Education* 62 (3): 100871.

Androutsopoulos, J. & K. Juffermans. 2014. Digital language practices in superdiversity. Introduction. *Discourse, Context and Media* 4–5: 1–6.

Androutsopoulos, J & K. V. Lexander. 2021. Digital polycentricity and diasporic connectivities: A Norwegian-Senegalese case study. *Journal of Sociolinguistics* 25 (5): 720–736.

Androutsopoulos, J & A. Stæhr. 2018. Moving methods online. Researching digital language practices. In *The Routledge handbook of language and superdiversity*, edited by A. Creese & A. Blackledge, 118–132. London, Routledge.

Appadurai, A. 1996. *Modernity at large: Cultural dimensions of globalization*. Minneapolis, University of Minnesota Press.

Arminen, I., C. Licoppe, & A. Spagnolli. 2016. Respecifying mediated interaction. *Research on Language and Social Interaction* 49 (4): 290–309.

Arnaut, K. 2016. Superdiversity: Elements of an emerging perspective. In *Language and superdiversity*, edited by K. Arnaut, J. Blommaert, B. Rampton, & M. Spotti, 49–70. New York, Routledge.

Artamonova, O. & J. Androutsopoulos. 2019. Smartphone-based language practices among refugees: Mediational repertoires in two families. *Journal für Medienlinguistik* 2 (2): 60–89. https://doi.org/10.21248/jfml.2019.14

Auer, P. 1984. *Bilingual conversation*. Amsterdam, John Benjamins.

Auer, P. 1995. The pragmatics of code-switching: A sequential approach. In *One speaker, two languages*, edited by L. Milroy & P. Muysken, 115–135. West Nyack, Cambridge University Press.

Auer, P. 1998. Introduction: 'Bilingual conversation' revisited. In *Code-switching in conversation: Language, interaction and identity*, edited by P. Auer, 1–24. London/New York, Routledge.
Auer, P. 1999. From codeswitching via language mixing to fused lects. Toward a dynamic typology of bilingual speech. *International Journal of Bilingualism* 3 (4): 309–32.
Auer, P. 2000. Why should we and how can we determine the 'base language' of a bilingual conversation? *Estudios de Sociolingüística* 1 (1): 129–144.
Auer, P. 2022. 'Translanguaging' or 'doing languages'? Multilingual practices and the notion of codes. In *Multilingual perspectives on translanguaging*, edited by J. MacSwan. Clevedon, Multilingual Matters.
Auzanneau, M. 2001. Identités africaines: le rap comme lieu d'expression. *Cahiers d'études africaines* 41 (163–164): 711–734.
Bailey, B. 2007. Heteroglossia and boundaries. In *Bilingualism: A social approach*, edited by M. Heller, 257–274. London, Palgrave Macmillan.
Bakhtin, M. 1981. *The dialogic imagination: Four essays*. Edited by M. Holquist, translated by M. Holquist & C. Emerson. Austin, University of Texas Press.
Bakhtin, M. 1999. *Esthétique et théorie du roman*. Paris, Gallimard. (1st ed. 1975, 1st French version 1978).
Baldassar, L. 2007. Transnational families and the provision of moral and emotional support: the relationship between truth and distance. *Identities: Global Studies in Culture and Power* 14 (4): 1–25.
Baldassar, L. 2008. Missing kin and longing to be together: Emotions and the construction of co-presence in transnational relationships. *Journal of Intercultural Studies* 29 (3): 247–266.
Baldassar, L. 2016. De-demonizing distance in mobile family lives: Co-presence, care circulation and polymedia as vibrant matter. *Global Networks* 16 (2): 145–163.
Baldassar, L., C. Baldock & R. Wilding. 2007. *Families caring across borders: Migration, ageing and transnational caregiving*. London, Palgrave Macmillan.
Baldassar, L. & L. Merla (eds.). 2014a. *Transnational families, migration and the circulation of care: Understanding mobility and absence in family life*. New York/London, Routledge.
Baldassar, L. & L. Merla. 2014b. Introduction. Transnational family caregiving through the lens of circulation. In *Transnational families, migration and the circulation of care: Understanding mobility and absence in family life*, edited by L. Baldassar & L. Merla, 3–24. New York/London, Routledge.
Baldassar, L., R. Wilding, P. Boccagni, & L. Merla. 2017. Aging in place in a mobile world: New media and older people's support networks. *Transnational Social Review* 7 (1): 2–9.
Barton, D. 2007. *Literacy: An introduction to the ecology of written language* (2nd ed.). Malden, MA, Blackwell.
Barton, D. & M. Hamilton. 1998. *Local literacies: Reading and writing in one community*. London, Routledge.
Barton, D. & C. Lee. 2013. *Language online*. London, Routledge.
Bava, S. 2002. Entre Touba et Marseille: le mouride migrant et la société locale. In *La société sénégalaise entre le local et le global*, edited by M.-C. Diop, 579–594. Paris, Karthala.

Baym, N. 2010. *Personal connections in the digital age.* Cambridge, Polity.
Beauchemin, C., K. Caarls, & V. Mazzucato. 2018. Senegalese families between here and there. In *Migration between Africa and Europe*, edited by C. Beauchemin, 423–453. Cham, Springer.
Bello-Rodzen, I. 2016. Multilingual upbringing as portrayed in the blogosphere: On parent-bloggers' profile. *Theory and Practice of Second Language Acquisition* 2 (2): 27–47.
Ben-Rafael, E. & M. Ben-Rafael. 2019. *Multiple globalizations: Linguistic landscapes in world-cities.* Leiden, Brill.
Berckmoes, L. H. & V. Mazzucato. 2018. Resilience among Nigerian transnational parents in the Netherlands: A strength-based approach to migration and transnational parenting. *Global Networks* 18 (4): 589–607.
Blackledge, A. & A. Creese. 2014. *Heteroglossia as practice and pedagogy.* Dordrecht, Springer.
Blackledge, A. & A. Creese. 2020. Heteroglossia. In *The Routledge handbook of linguistic ethnography*, edited by K. Tusting, 97–108. Milton, Routledge.
Blackledge, A., A. Creese, & J. Kaur Takhi. 2014. Voice, register and social position. *Multilingua* 33 (5): 485–504.
Blackledge, A., A. Creese, T. Baraç, A. Bhatt, S. Hamid, V. Lytra, P. Martin, C. J. Wu, & D. Yagcioglu. 2008. Contesting 'language' as 'heritage': Negotiation of identities in late modernity. *Applied Linguistics* 29 (4): 533–554.
Blommaert, J. 2003. Commentary: A sociolinguistics of globalization. *Journal of Sociolinguistics* 7 (4): 607–623.
Blommaert, J. 2005. *Discourse: A critical introduction.* Cambridge, Cambridge University Press.
Blommaert, J. 2007. Sociolinguistics and discourse analysis: Orders of indexicality and polycentricity. *Journal of Multicultural Discourses* 2: 115–130.
Blommaert, J. 2010. *The sociolinguistics of globalization.* Cambridge, Cambridge University Press.
Blommaert, J. 2013. Complexity, accent and conviviality: Concluding comments. *Applied Linguistics* 34 (5): 613–622. https://doi.org/10.1093/applin/amt028
Blommaert, J. 2017. Society through the lens of language: A new look at social groups and integration. *Tilburg Papers in Culture Studies* 178: 1–25. https://research.tilburguniversity.edu/files/32303872/TPCS_178_Blommaert.pdf
Blommaert, J. 2019. Sociolinguistic restratification in the online-offline nexus: Trump's viral errors. *Tilburg Papers in Culture Studies* 234: 1–20. https://research.tilburguniversity.edu/files/48995544/TPCS_234_Blommaert.pdf
Blommaert, J. & A. Backus. 2013. Superdiverse repertoires and the individual. In *Multilingualism and multimodality. Current challenges for educational studies*, edited by I. de Saint-Georges & J.-J. Weber, 11–32. Rotterdam, Sense.
Blommaert, J., J. Collins, & S. Slembrouck. 2005a. Polycentricity and interactional regimes in 'global neighborhoods'. *Ethnography* 6 (2): 205–235.
Blommaert, J., J. Collins, & S. Slembrouck. 2005b. Spaces of multilingualism. *Language & Communication* 25 (3): 197–216.
Blommaert, J. & B. Rampton. 2011. Language and superdiversity. *Diversities* 13 (2): 1–21.
Boczkowski, P. J., M. Matassi, & E. Mitchelstein. 2018. How young users deal with multiple platforms: The role of meaning-making in social media repertoires. *Journal of Computer-Mediated Communication* 23 (5): 245–259.

Bourdieu, P. 1982. *Ce que parler veut dire: l'économie des échanges linguistiques*. Paris, Fayard.
Brandehof, J. 2014. Superdiversity in a Cameroonian diaspora community in Ghent: The social structure of superdiverse networks. Master thesis, Tilburg University. http://arno.uvt.nl/show.cgi?fid=136106
Brinkerhoff, J. M. 2009. *Digital diasporas: Identity and transnational engagement*. Cambridge, Cambridge University Press.
Brubaker, R. 2005. The 'diaspora' diaspora. *Ethnic and Racial Studies* 28: 1–19.
Bryceson, D. & U. Vuorela. 2002. *Transnational family*. London, Bloomsbury.
Bucher, T. & A. Helmond. 2019. The affordances of social media platforms. In *The SAGE Handbook of Social Media*, edited by J. Burgess, T. Poell, & A. Marwick, 233–253. London/New York, Sage.
Bucholtz, M. & K. Hall. 2005. Identity and interaction: A sociocultural linguistic approach. *Discourse Studies* 7 (4–5): 585–614.
Burdelski, M. & H. Cook. 2012. Formulaic language in language socialization. *Annual Review of Applied Linguistics* 32: 173–188.
Busch, B. 2012. Linguistic repertoire revisited. *Applied Linguistics* 33 (5): 503–523.
Busch, B. 2013. *Mehrsprachigkeit*. Wien, Facultas (UTB).
Busch, B. 2016. Biographical approaches to research in multilingual settings: Exploring linguistic repertoires. In *Researching multilingualism*, edited by M. Martin-Jones & D. Martin, 60–73. London, Routledge.
Busch, B. 2017. Expanding the notion of the linguistic repertoire: On the concept of *Spracherleben* – The lived experience of language. *Applied Linguistics* 38 (3): 340–358.
Busch, F. 2018. Digital writing practices and media ideologies of German adolescents. *The Mouth. Critical Studies in Language, Culture and Society* 3: 85–103.
Busch, F. 2021. The interactional principle in digital punctuation. *Discourse, Context & Media* 40: 1–10.
Calvet, L. 1999. *La guerre des langues et les politiques linguistiques*. 2nd ed. Paris, Payot.
Canagarajah, A. S. 2008. Language shift and the family: Questions from the Sri Lankan Tamil diaspora. *Journal of Sociolinguistics* 12 (2): 143–176.
Canagarajah, A. S. 2012. Styling one's own in the Sri Lankan Tamil diaspora: Implications for language and ethnicity. *Journal of Language, Identity & Education* 11: 124–135.
Canagarajah, A. S. 2013a. *Translingual practice: Global Englishes and cosmopolitan relations*. New York, Routledge.
Canagarajah, A. S. 2013b. *Literacy as translingual practice*. New York, Routledge.
Canagarajah, A. S. 2013c. Negotiating translingual literacy: An enactment. *Research in the Teaching of English* 48 (1): 40–67.
Canagarajah, A. S. 2018. Translingual practice as spatial repertoires: Expanding the paradigm beyond structuralist orientations. *Applied Linguistics* 39 (1): 31–54.
Canagarajah, A. S. 2019. Changing orientations to heritage language: The practice-based ideology of Sri Lankan Tamil diaspora families. *International Journal of the Sociology of Language* 255: 9–44.
Canagarajah, S. & S. Silberstein. 2012. Diaspora identities and language. *Journal of Language, Identity & Education* 11: 81–84.

Cho, G., K. S. Cho, & L. Tse. 1997. Why ethnic minorities want to develop their heritage language: The case of Korean-Americans. *Language, Culture and Curriculum* 10 (2): 106–112.
Christensen, T. 2009. 'Connected presence' in distributed family life. *New Media & Society* 11 (3): 433–451.
Cissé, M. 2005. Langues, Etat et société au Sénégal. *Sudlangues* 5: 99–133.
Clyne, M. 1992. *Pluricentric languages. Differing norms in different nations.* Berlin, Mouton de Gruyter.
Coetzee, F. 2018. 'Hy leer dit nie hier nie ("he doesn't learn it here")': Talking about children's swearing in extended families in multilingual South Africa. *International Journal of Multilingualism* 15 (3): 291–305.
Collot, M. & N. Belmore. 1996. Electronic language as a new variety of English. In *Computer-mediated communication: Linguistic, social and cross-cultural perspectives*, edited by S. C. Herring, 13–28. Amsterdam/Philadelphia, Benjamins.
Conradson, D. & D. Mckay. 2007. Translocal subjectivities: Mobility, connection, emotion. *Mobilities* 2 (2): 167–174.
Coupland, N. 2003. Introduction: Sociolinguistics and globalisation. *Journal of Sociolinguistics* 7 (4): 465–472.
Creese, A. & A. Blackledge. 2018. *The Routledge handbook of language and superdiversity.* London, Routledge.
Cuban, S. 2014. Transnational families, ICTs and mobile learning. *International Journal of Lifelong Learning* 33 (6): 737–754.
Curdt-Christiansen, X. L. 2009. Invisible and visible language planning: Ideological factors in the family language policy of Chinese immigrant families in Quebec. *Language Policy* 8 (4): 351–375.
Curdt-Christiansen, X. L. 2013. Family Language Policy: Sociopolitical reality versus linguistic continuity. *Language Policy* 12 (1): 1–6.
Curdt-Christiansen, X. L. 2016. Conflicting language ideologies and contradictory language practices in Singaporean multilingual families. *Journal of Multilingual and Multicultural Development* 37 (7): 694–709.
Curdt-Christiansen, X. L. 2018. Family language policy. In *The Oxford handbook of language policy and planning*, edited by J. W. Tollefson & M. Perez-Milans, 420–441. New York, Oxford University Press.
Curdt-Christiansen, X. L. 2021. Multilingual digital practices in transnational families, Conference paper, *International Symposium on Bilingualism 13*, Warsaw, online 10–14 July.
Curdt-Christiansen, X. L., H. Zhu, & L. Wei. 2021. Introduction: The changing faces of transnational communities in Britain. *International Journal of the Sociology of Language* 269: 3–13.
Curdt-Christiansen, X. L. & J. Huang. 2020. Factors influencing family language policy. In *Handbook of social and affective factors in home language maintenance and development*, edited by A. C. Schalley & S. A. Eisenchlas, 174–193. Boston, De Gruyter Mouton.
Curdt-Christiansen, X. L. & E. Lanza. 2018. Language management in multilingual families: Efforts, measures and challenges. *Multilingua* 37 (2): 123–130.
Cutler, C. & U. Røyneland. 2018. Multilingualism in the digital sphere: The diverse practices of youth online. In *Multilingual youth practices in computer mediated communication*, edited by C. Cutler & U. Røyneland, 3–26. Cambridge, Cambridge University Press.

Danet, B. 2001. *Cyberpl@y: Communicating online*. New York, Berg.
Danet, B. & S. C. Herring (eds.) 2007. *The multilingual Internet: Language, culture, and communication online*. New York, Oxford University Press.
Dang, X. T., H. Nicholas, & D. Starks. 2019. Multimedia and layers of transnational family communication. *Migration, Mobility, & Displacement* 4 (1): 23–47.
De Fina, A. 2012. Family interaction and engagement with the heritage language: A case study. *Multilingua – Journal of Cross-Cultural and Interlanguage Communication* 31 (4): 349–379.
De Fina, A. 2015. Language ideologies and practices in a transnational community: Spanish language radio and Latino identities in the US. In *A sociolinguistics of diaspora: Latino practices, identities and ideologies*, edited by R. Marquez Reiter & L. Rojo, 48–65. London, Routledge.
De Meulder, M., A. Kusters, E. Moriarty, & J. Murray. 2019. Describe, don't prescribe. The practice and politics of translanguaging in the context of deaf signers. *Journal of Multilingual and Multicultural Development* 40 (10): 892–906.
De Meulder, M., A. Kusters, & J. Napier. 2021. Researching family language policy in multilingual deaf-hearing families: Using autoethnographic, visual and narrative methods. In *Diversifying family language policy* edited by L. Wright & C. Higgins, 165–188. London, Bloomsbury.
Descemet, Louis. 1864. *Recueil d'environ 1,200 phrases françaises usuelles avec leur traduction en regard en oulouf de Saint-Louis*. Saint-Louis, Imprimerie du Gouvernement.
Deumert, A. 2014a. *Sociolinguistics and mobile communication*. Edinburgh, Edinburgh University Press.
Deumert, A. 2014b. Sites of struggle and possibility in cyberspace. Wikipedia and Facebook in Africa. In *Mediatization and Sociolinguistic Change*, edited by J. Androutsopoulos, 487–514. Berlin, de Gruyter.
Deumert, A. & K. V. Lexander. 2013. Texting Africa: Writing as performance. *Journal of Sociolinguistics* 17 (4): 522–546.
Dewaele, J. 2004. The emotional force of swearwords and taboo words in the speech of multilinguals. *Journal of Multilingual and Multicultural Development* 25 (2–3): 204–222.
Dewaele, J. 2010. *Emotions in multiple languages*. London, Palgrave Macmillan.
Dia, H. 2007. Le téléphone portable dans la vallée du fleuve Sénégal. *Agora débats/jeunesses* 46 (4): 70–80.
Diallo, N. S. 2013. Le réseau national d'origine comme ressource pour l'intégration à la société norvégienne. Le cas des Sénégalais à Oslo. Unpublished master thesis, University of Oslo.
Diminescu, D. 2008. The connected migrant: An epistemological manifesto. *Social Science Information* 47 (4): 565–579.
Diop, A. B. 1985. *La famille wolof. Tradition et changement*. Paris, Karthala.
Diop, M.-C. (ed.) 2008. *Le Sénégal des migrations: mobilités, identités et sociétés*. Paris, Karthala.
Diop, S. 2020. *La diaspora africaine en Norvège. Immigration et intégration en Europe/The African diaspora in Norway. Immigration and integration in Europe*. Paris, l'Harmattan.
Diouf, M. 1994. *Sénégal. Les ethnies et la nation*. Paris, l'Harmattan.
Diouf, M. 2001. *Histoire du Sénégal. Le modèle islamo-wolof et ses périphéries*. Paris, Maisonneuve & Larose.

Dorleijn, M. & J. Nortier. 2009. Code-switching and the internet. In *The Cambridge handbook of linguistic code-switching*, edited by B. E. Bullock & A. J. Toribio, 127–141. Cambridge, Cambridge University Press.

Dovchin, S. 2015. Language, multiple authenticities and social media: The online language practices of university students in Mongolia. *Journal of Sociolinguistics* 19 (4): 437–459.

Dovchin, S. 2016. The ordinariness of youth linguascapes in Mongolia. *International Journal of Multilingualism* 14 (2): 144–159. DOI: 10.1080/14790718.2016.1155592

Drahota, A. & A. Dewey. 2008. The sociogram. A useful tool in the analysis of focus groups. *Nursing Research* 57 (4): 293–297.

Dresner, E. & S. Herring, 2010. Functions of the nonverbal in CMC: Emoticons and illocutionary force. *Communication Theory* 20 (3): 249–268.

Dreyfus, M. & C. Juillard. 2004. *Le plurilinguisme au Sénégal: Langues et identités en devenir*. Paris, Karthala.

Ducu, V. 2018. *Romanian transnational families. gender, family practices and difference*. Cham, Springer.

Ducu, V. 2020. Displaying grandparenting within Romanian transnational families. *Global Networks* 20 (2): 380–395.

Duff, P. A. 2012. Second language socialization. In *Handbook of language socialization*, edited by A. Duranti, E. Ochs, & B. Schieffelin, 564–586. Malden, MA, Wiley-Blackwell.

Dynel, M. 2014. Participation framework underlying YouTube interaction. *Journal of Pragmatics* 73: 37–52.

Eisenchlas, S. A., A. C. Schalley, & G. Moyes. 2016. Play to learn: Self-directed home language literacy acquisition through online games. *International Journal of Bilingual Education and Bilingualism* 19 (2): 136–152.

Elul, E. B. 2020. Noisy polymedia in urban Ghana: Strategies for choosing and switching between media under unstable infrastructures. *New Media & Society* 23 (7): 1953–1970.

Evans, R. 2020. Picturing translocal youth: Self-portraits of young Syrian refugees and young people of diverse African heritages in South-East England. *Population Space and Place* 26 (6): N/a.

Fagerberg-Diallo, S. 2001. Constructive interdependence: The response of a Senegalese community to the question of why become literate. In *The making of literate societies*, edited by D. Olson & N. Torrance, 153–177. Oxford, Blackwell.

Ferrara, K., H. Brunner, & G. Whittemore. 1991. Interactive written discourse as an emergent register. *Written Communication* 8 (1): 8–34.

Finch, J. 2007. Displaying families. *Sociology* 41 (1): 65–81.

Fishman, J. A. 1965. Who speaks what language to whom and when? *La Linguistique* 1 (2): 67–88.

Fishman, J. A. 1991. *Reversing language shift: Theoretical and methodological implications*. Clevedon, Multilingual Matters.

Fishman, J. A. 2001. *Can threatened languages be saved?: Reversing language shift, revisited: A 21st century perspective*. Clevedon, Multilingual Matters.

Fitzgerald, M. & R. Debski. 2006. Internet use of Polish by Polish Melburnians: Implications for maintenance and teaching. *Language Learning & Technology* 10 (1): 87–109.

Flewitt, R. 2019. Ethics and researching young children's digital literacy practices. In *The Routledge handbook of digital literacies in early childhood*, edited by O. Erstad, R. Flewitt, B. Kuemmerling-Meibauer, & I. Pires Pereira, 64–78. New York, Routledge.

Fogle, L. W. 2012. *Second language socialization and learner agency: Adoptive family talk*. Bristol, Multilingual Matters.

Fogle, L. W. 2013. Parental ethnotheories and family language policy in transnational adoptive families. *Language Policy* 12 (1): 83–102.

Fogle, L. W. & K. A. King. 2013. Child agency and policy in transnational families. *Issues in Applied Linguistics* 19 (1): 1–25.

Fogle, L. W. & K. A. King. 2017. Bi- and multilingual family language socialization. In *Language socialization*, edited by P. A. Duff & S. May, 79–95. Cham, Springer.

Francisco, V. 2015. 'The internet is magic': Technology, intimacy and transnational families. *Critical Sociology* 41 (1): 173–190.

Frøyland, L. R. & C. Gjerustad. 2012. *Vennskap, utdanning og framtidsplaner. NOVA Rapport 5/12*. Research report, Oslo Metropolitan University, Norwegian Social Research (NOVA).

Fung, L. & R. Carter. 2007. New varieties, new creativities: ICQ and English–Cantonese e-discourse. *Language and Literature* 16 (4): 345–366. DOI: 10.1177/0963947007079112

Gafaranga, J. 2010. Medium request: Talking language shift into being. *Language in Society* 39 (2): 241–270.

García, O. 2009. *Bilingual education in the 21st century: A global perspective*. Chichester, Wiley-Blackwell.

García, O. & W. Li. 2014. *Translanguaging: Language, bilingualism and education*. Basingstoke, Palgrave Macmillan.

Gasser, G. 2002. 'Manger ou s'en aller': que veulent les opposants armés casamançais? In *Le Sénégal contemporain*, edited by M.-C. Diop, 459–498. Paris, Karthala.

Gawne, L. & G. McCulloch. 2019. Emoji as digital gestures. *Language@Internet*, 17: article 2. urn:nbn:de:0009-7-48882.

Georgakopoulou, A. 1997. Self-presentation and interactional alliances in e-mail discourse: The style-and code-switches of Greek messages. *International Journal of Applied Linguistics* 7 (2): 141–164.

George, R. 2019. Simultaneity and the refusal to choose: The semiotics of Serbian youth identity on Facebook. *Language in Society* 49 (3): 399–423.

Gershon, I. 2010. Media ideologies. An introduction. *Journal of Linguistic Anthropology* 20: 283–293.

Giaxoglou, K. 2015. Entextualising mourning on Facebook: Stories of grief as acts of sharing. *The New Review of Hypermedia and Multimedia* 21 (1–2): 87–105.

Gibson, J. 1986. *The ecological approach to visual perception*. Hillsdale, NJ, Lawrence Erlbaum.

Glick-Schiller, N., L. Basch, & C. Blanc-Szanton. 1992. Towards a definition of transnationalism. Introductory remarks and research questions. *Annals of the New York Academy of Sciences* 645: ix–xiv.

Glick-Schiller, N., L. Basch, & C. Blanc-Szanton. 1995. From immigrant to transmigrant: Theorizing transnational migration. *Anthropological Quarterly* 68 (1): 48–63.

Goffman, E. 1986. *Frame analysis: An essay on the organization of experience.* Boston, Northeastern University Press (first published 1974).

Goodchild, S. 2016. 'Which language(s) are you for?' 'I am for all the languages.' Reflections on breaking through the ancestral code: Trials of sociolinguistic documentation. In *SOAS working papers in linguistics 18*, edited by L. Lu & S. Ritchie, 75–91. London, SOAS.

Gordon, C. 2008. A(p)parent play: Blending frames and reframing in family talk. *Language in Society* 37 (3): 319–349.

Gordon, C. 2009. *Making meanings, creating family: Intertextuality and framing in family interactions.* New York, Oxford University Press.

Greschke, H. 2021. Idioms of polymediated practices and the techno-social accomplishment of co-presence in transnational families. *Pragmatics and Society* 12 (5): 828–850.

Guardado, M. 2018. *Discourse, ideology and heritage language socialization: Micro and macro perspectives.* Boston, De Gruyter Mouton.

Gumperz, J. J. 1964. Linguistic and social interaction in two communities. *American Anthropologist* 66 (6): 137–153.

Gumperz, J. J. 1982. *Discourse strategies.* Cambridge, Cambridge University Press.

Hanks, W. F. 1996. *Language and communicative practice.* Oxford & Boulder, Westview.

Hanks, W. F. 2005. Pierre Bourdieu and the practices of language. *Annual Review of Anthropology* 34 (1): 67–83.

Hannaford, D. 2015. Technologies of the spouse: Intimate surveillance in Senegalese transnational marriages. *Global Networks* 15 (1): 43–59.

Hannaford, D. 2017. *Marriage without borders: Transnational spouses in neoliberal Senegal.* Philadelphia, University of Pennsylvania Press.

Haque, S. 2012. Etude de cas sociolinguistique et ethnographique de quatre familles indiennes immigrantes en Europe: pratiques lagagières et politiques linguistiques nationales et familiales. Thèse de doctorat, Université de Grenoble.

Hatoss, A. 2020. Transnational grassroots language planning in the era of mobility and the Internet. In *Handbook of home language maintenance and development: Social and affective factors*, edited by A. C. Schalley & S. A. Eisenchlas, 274–292. Boston, De Gruyter.

Haythornthwaite, C. 2005. Social networks and Internet connectivity effects. *Information, Community & Society* 8 (2): 125–147.

He, A. W. 2008. Heritage language learning and socialization. In *Encyclopedia of language and education. Volume 8: Language socialization*, edited by P. Duff & N. Hornberger, 201–213. New York, Springer.

He, A. W. 2012. Heritage language socialization. In *Handbook of language socialization*, edited by A. Duranti, E. Ochs, & B. Schieffelin, 587–609. Malden, MA, Wiley-Blackwell.

He, A. W. 2016. Discursive roles and responsibilities: A study of interactions in Chinese immigrant households. *Journal of Multilingual and Multicultural Development: Multilingual Encounters in Transcultural Families* 37 (7): 667–679.

Heller, M. 2007. *Bilingualism. A social approach.* Basingstoke & New York, Palgrave Macmillan.

Hepp, A., C. Roitsch, & M. Berg. 2016. Investigating communication networks contextually. Qualitative network analysis as cross-media research. *MedieKultur, Journal of Media and Communication Research* 32 (60): 87–106.
Hernández-Carretero, M. 2015. Renegotiating obligations through migration: Senegalese transnationalism and the quest for the right distance. *Journal of Ethnic and Migration Studies* 41 (12): 2021–2040.
Herring, S. C. 1996. *Computer-mediated communication: Linguistic, social, and cross-cultural perspectives*. Amsterdam/Philadelphia, Benjamins.
Hillewaert, S. 2015. Writing with an accent: Orthographic practice, emblems, and traces on Facebook. *Journal of Linguistic Anthropology* 25 (2): 195–214.
Hiratsuka, A. & A. Pennycook. 2020. Translingual family repertoires: 'no, Morci is itaiitai panzita, amor'. *Journal of Multilingual and Multicultural Development* 41 (9): 749–763.
Hogan, B., J.-A. Carrasco, & B. Wellman. 2007. Visualizing personal networks: Working with participant-aided sociograms. *Field Methods* 19 (2): 116–144.
Huang, W., S. Hong, & P. Eades. 2006. How people read sociograms: A questionnaire study. *APVIS* 60, 199–206.
Humery-Dieng, M.-E. 2001. Le Paradis, le mariage et la terre: Des langues de l'écrit en milieu fuutanke (arabe, français et pulaar). *Cahiers d'études africaines* 41 (3–4): 565–594.
Hutchby, I. 2001. *Conversation and technology: From the telephone to the Internet*. Cambridge, Polity.
Ivan, L. & S. Hebblethwaite. 2016. Grannies on the Net: Grandmothers' experiences of Facebook in family communication. *Romanian Journal of Communication and Public Relations* 18 (1): 11–25.
Jackson, K. M. 2005. *Rituals and patterns in children's lives*. Madison WI, University of Wisconsin Press.
Jacquemet, M. 2005. Transidiomatic practices: Language and power in the age of globalisation. *Language and Communication* 25: 257–277.
Johnsen, R. V. 2021. 'Then suddenly I spoke a lot of Spanish' – Changing linguistic practices and heritage language from adolescents' points of view. *International Multilingual Research Journal* 15 (2): 105–125.
Jones, R. H. & C. A. Hafner. 2012. *Understanding digital literacies*. London, Taylor & Francis.
Jones, R., A. Chik, & C. A. Hafner. 2015. *Discourse and digital practices*. London, Routledge.
Jonsson, C. & A. Muhonen, A. 2014. Multilingual repertoires and the relocalization of manga in digital media. *Discourse, Context and Media* 4–5: 87–100.
Joof, C. L. 2018. *Eg snakkar om det heile tida: ['I talk about it all the time']*. Oslo, Samlaget.
Jørgensen, J. N. 2008. Polylingual languaging around and among children and adolescents. *International Journal of Multilingualism* 5 (3): 161–176.
Jørgensen, J. N., M. S. Karrebæk, L. M. Madsen, & J. S. Møller. 2011. Polylanguaging in superdiversity. *Diversities* 13 (2): 23–38.
Juffermans, K. 2015. *Local languaging, literacy and multilingualism in a West African society*. Bristol, Channel View Publications.
Juillard, C. 1990. Répertoires et actes de communication en situation plurilingue: le cas de Ziguinchor au Sénégal. *Langage et société* 54 (1): 65–82.

Juillard, C. 1995. *Sociolinguistique urbaine. La vie des langues à Ziguinchor (Sénégal)*. Paris, CNRS.
Juillard, C. 2005. Hétérogénéité des plurilinguismes en Afrique à partir du terrain sénégalais. *La linguistique* 41 (2): 23–36.
Kane, O. 2011. *The homeland is the arena: Religion, transnationalism, and the integration of Senegalese immigrants in America*. Oxford, Oxford University Press.
Karrebæk, M. S. 2016. Arabs, Arabic and urban languaging: Polycentricity and incipient enregisterment among primary school children in Copenhagen, in *Everyday languaging*, edited by L. M. Madsen, M. S. Karrebæk, & J. S. Møller, 19–48. Berlin, De Gruyter.
Kasanga, L. A. 2008. 'Cheap' c'est quoi? Immigrant teenagers in quest of multilingual competence and identity. *International Journal of Multilingualism* 5 (4): 333–356.
Keating, C., O. Solovova, & O. Barradas. 2015. Migrations, multilingualism and language policies in Portugal and in the UK: A polycentric approach. In *Global Portuguese* edited by L. P. Moita-Lopes, 144–162. New York, Routledge.
Kébé, A. B. & F. Leconte. 2020. In-sécurité et légitimités linguistiques dans la vallée du fleuve Sénégal. In *(In)sécurité linguistique en Francophonies: Perspectives in(ter)disciplinaires*, edited by V. Feussi & J. Lorilleux, 77–92. Paris, L'Harmattan.
Kędra, J. 2020. Performing transnational family with the affordances of mobile apps: A case study of Polish mothers living in Finland. *Journal of Ethnic and Migration Studies* 47 (13): 2877–2896.
Kędra, J. 2021. Virtual proximity and transnational familyhood: A case study of the digital communication practices of Poles living in Finland. *Journal of Multilingual and Multicultural Development* 42 (5): 426–474.
Kelly, R. M. & L. A. Watts. 2015. Characterizing the inventive appropriation of emoji as relationally meaningful in mediated close personal relationships. In *Proceedings of experiences of technology appropriation: Unanticipated users, usage, circumstances, and design (workshop held at ECSCW 2015)*. https://researchportal.bath.ac.uk/files/130966701/emoji_relational_value.pdf
Kendall, S. 2006. 'Honey, I'm home!': Framing in family dinnertime homecomings. *Text and Talk: An Interdisciplinary Journal of Language, Discourse and Communication Studies* 26 (4): 411–441.
Kenner, C., M. Ruby, J. Jessel, E. E. Gregory, & T. Arju. 2008. Intergenerational learning events around the computer: A site for linguistic and cultural exchange. *Language and Education* 22 (4): 298–319.
Kheirkhah, M. & A. Cekaite. 2017. Siblings as language socialization agents in bilingual families. *International Multilingual Research* 12 (4): 255–272.
King, K. A. 2013. A tale of three sisters: Language ideologies, identities, and negotiations in a bilingual, transnational family. *International Multilingual Research Journal* 7 (1): 49–65.
King, K. A. 2016. Language policy, multilingual encounters, and transnational families. *Journal of Multilingual and Multicultural Development* 37 (7): 726–733.
King, K. A., L. Fogle, & A. Logan-Terry. 2008. Family language policy. *Language and Linguistics Compass* 2 (5): 907–922.
King, K. A. & E. Lanza. 2019. Ideology, agency and imagination in multilingual families: An introduction. *International Journal of Bilingualism* 23 (3): 717–723.

King-O'Riain, R. C. 2015. Emotional streaming and transconnectivity: Skype and emotion practices in transnational families in Ireland. *Global Networks* 15 (2): 256–273.
Kluge, B. 2015. The joint construction of a supra-national identity in the Latin American blogging community in Quebec. In *A sociolinguistics of diaspora: Latino practices, identities and ideologies*, edited by R. Marquez Reiter & L. Martin Rojo, 181–195. London, Routledge.
König, K. & T. M. Hector. 2019. Neue Medien – neue Mündlichkeit? Zur Dialogizität von WhatsApp-Nachrichten. In *Interaktion und Medien. Interaktionsanalytische Zugänge zu medienvermittelter Kommunikation*, edited by K. Marx & A. Schmidt, 59–84. Heidelberg, Winter.
Koven, M. & I. Simões Marques. 2015. Performing and evaluating (non)modernities of Portuguese migrant figures on YouTube: The case of Antonio de Carglouch. *Language in Society* 44 (2): 213–242.
Kozminska, K. & H. Zhu. 2021. The promise and resilience of multilingualism: language ideologies and practices of Polish-speaking migrants in the UK post the Brexit vote. *Journal of Multilingual and Multicultural Development* 42 (5): 444–461.
Kubaniyova, M. 2008. Rethinking research ethics in contemporary applied linguistics: The tension between macroethical and microethical perspectives in situated research. *The Modern Language Journal* 92 (4): 503–518.
Kulbrandstad, L. A. 2007. Dialekt og aksentpreget norsk – en språkholdningsstudie. In: *A sjå samfunnet gjennom språket*, edited by G. Akselberg & J. Myking, 115–123. Oslo, Novus Forlag.
Kulbrandstad, L. I. 2017. Integration and language education in Norwegian policy documents 1980–2016. *Apples – Journal of Applied Language Studies* 11 (3): 101–120.
Kulbrandstad, L. A. 2020. Minoritetsspråk i Norge – brukere og bruk. In *Språkreiser. Festskrift til Anne Golden på 70-årsdagen 14. juli 2020*, edited by L. A. Kulbrandstad & G. B. Steien, 200–234. Oslo, Novus Forlag.
Kusters, A. 2021. Introduction: the semiotic repertoire: Assemblages and evaluation of resources. *International Journal of Multilingualism* 18 (2): 183–189.
Kusters, A., M. De Meulder, & J. Napier. 2021. Family language policy on holiday: Four multilingual signing and speaking families travelling together. *Journal of Multilingual and Multicultural Development* 42 (8): 698–715.
Kusters, A., M. Spotti, R. Swanwick, & E. Tapio. 2017. Beyond languages, beyond modalities: Transforming the study of semiotic repertoires. *International Journal of Multilingualism* 14 (3): 219–232.
Kytölä, S. 2016. Translocality. In *The Routledge handbook of language and digital communication*, edited by A. Georgakopoulou, & T. Spilioti, 371–388. Abingdon, Routledge.
Lam, S. 2013. ICT's impact on family solidarity and upward mobility in translocal China. *Asian Journal of Communication* 23 (3): 322–340.
Lanza, E. 1997. *Language mixing in infant bilingualism: A sociolinguistic perspective*. Oxford, Clarendon Press.
Lanza, E. 2004. Language socialization of infant bilingual children in the family: Quo vadis? In *Bilingualism and education from the family to the school*, edited by X. Rodríguez-Yáñez, A. Suárez, & F. Ramallo, 21–39. Munich, Lincom Europa.

Lanza, E. 2007. Multilingualism in the family. In *Handbook of multilingualism and multilingual communication*, edited by P. Auer & W. Li, 45–67. New York, Mouton de Gruyter.

Lanza, E. 2020. Digital storytelling: Multilingual parents' blogs and vlogs as narratives of family language policy. In *Språkreiser*, edited by L. A. Kulbrandstad & G. B. Steien, 177–192. Oslo, Novus Forlag.

Lanza, E. 2021. The family as a space: Multilingual repertoires, language practices and lived experiences. *Journal of Multilingual and Multicultural Development* 42 (8): 763–771.

Lanza, E. & R. L. Gomes. 2020. Family language policy: Foundations, theoretical perspectives and critical approaches. In *Handbook of home language maintenance and development: social and affective factors*, edited by A. C. Shalley & S. A. Eisenchlas, 153–173. Berlin, De Gruyter.

Lanza, E. & K. V. Lexander. 2019. Family language practices in multilingual transcultural families. In *Transdisciplinary perspectives on multilingualism*, edited by S. Montanari & S. Quay, 229–251. Berlin/New York, De Gruyter.

Lave, J. & E. Wenger. 1991. *Situated learning: Legitimate peripheral participation*. Cambridge, Cambridge University Press.

Lawrence, P. O. 2009. Le rôle du sport pour les jeunes sénégalais: étudiants amateurs à Saint-Louis et footballeurs professionels en Norvège. Unpublished master thesis. University of Oslo.

Leconte, F. 1997. *La famille et les languges. Une étude sociolinguistique de la deuxième génération de l'immigration africaine dans l'agglomération rouennaise*. Paris, l'Harmattan.

Leconte, F. 2001. Familles africaines en France entre volonté d'insertion et attachement au patrimoine langagier d'origine. *Langage et société* 98: 77–103.

Leconte F. & A. B. Kébé. 2013. Répertoires trilingues et alternances pulaar/wolof/français en France. In *Travaux du CLAIX / Travaux – Cercle linguistique d'Aix-en-Provence vol. 24 – Contacts de langues et langues en contact*, edited by S. Kriegel & D. Veronique, 59–72. Publications de l'Aix-Marseille Université.

Lee, C. 2007. Affordances and text-making practices in online instant messaging. *Written Communication* 24 (3): 223–249.

Lee, C. 2017. *Multilingualism online*. London, Routledge.

Lee, J. S. 2006. Exploring the relationship between electronic literacy and heritage language maintenance. *Language Learning and Technology* 10 (2): 93–113.

Lee, H., M. Pang, & J. Park. 2021. Translanguaging and family language policy: An investigation of Korean short-term stayers' language practice at home. *Journal of Language, Identity, and Education*, online first: 1–16.

Léglise, I. 2019. Documenter les parcours de familles transnationales: Généalogies, biographies langagières et pratiques langagières familiales. In *Family language policy: Dynamics in language transmission under a migratory context/ Politique Linguistique familiale: Enjeux dynamiques de la transmission linguistique dans un contexte migratoire*, edited by S. Haque & F. Lelièvre, 159–182. Munich, LINCOM.

Lenihan, A. 2011. 'Join our community of translators' Language ideologies and/in Facebook. In *Digital discourse: Language in the new media*, edited by C. Thurlow & K. Mroczek, 48–64. New York/London, Oxford University Press.

Leppänen, S. & S. Peuronen. 2012. Multilingualism on the internet. In *Handbook of research on multilingualism*, edited by M. Martin-Jones, A. Blackledge, & A. Creese, 384–402. London, Routledge.

Leppänen, S., A. Pietkänen-Huhta, A. Piirjanen-Marsch, T. Nikula, & S. Peuronen. 2009. Young people's translocal new media uses: A multiperspective analysis of language choice and heteroglossia. *Journal of Computer-Mediated Communication* 14 (4): 1080–1107.

Leurs, K. 2015. *Digital passages: Migrant youth 2.0; diaspora, gender and youth cultural intersections*. Amsterdam, Amsterdam University Press.

Lexander, K. V. 2010. Vœux plurilingues électroniques – nouvelles pratiques, nouvelles fonctions pour les langues africaines? *Journal of Language Contact THEMA* 3: 228–246.

Lexander, K. V. 2011. Texting and African language literacy. *New Media & Society* 13 (3): 427–443.

Lexander, K. V. 2012. Analyzing multilingual texting in Senegal: An approach for the study of mixed-language SMS. In *Language mixing and code-switching in writing*, edited by M. Sebba, S. Mahootian, & C. Jonsson, 146–169. New York, Routledge.

Lexander, K. V. 2013. Le SMS amoureux. *Journal des africanistes* 83 (1): 70–91.

Lexander, K. V. 2018. Nuancing the *jaxase* – Young and urban texting in Senegal. In *Multilingual youth practices in computer mediated communication*, edited by C. Cutler & U. Røyneland, 68–86. Cambridge, Cambridge University Press.

Lexander, K. V. 2020a. Norsk som digitalt samhandlingsspråk i fire familier med innvandrerbakgrunn – identitet og investering. *Nordand – nordisk tidsskrift for andrespråksforskning* 15 (1): 4–21.

Lexander, K. V. 2020b. Literacies in contact when writing Wolof – orthographic repertoires in digital communication. *Written Language and Literacy* 23 (2): 194–213.

Lexander, K. V. 2021a. Polymedia and family multilingualism: Linguistic repertoires and relationships in digitally mediated interaction. *Pragmatics and Society* 12 (5): 782–804.

Lexander, K. V. 2021b. Rural Norway in flux – multilingualism in Lithuanian labour migrants' digital interaction with employers and colleagues, conference paper *International Symposium on Bilingualism* 13, online 10–14 July.

Lexander, K. V. & D. Alcón-López. Forthcoming. Digital language practices and new configurations of multilingualism: Writing in a Senegal-based discussion forum. In *The Oxford guide to the Atlantic languages of West Africa*, edited by F. Lüpke, p. xxx–xxx. Oxford, Oxford University Press.

Lexander, K. V. & J Androutsopoulos. 2021. Working with mediagrams: A methodology for collaborative research on mediational repertoires in multilingual families. *Journal of Multilingual and Multicultural Development* 42 (1): 1–18.

Lexander, K. V. & R. Watson. 2022. Things you cannot do in Norway: Multilingual transnational action and interaction in digital communication. *Nordic Journal of African Studies* 31 (1): 45–71.

Li, W. 2011. Moment Analysis and translanguaging space: Discursive construction of identities by multilingual Chinese youth in Britain. *Journal of Pragmatics* 43 (5): 1222–1235.

Li, W. 2018. Translanguaging as a practical theory of language. *Applied Linguistics* 39 (1): 9–30.

Li, J. & Juffermans, K. 2015. Polycentric repertoires. Constructing Dutch-Chinese youth identities in the classroom and online. In *Multilingualism in the Chinese diaspora worldwide*, edited by W. Li, 32–46. London, Routledge.

Li W. & H. Zhu. 2019a. Imagination as a key factor in LMLS in transnational families. *International Journal of the Sociology of Language* 255: 73–107.

Li, W. & H. Zhu. 2019b. Tranßcripting: Playful subversion with Chinese characters. *International Journal of Multilingualism* 16 (2): 1–17.

Licoppe, C. 2004. 'Connected' presence: The emergence of a new repertoire for managing social relationships in a changing communication technoscape. *Environment and Planning D* 22 (1): 135–156.

Lindquist, H. & N. G. Garmann. 2021. Toddlers and their translingual practicing homes. *International Journal of Multilingualism* 18 (1): 59–72.

Ling, R., & C. Lai. 2016. Microcoordination 2.0: Social coordination in the age of smartphones and messaging apps. *Journal of Communication* 66 (5): 834–856.

Little, S. 2019. 'Is there an app for that?' Exploring games and apps among heritage language families. *Journal of Multilingual and Multicultural Development* 40 (3): 218–229.

Little, S. 2020a. Whose heritage? What inheritance? Conceptualising family language identities. *International Journal of Bilingual Education and Bilingualism* 23 (2): 198–212.

Little, S. 2020b. Social media and the use of technology in home language maintenance. In *Handbook of home language maintenance and development: Social and affective factors*, edited by A. C. Schalley & S. A. Eisenchlas, 257–273. Boston, De Gruyter.

Little S. & T. Little. 2022. An un/familiar space: Children and parents as collaborators in autoethnographic family research. *Qualitative Research* 22 (4): 632–648.

Lo, S. 2008. The nonverbal communication functions of emoticons in computer-mediated communication. *CyberPsychology & Behavior* 11: 595–597.

Lobinger, K. 2016. Photographs as things – photographs of things. A texto-material perspective on photo-sharing practices. *Information, Communication & Society* 19 (4): 475–488.

Lomeu Gomes, R. 2018. Family language policy ten years on: A critical approach to family multilingualism. *Multilingual Margins* 5 (2): 54–76.

Lomeu Gomes, R. 2020. Talking multilingual families into being: Language practices and ideologies of a Brazilian-Norwegian family in Norway. *Journal of Multilingual and Multicultural Development*, online first: 1–21. DOI: 10.1080/01434632.2020.1788037

Lüpke, F. 2016. Uncovering small-scale multilingualism. *Critical Multilingualism Studies* 4: 35–74.

Lüpke, F. 2018. Escaping the tyranny of writing: West African regimes of writing as a model for multilingual literacy. In *The tyranny of writing: Ideologies of the written word*, edited by C. Weth & K. Juffermans, 129–148. London, Bloomsbury.

Lüpke, F. 2021. Patterns and perspectives shape perceptions: Epistemological and methodological reflections on the study of small-scale multilingualism. *The International Journal of Bilingualism: Cross-disciplinary, Cross-linguistic Studies of Language Behavior* 25 (4): 878–900.

Lüpke, F. & S. Bao-Diop. 2014. Beneath the surface? Contemporary Ajami writing in West Africa exemplified through Wolofal. In *African literacies: Ideologies, scripts, education*, edited by K. Juffermans, Y. M. Asfaha, & A. Abdulhay, 88–117. Newcastle upon Tyne, Cambridge Scholars Publishing.

Lüpke, F., K. Stenzel, F. D. Cabalzar, T. Chacon, A. da Cruz, B. Franchetto, A. Guerreiro, S. Meira, G. R. da Silva, W. Silva, L. Storto, L. Valentino, H. van der Voort, & R. Watson. 2020. Comparing rural multilingualism in Lowland South America and Western Africa. *Anthropological Linguistics* 60 (1): 3–57.

Lüpke, F. & A. Storch. 2013. *Repertoires and choices in African languages*. Berlin/Boston, De Gruyter.

MacSwan, J. 2017. A multilingual perspective on translanguaging. *American Educational Research Journal* 54 (1), 167–201.

Madianou, M. 2014a. Polymedia communication and mediatized migration: An ethnographic approach. In *Mediatization of communication*, edited by K. Lundby, 323–348. Berlin, De Gruyter.

Madianou, M. 2014b. Smartphones as polymedia. *Journal of Computer-Mediated Communication* 19 (3): 667–680.

Madianou, M. 2016. Ambient co-presence: Transnational family practices in polymedia environments. *Global Networks* 16 (2): 183–201.

Madianou, M. 2017. 'Doing family' at a distance. In *The Routledge companion to digital ethnography*, edited by L. Hjorth, H. Horst, A. Galloway, & G. Bell, 102–112. London, Routledge.

Madianou, M. 2019. Migration, transnational families, and new communication technologies. In *The Handbook of diasporas, media, and culture*, edited by J. Retis & R. Tsagarousianou, 577–590. Hoboken, NJ, John Wiley & Sons.

Madianou, M. & D. Miller. 2012a. *Migration and new media. Transnational families and polymedia*. London, Routledge.

Madianou, M. & D. Miller. 2012b. Polymedia: Towards a new theory of digital media in interpersonal communication. *International Journal of Cultural Studies* 16 (2): 169–187.

Mainsah, H. 2011. Transcending the national imagery: Digital online media and the transnational networks of ethnic minority youth in Norway. In *Media in motion: Cultural complexity and migration in the Nordic region*, edited by E. Eide, 201– 218. London, Routledge.

Mainsah, H. 2014. Young African Norwegian women and diaspora: Negotiating identity and community through digital social networks. *Crossings: Journal of Migration & Culture* 5 (1): 105–119.

Makoni, S. 2011. Sociolinguistics, colonial and postcolonial: An integrationist perspective. *Language Sciences* 33 (4): 680–688.

Makoni, S. 2015. Book review: Repertoires and choices in African languages. *Journal of Multilingual and Multicultural Development* 36: 216–217.

Makoni, S. & A. Pennycook. 2007. *Disinventing and reconstituting languages*. Clevedon, Multilingual Matters.

Marino, S. 2015. Making space, making place: Digital togetherness and the redefinition of migrant identities online. *Social Media + Society* 1 (2): 1–9.

Marino, S. 2019. Cook it, eat it, Skype it: Mobile media use in re-staging intimate culinary practices among transnational families. *International Journal of Cultural Studies* 22 (6): 788–803.

Marley, D. 2013. The role of online communication in raising awareness of bilingual identity. *Multilingua – Journal of Cross-Cultural and Interlanguage Communication* 32 (4): 485–505.

Marquez Reiter, R. & L. Martin Rojo (eds.). 2015. *A sociolinguistics of diaspora: Latino practices, identities and ideologies*. London, Routledge.

Mbodj-Pouye, A. & S. Le Courant. 2017. Living away from family is not good but living with it is worse: Debating conjugality across generations of West African migrants in France. *Mande Studies* 19: 109–130.

Mc Laughlin, F. 1995. Haalpulaar identity as a response to Wolofization. *African Languages and Cultures* 8 (2): 153–168.

Mc Laughlin, F. 2001. Dakar Wolof and the configuration of an urban identity. *Journal of African Cultural Studies* 14 (2): 153–172.

Mc Laughlin, F. 2008a. Senegal: The emergence of a national lingua franca. In *Language and national identity in Africa*, edited by A. Simpson, 79–97. Oxford, Oxford University Press.

Mc Laughlin, F. 2008b. On the origins of urban Wolof: Evidence from Louis Decemet's 1864 phrase book. *Language in Society* 37 (5): 713–735.

Mc Laughlin, F. 2014. Senegalese digital repertoires in superdiversity: A case study from Seneweb. *Discourse, Context & Media* 4/5: 29–37.

Mc Laughlin, F. 2022. Senegal: Urban Wolof then and now. In *Urban contact dialects and language change: Insights from the Global North and South*, edited by P. Kerswill & H. Wiese, 47–65. London, Routledge.

Meredith, J. 2017. Analysing technological affordances of online interactions using conversation analysis. *Journal of Pragmatics* 115: 42–55. http://dx.doi.org/10.1016/j.pragma.2017.03.001

Meyers, C. & P. Rugunanan. 2020. Mobile-mediated mothering from a distance: A case study of Somali mothers in Port Elizabeth, South Africa. *International Journal of Cultural Studies* 23 (5): 656–673.

Milroy, L. 1980. *Language and social networks*. Oxford, Blackwell.

Ministry of Education and Research. 2017. *Core curriculum – values and principles for primary and secondary education*. Online publication. www.regjeringen.no/en/dokumenter/verdier-og-prinsipper-for-grunnopplaringen---overordnet-del-av-lareplanverket/id2570003/

Mirvahedi, S. 2021. Examining family language policy through realist social theory. *Language in Society* 50 (3): 389–410.

Monz, K. 2020. Decolonizing decolonization? Desiring pure language in Mali. In *Colonial and decolonial linguistics: Knowledge and epistemes*, edited by A. Deumert, A. Storch, & N. Shepherd, 260–273. Oxford, Oxford Linguistics.

Morgan, D. 1996. *Family connections*. Cambridge, Polity Press.

Myers-Scotton, C. 1993. *Social motivations for codeswitching: Evidence from Africa*. Oxford, Clarendon Press.

N'Diaye Corréard, G., M. Daff, A. Mbaye, M. Ndiaye, A. N. Seck, & C. H. Traoré. 2006. *Les mots du patrimoine: le Sénégal*. Paris, Editions des archives contemporaines.

Nag, W., R. Ling, & M. H. Jakobsen. 2016. Keep out! Join in! Cross-generation communication on the mobile internet in Norway. *Journal of Children and Media* 10 (4): 411–425.

Nedelcu, M. & M. Wyss. 2016. 'Doing family' through ICT-mediated ordinary co-presence: transnational communication practices of Romanian migrants in Switzerland. *Global Networks* 16 (2): 202–218.

Nedelcu, M. & M. Wyss. 2020. Transnational grandparenting: An introduction. *Global Networks* 20 (2): 292–307.
Nemcová, M. 2016. Rethinking integration: Superdiversity in the networks of transnational individuals. *Tilburg Papers in Culture Studies* 167.
Ngom, F. 2002. Linguistic resistance in the Murid speech community in Senegal. *Journal of Multilingual and Multicultural Development* 23: 214–226.
Norton, B. 2013. *Identity and language learning: Extending the conversation*. 2nd edition. Bristol, Multilingual Matters.
Norton, B. 2016. Identity and language learning: Back to the future. *TESOL Quarterly* 50 (2): 475–479.
O'Brien, D. 1998. The shadow-politics of Wolofisation. *The Journal of Modern African Studies* 36 (1): 25–46
Obojska, M. 2018. Between duty and neglect: Language ideologies and stancetaking among Polish adolescents in Norway. *Lingua* 208: 82–97.
Obojska, M. 2019. 'Ikke snakke norsk?' – Transnational adolescents and negotiations of family language policy explored through family interview. *Multilingua* 38 (6): 653–674.
Obojska, M. & J. Purkarthofer. 2018. 'And all of a sudden, it became my rescue': Language and agency in transnational families in Norway. *International Journal of Multilingualism* 15 (3): 249–261.
Ochs, E. 1992. Indexing gender. In *Rethinking context: Language as an interactive phenomenon*, edited by A. Duranti & C. Goodwin, 335–358. Cambridge, Cambridge University Press.
Ochs, E. & T. Kremer-Sadlik. 2007a. Introduction: Morality as family practice. *Discourse & Society* 18 (1): 5–10.
Ochs, E. & T. Kremer-Sadlik. 2007b. Morality as family practice. Special issue. *Discourse & Society* 18 (1).
Ochs E. & T. Kremer-Sadlik. 2015. How postindustrial families talk. *Annual Review of Anthropology* 44: 87–103.
Opsahl, T. 2009. Wolla I swear this is typical for the conversational style of adolescents in multiethnic areas in Oslo. *Nordic Journal of Linguistics* 32 (2): 221–244.
Opsahl, T. & U. Røyneland. 2016. Reality rhymes – recognition of rap in multicultural Norway. *Linguistics and Education* 36: 45–54.
Otheguy, R., O. García, & W. Reid. 2015. Clarifying translanguaging and deconstructing named languages: A perspective from linguistics. *Applied Linguistics Review* 6 (3): 281–307.
Otsuji, E. & A. Pennycook. 2010. Metrolingualism: fixity, fluidity and language in flux. *International Journal of Multilingualism* 7 (3): 240–254.
Palviainen, Å. 2020a. Video calls as a nexus of practice in multilingual translocal families. *Zeitschrift Für Interkulturellen Fremdsprachenunterricht* 25 (1): 85–108.
Palviainen, Å. 2020b. Faces and spaces: Doing multilingual family life through digital screens. In *Språkreiser. Festskrift til Anne Golden på 70-årsdagen 14. juli 2020*, edited by L. A. Kulbrandstad & G. B. Steien, 193–208. Oslo, Novus.
Palviainen, Å. 2020c. Future prospects and visions for family language policy research. In *Handbook of home language maintenance and development: Social and affective factors*, edited by A. C. Schalley & S. A. Eisenchlas, 236–253. Boston, De Gruyter Mouton.

Palviainen, Å. & J. Kędra. 2020. What's in the family app? Making sense of digitally mediated communication within multilingual families. *Journal of Multilingual Theories and Practices* 1 (1): 89–111.
Panckhurst, R. & L. A. Cougnon. 2019. Youth digital practices: Results from Belgian and French projects. *TechTrends* 63: 741–750.
Paolillo, J. C. 1996. Language choice on soc. culture. punjab. *Electronic Journal of Communication/La revue électronique de communication* 6 (3).
Parven, A. 2016. A young child's intergenerational practices through the use of visual screen-based multimodal communication to acquire Qur'anic literacy. *Language and Education* 30 (6): 500–518.
Pavlenko, A. 2004. 'Stop doing that, la komu skazala!': Language choice and emotions in parent–child communication. *Journal of Multilingual and Multicultural Development* 25 (2–3): 179–203.
Pavlenko, A. 2005. *Emotions and multilingualism*. New York, Cambridge University Press.
Pavlenko, A. 2012. Multilingualism and emotions. In *The Routledge handbook of multilingualism*, edited by M. Martin-Jones, A. Blackledge, & A. Creese, 454–469. London, Routledge.
Pennycook, A., 2010. *Language as a local practice* (1st ed.). London, Routledge.
Pennycook, A. 2016. Mobile times, mobile terms: The trans-super-poly-metro movement. In *Sociolinguistics: Theoretical debates*, edited by N. Coupland, 201–216. Cambridge, Cambridge University Press.
Pennycook, A. 2017. Translanguaging and semiotic assemblages. *International Journal of Multilingualism* 14 (3): 269–282.
Pennycook, A. 2018. Repertoires, registers and linguistic diversity. In *The Routledge handbook of language and superdiversity*, edited by A. Creese & A. Blackledge, 3–15. London, Routledge.
Pennycook, A. & E. Otsuji. 2014. Metrolingual multitasking and spatial repertoires: 'Pizza mo two minutes coming'. *Journal of Sociolinguistics* 18 (2): 161–184.
Pennycook, A. & E. Otsuji. 2015. *Metrolingualism: Language in the city*. New York, Routledge.
Pérez-Sabater, C. 2018. Emoticons in relational writing practices on WhatsApp: Some reflections on gender. In *Analyzing digital discourse*, edited by P. Bou-Franch & P. Garcés-Conejos Blitvich, 163–189. Cham, Springer & Palgrave Macmillan.
Pfeifer, S. & U. Neumann. 2021. In/Visible images of mobility: sociality and analog–digital materiality in personal archives of transnational migration. *Visual Anthropology* 34 (4): 317–338. DOI: 10.1080/08949468.2021.1944770
Pietikäinen, S. 2010. Sámi language mobility: Scales and discourses of multilingualism in a polycentric environment. *International Journal of the Sociology of Language* 20: 79–101.
Ponzanesi, S. (2020) Digital diasporas: Postcoloniality, media and affect. *Interventions* 22 (8): 977–993. https://doi.org/10.1080/1369801X.2020.1718537
Porter, G., K. Hampshire, A. Abane, A. Munthali, E. Robson, A. Tanle, S. Owusu, A. de Lannoy, & A. Bango. 2018. Connecting with home, keeping in touch: Physical and virtual mobility across stretched families in sub-Saharan Africa. *Africa* 88 (2): 404–424.

References 225

Pratt, M. L. 1991. Arts of the contact zone. *Profession* 33–40. www.jstor.org/stable/25595469

Prieto Blanco, P. 2016. Digital photography, experience and space in transnational families. a case study of Spanish-Irish families living in Ireland. In *Digital photography and everyday life: Empirical studies on material visual practices*, edited by A. Lehmuskallio & E. G. Cruz, 122–141. London, Routledge.

Purkarthofer, J. 2018. Children's drawings as part of School Language Profiles: Heteroglossic realities in families and schools. *Applied Linguistics Review* 9 (2–3): 201–223.

Purkarthofer, J. 2019. Building expectations: Imagining family language policy and heteroglossic social spaces. *International Journal of Bilingualism* 23 (3): 724–739.

Purkarthofer, J. 2021. Navigating partially shared linguistic repertoires: Attempts to understand centre and periphery in the scope of family language policy. *Journal of Multilingual and Multicultural Development* 42 (8): 732–746.

Purkarthofer, J. & G. B. Steien. 2019. 'Prétendre comme si on ne connaît pas une autre langue que le swahili': Multilingual parents in Norway on change and continuity in their family language policies. *International Journal of the Sociology of Language* 255: 109–131.

Quist, P. & N. Jørgensen. 2008. Crossing – negotiating social boundaries. In *Handbook of multilingualism and multilingual communication*, edited by P. Auer & W. Li, 371–390. Berlin/New York, De Gruyter Mouton.

Rampton, B. 1995. *Crossing: Language and ethnicity among adolescents*. London, Longman.

Reershemius, G. 2017. Autochthonous heritage languages and social media: Writing and bilingual practices in Low German on Facebook. *International Journal of Multilingual and Multicultural Development* 38 (1): 35–49.

Reynolds, T. & E. Zontini. 2014. Care circulation in transnational families: Social and cultural capitals in Italian and Caribbean migrant communities in Britain. In *Transnational families, migration and the circulation of care: Understanding mobility and absence in family life*, edited by L. Baldassar & L. Merla, 203–219. New York/London, Routledge.

Riccio, B. 2001. From 'ethnic group' to 'transnational community'?: Senegalese migrants' ambivalent experiences and multiple trajectories. *Journal of Ethnic and Migration Studies* 27 (4): 583–599.

Riccio, B. 2002. Senegal is our home: The anchored nature of Senegalese transnational networks. In *New approaches to migration: Transnational communities and the transformation of home*, edited by K. Koser & N. Al-Ali, 68–83. London, Routledge.

Riccio, B. 2008. West African transnationalisms compared: Ghanaians and Senegalese in Italy. *Journal of Ethnic and Migration Studies* 34 (2): 217–234.

Riccio, B. 2011. Rehearsing transnational citizenship: Senegalese associations, co-development and simultaneous inclusion. *African Diaspora* 4 (1): 97–113.

Riccio, B. & S. degli Uberti. 2013. Senegalese migrants in Italy: Beyond the assimilation/transnationalism divide. *Urban Anthropology and Studies of Cultural Systems and World Economic Development* 42 (3/4): 207–254.

Rindal, U. 2015. Who owns English in Norway? L2 attitudes and choices among learners. In *Attitudes towards English in Europe*, edited by A. Linn, N. Bernard, & G. Ferguson, 241–270. Boston, De Gruyter.

Riordan, M. 2017. The communicative role of non-face emojis: Affect and disambiguation. *Computers in Human Behavior* 76: 75–86.

Rosa, J. & S. Trivedi. 2017. Diaspora and language. In *The Routledge handbook of migration and language*, edited by S. Canagarajah, 330–346. New York/London, Routledge.

Rotevatn, A. G. 2014. Språk i spagaten. Facebook-språket. Om normert språk og dialekt blant vestlandselevar. Unpublished master thesis. Volda University College.

Røyneland, U. 2017. Kva skal til for å høres ut som du hører til? Forestillinger om dialektale identiteter i det senmoderne Norge. *Nordica Helsingiensia* 48: 91–106.

Røyneland, U. 2018. Virtually Norwegian: Negotiating language and identity on YouTube. In *Multilingual youth practices in computer mediated communication*, edited by C. Cutler & U. Røyneland, 145–168. Cambridge, Cambridge University Press.

Røyneland, U. & B. Uri. 2020. Dialect acquisition and migration in Norway – questions of authenticity, belonging and legitimacy. *Journal of Multilingual and Multicultural Development*, online first: 1–17. DOI: 10.1080/01434632.2020.1722679

Said, F. & H. Zhu, 2019. 'No, no Maama! say "shaatir ya ouledee shaatir"!': Children's agency and creativity in language use and socialisation. *International Journal of Bilingualism* 23 (3): 771–785.

Said, F. S. 2021. '*Ba*-SKY-*aP* with her each day at dinner': Technology as supporter in the learning and management of home languages. *Journal of Multilingual and Multicultural Development* 42 (8): 747–762.

Sall, A. 2021. De la phrase au texte: présentation et analyse des marqueurs de la cohérence en wolof. Unpublished Ph.D. thesis. Dakar, Université Cheikh Anta Diop.

Sall, D. 2020. Selective acculturation among low-income second-generation West Africans. *Journal of Ethnic and Migration Studies* 46 (11): 2199–2217.

Schalley, A. C. & S. A. Eisenchlas. 2020. Social and affective factors in home language maintenance and development: Setting the scene. In *Handbook of home language maintenance and development: Social and affective factors*, edited by A. C. Schalley & S. A. Eisenchlas, 1–13. Boston, De Gruyter.

Schatzki, T. R., K. Knorr-Cetina, & E. Von Savigny (eds.). 2001. *The practice turn in contemporary theory*. London, Routledge.

Schieffelin, B. & E. Ochs. 1986. Language socialization. *Annual Review of Anthropology* 15: 163–191.

Schreiber, B. R. 2015. 'I am what I am'. Multilingual identity and digital translanguaging. *Language Learning & Technology* 19 (3): 69–87.

Scollon, R. 2001. *Mediated discourse: The nexus of practice*. London, Routledge.

Seargeant, P., C. Tagg, & W. Ngampramuan. 2012. Language choice and addressivity strategies in Thai–English social network interactions. *Journal of Sociolinguistics* 16 (4): 510–531.

Shakar, Z. 2017. *Tante Ulrikkes vei: Roman*. Oslo, Gyldendal.

Shankar, S. 2004. Reel to real: Desi teens' linguistic engagements with Bollywood. *Pragmatics* 14: 317–335.

Shannon, C. S. 2019. #Family: Exploring the display of family and family leisure on Facebook and Instagram. *Leisure Sciences*: 1–17.

Share, M., C. Williams, & L. Kerrins. 2018. Displaying and performing: Polish transnational families in Ireland Skyping grandparents in Poland. *New Media & Society* 20 (8): 3011–3028.

Sharma, D. 2017. Scalar effects of social networks on language variation. *Language Variation and Change* 29 (3): 393–418.

Sinanan, J. 2019. Visualising intimacies: The circulation of digital images in the Trinidadian context. *Emotion, Space and Society* 31: 93–101.

Sindoni, M. 2013. *Spoken and written discourse in online interactions: A multimodal approach*. New York, Routledge.

Sindoni, M. 2021. Mode-switching in video-mediated interaction: Integrating linguistic phenomena into multimodal transcription tasks. *Linguistics and Education* 62, 100738. https://doi.org/10.1016/j.linged.2019.05.004

Skaranger, M. N. 2015. *Alle utlendinger har lukka gardiner: Roman*. Oslo, Oktober.

Skjekkeland, M. 2010. *Dialektlandet*. Kristiansand, Portal.

Skog, B. 2009. Språket på Facebook. *Språknytt* 37 (1): 23–25.

Smith, M. 2019. *Senegal abroad: Linguistic borders, racial formations, and diasporic imaginaries*. Madison, University of Wisconsin Press.

Smith-Christmas, C. 2014. Being socialised into language shift: The impact of extended family members on family language policy. *Journal of Multilingual and Multicultural Development* 35 (5): 511–526.

Smith-Christmas, C. 2018. 'One cas, two cas': Exploring the affective dimensions of family language policy. *Multilingua* 37 (2): 131–152.

Smith-Christmas, C. 2019. When X doesn't mark the spot: The intersection of language shift, identity and family language policy. *International Journal of the Sociology of Language* 255: 133–158.

Søndergaard, B. 1991. Switching between seven codes within one family – A linguistic resource. *Journal of Multilingual and Multicultural Development* 12 (1&2): 85–92.

Sow, N. 2016. Le code mixte chez les jeunes scolarisés à Ziguinchor: un signe d'urbanité? In *Les sciences sociales au Sénégal: Mise à l'épreuve et nouvelles perspectives*, edited by M. Diouf & S. B. Diagne, 247–272. Dakar, CODESRIA.

Spolsky, B. 2004. *Language policy*. Cambridge, Cambridge University Press.

Stæhr, A. 2016. Languaging and normativity on Facebook. In *Engaging superdiversity*, edited by K. Arnaut, M. S. Karrebæk, M. Spotti, & J. Blommaert, 170–195. Bristol, Multilingual Matters.

Stæhr, A. & T. Nørreby. 2021. The metapragmatics of mode alternation. *Pragmatics and Society* 12 (5): 756–781.

Staksrud. E. 2019. Top ten types of informed consent your supervisor never told you about. *Journal of Children and Media* 13 (4): 490–493.

Statistics Norway. 2021. *Innvandrere og norskfødte med innvandrerforeldre [Immigrants and Norwegian born with immigrant parents]*. www.ssb.no/befolkning/statistikker/innvbef.

Statistics Norway. 2022. *Statistikkbanken Table 09817: Immigrants and Norwegian-born to immigrant parents by immigration category, country background and percentages of the population (M) 2010–2022*. www.ssb.no/en/statbank/table/09817

Strand, T. 2019. Tradition as innovation: Dialect revalorization and maximal orthographic distinction in rural Norwegian writing. *Multilingua* 38 (1): 51–68.

Street, B. 1984. *Literacy in theory and practice*. Cambridge, Cambridge University Press.
Svendsen, B. & U. Røyneland. 2008. Multiethnolectal facts and functions in Oslo, Norway. *The International Journal of Bilingualism: Cross-disciplinary, Cross-linguistic Studies of Language Behavior* 12 (1–2): 63–83.
Swigart, L. 1990. Wolof, langue ou ethnie: le développement d'une identité nationale. In *Des langues et des villes*, edited by E. Gouaini & N. Thiam, 545–552. Paris, Agence de la coopération culturelle et technique, Didier Erudition.
Swigart, L.1992. Two codes or one? The insider's view and the description of codeswitching in Dakar. In *Codeswitching*, edited by C. Eastman, 83–102. Clevedon, Multilingual Matters.
Szecsi, T. & J. Szilagyi. 2012. Immigrant Hungarian families' perceptions of new media technologies in the transmission of heritage language and culture. *Language, Culture and Curriculum* 25 (3): 265–281.
Tagg, C. 2016. Heteroglossia in text-messaging: Performing identity and negotiating relationships in a digital space. *Journal of Sociolinguistics* 20 (1): 59–85.
Tagg, C. & A. Lyons. 2017. Mobile messaging by micro-enterpreneurs in contexts of superdiversity. In *The Routledge handbook of language and superdiversity*, edited by A. Creese & A. Blackledge, 312–328. Abingdon, Routledge.
Tagg, C. & A. Lyons. 2021a. Polymedia repertoires of networked individuals. A day-in-the-life approach. *Pragmatics and Society* 12 (5): 725–755.
Tagg, C. & A. Lyons. 2021b. Repertoires on the move: Exploiting technological affordances and contexts in mobile messaging interactions. *International Journal of Multilingualism* 18 (2): 244–266.
Tagg, C. & P. Seargeant. 2021. Context design and critical language/media awareness: Implications for a social digital literacies education. *Linguistics and Education* 62, 100776. https://doi.org/10.1016/j.linged.2019.100776
Tagliamonte, S. 2016. So sick or so cool? The language of youth on the internet. *Language in Society* 45 (1): 1–32.
Tandoc, E. C. Jr., C. Lou, & V. L. H. Min. 2019. Platform-swinging in a poly-social-media context: How and why users navigate multiple social media platforms. *Journal of Computer-Mediated Communication* 24 (1): 21–35.
Tannen, D. 1994. *Gender and discourse*. Cary, Oxford University Press.
Tannen, D. 2006. Intertextuality in interaction: Reframing family arguments in public and private. *Text and Talk: An Interdisciplinary Journal of Language, Discourse and Communication Studies* 26 (4): 597–617.
Tannen, D. 2007. Power maneuvers and connection maneuvers in family interaction. In *Family talk: Discourse and identity in four American families*, edited by D. Tannen, S. Kendall, & C. Gordon, 27–48. New York, Oxford University Press.
Tannen, D., S. Kendall, & C. Gordon. 2007. *Family talk. Discourse and identity in four American families*. New York, Oxford University Press.
Tazanu, P. M. 2012. *Being available and reachable: New media and Cameroonian transnational sociality*. Cameroon, Langaa RPCIG.
Theodoropoulou, I. 2021. Nostalgic diaspora or diasporic nostalgia? Discursive and identity constructions of Greeks in Qatar. *Lingua 263*, November 2021. https://doi.org/10.1016/j.lingua.2019.05.007
Thiam, N. 1994. La variation sociolinguistique du code mixte wolof-français à Dakar: une première approche. *Langage et Société* 68: 11–34.

References

Thiam, N. 1998. Repérage sociolinguistique dans les désignations de la ville de Dakar (Sénégal). *Revue Parole* 5 (6): 113–139.
Tsagarousianou, R. 2016. European Muslim diasporic geographies: Media use and the production of translocality. *Middle East Journal of Culture and Communication* 9: 62–86.
Tseng, A. & L. Hinrichs. 2021. Introduction: Mobility, polylingualism, and change: Toward an updated sociolinguistics of diaspora. *Journal of Sociolinguistics* 25 (5): 649–661.
Tsiplakou, S. 2009. Doing (bi)lingualism: Language alternation as performative construction of online identities. *Pragmatics* 19 (3): 361–391.
Tubaro, P., A. A. Casilli, & L. Mounier. 2014. Eliciting personal network data in web surveys through participant-generated sociograms. *Field Methods* 26 (2): 107–125.
Tudini, V. 2007. Negotiation and intercultural learning in Italian native speaker chat rooms. *Modern Language Journal* 91 (4): 577–601.
Tusting, K. 2020. *The Routledge handbook of linguistic ethnography*. Milton, Routledge.
Van Mensel, L. 2018.'Quiere koffie?' The multilingual familylect of transcultural families. *International Journal of Multilingualism* 15 (3): 233–248.
Vandekerckhove, R. & J. Nobels. 2010. Code eclecticism: Linguistic variation and code alternation in the chat language of Flemish teenagers. *Journal of Sociolinguistics* 14 (5): 657–677.
Vassenden, K. 1999. Norge et innvandringsland siden 1971. *Statistikk mot år 2000: 1970–1971*. Statistics Norway. www.ssb.no/befolkning/artikler-og-publikasjoner/norge-et-innvandringsland-siden-1971
Velghe, F. & J. Blommaert. 2016. Emergent new literacies and the mobile phone: Informal language learning, voice and identity in a South African township. In *Intercultural contact, language learning and migration*, edited by J. Blommaert, B. Geraghty, & J. Conacher, 89–111. London, Bloomsbury.
Vertovec, S. 2001. Transnationalism and identity. *Journal of Ethnic and Migration Studies* 27 (4): 573–582.
Vertovec, S. 2004. Cheap calls: The social glue of migrant transnationalism. *Global Networks* 4 (2): 219–224.
Vertovec, S. 2007. Super-diversity and its implications. *Ethnic and Racial Studies* 30 (6): 1024–1054.
Villi, M. 2010. Visual mobile communication. Camera phone photo messages as ritual communication and mediated presence. Unpublished Ph.D. thesis. Aalto University.
Villi, M. & M. Stocchetti. 2011. Visual mobile communication, mediated presence and the politics of space. *Visual Studies* 26 (2): 102–112.
Vincent, J. 2015. Staying in touch with my mobile phone in my pocket and Internet in the cafes. In *A sociolinguistics of diaspora: Latino practices, identities and ideologies*, edited by R. Marquez Reiter & L. Martin Rojo, 169–180. London, Routledge.
Vives, L. & I. V. Silva. 2017. Senegalese migration to Spain: Transnational mothering practices. *Journal of Ethnic and Migration Studies* 43 (3): 495–512.
Voltelen, B., H. Konradsen, & B. Østergaard. 2018. Ethical considerations when conducting joint interviews with close relatives or family: An integrative review. *Scandinavian Journal of Caring Sciences* 32 (2): 515–526.

Vorobeva, P. 2021. Families in flux: At the nexus of fluid family configurations and language practices. *Journal of Multilingual and Multicultural Development*, online first: 1–15.
Watson, R. 2018. Patterns of lexical correlation and divergence in Casamance. *Language & Communication* 62: 170–183.
Weidl, M. 2018. The role of Wolof in multilingual conversations in the Casamance: Fluidity of linguistic repertoires. Unpublished Ph.D. thesis. SOAS University of London.
Wikström, P. 2019. Acting out on Twitter: Affordances for animating reported speech in written computer-mediated communication. *Text and Talk* 39 (1): 121–145. https://doi.org/10.1515/text-2018-2021
Wilding, R. 2006. 'Virtual' intimacies? Families communicating across international contexts. *Global Networks* 6 (2): 125–142.
Wilding, R., L. Baldassar, S. Gamage, S. Worrell, & S. Mohamud. 2020. Digital media and the affective economies of transnational families. *International Journal of Cultural Studies* 23 (5): 639–655.
Wilhelmsen, M., B. A. Holth, Ø. Kleven, & T. Risberg. 2013. *Minoritetsspråk i Norge. En kartlegging av eksisterende datakilder og drøfting av ulike fremgangsmåter for statistikk og språk*. Documents 8/2013, Statistics Norway.
Wimmer, A. & N. Glick-Schiller. 2002. Methodological nationalism and beyond: Nation-state building, migration and the social sciences. *Global Networks* 2 (4): 301–334.
World Bank Data. 2019. https://data.worldbank.org/country/senegal?view=chart
Wright, L. 2020. *Critical perspectives on language and kinship in multilingual families*. London/New York, Bloomsbury.
Wright, L. 2022. The discursive functions of kinship terms in family conversation. In *Diversifying Family Language Policy*, edited by L. Wright & C. Higgins, 15–32. London, Bloomsbury.
Yoon, K. 2018. Multicultural digital media practices of 1.5-generation Korean immigrants in Canada. *Asian and Pacific Migration Journal* 27 (2): 148–165.
Yount-André, C. 2018. Gifts, trips and Facebook families: Children and the semiotics of kinship in transnational Senegal. *Africa* 88 (4): 683–701.
Zhao, S. 2019. Social media, video data and heritage language learning: Researching the transnational literacy practices of young children from immigrant families. In *The Routledge international handbook of learning with technology in early childhood*, edited by N. Kucirkova, J. Rowsell, & G. Falloon, 107–126. London/New York, Routledge.
Zhao, S. & R. Flewitt. 2020. Young Chinese immigrant children's language and literacy practices on social media: A translanguaging perspective. *Language and Education* 34 (3): 267–285.
Zhu, H. & W. Li. 2016. Transnational experience, aspiration and family language policy. *Journal of Multilingual and Multicultural Development* 37 (7): 655–666.

Index

Abdou (participant) 54, 65, 174, 178
affection 6, 106–7, 109, 124–30, 132–4, 198
affordance(s) 4, 7, 9, 15, 24, 31–4, 37, 39, 40, 73, 91–4, 113, 133, 138–9, 142, 146–8, 162, 196
agency 3, 17, 19, 76, 87, 189, 195–6, 200, 203
Agha, A. 15, 30, 107, 133, 163, 183
Arabic 4, 30, 47–8, 55–7, 59, 61, 66–7, 93, 98, 112, 116, 120, 134, 144, 149–56, 158, 160–3, 167–8, 171, 181, 189–90, 192, 203
Aida (participant) 53, 56–7, 64–6, 68, 73, 75, 98, 113, 115–16, 159, 189–90, 196
Androutsopoulos, J. 4, 10, 14, 23, 25–32, 43–4, 70, 73, 77, 82, 85, 113, 137–8, 141–2, 148, 159, 162–3, 165
Appadurai, A. 35, 137, 162
Astou (participant) 56, 58, 60–2, 65, 68, 78, 111–13, 115–16, 132–3, 142, 144–5, 147–8, 150, 158–9, 170, 178–9
Auer, P. 11–12, 25
Awa (participant) 56–9, 61, 64, 66–7, 80, 82, 88, 97–9, 104, 112–16, 133, 150, 170, 180–2, 186, 189–96, 200–1, 204

Bakhtin, M. 10, 21, 172
Baldassar, L. 2, 34–6, 106
banter 62, 124, 133; *see also* teasing
Barton, D. 9, 73, 85, 200
Baym, N. 133
Blackledge, A. 10, 15, 20, 88, 167
Blommaert, J. 3, 6, 12–14, 35, 86, 135, 137, 139–41, 162
Brubaker, R. 135–6, 142, 156

Busch, B. 3, 5–6, 14, 19, 71, 73, 166, 169, 172, 196, 200
Busch, F. 28, 45

Canagarajah, A. S. 11–12, 15, 20, 23, 29, 136–7, 162, 167, 195
chat 26, 33, 41, 113, 132, 135, 143, 163; dyadic 80, 142, 150; group 6, 28, 33, 39, 59, 66, 68, 80, 102–3, 113, 115–16, 132–5, 138, 142, 144–6, 150, 152–5, 161, 201; multi-party 31, 33, 113
Cheikh (participant) 54–5, 58–66, 75, 96, 100–3, 126–7, 142, 150, 154, 164, 166–70, 172, 177
Cissé, M. 46
code-switching 11–12, 24–5, 27–8, 30–1, 108, 140, 148, 181
communication: digitally mediated 8, 16, 19, 22–3, 31–4, 40, 42, 44, 51, 55, 66, 77, 137, 180, 198, 200; family 5, 6, 2, 39–40, 57, 73, 76, 106–7, 109, 133, 139, 142, 203–4; interpersonal mediated 9, 24, 32, 39, 166, 180; peer 195; transnational 5, 8, 23, 32, 38, 40, 65, 73, 91, 97–9, 104, 117, 133, 139, 179–80, 195, 197, 199
connected presence 2, 37, 138
co-presence: ambient 37–8, 94, 96; mediated 34, 36–7, 86, 97, 106; omnipresent 37, 96, 99, 104, 204; phatic 93; reinforced 37, 93–4; ritual 37, 96, 204; virtual 36, 93
Creese, A. 10, 15, 20, 88, 167
Curdt-Christiansen, X. L. 3, 17, 19, 36, 40, 70

Danet, B. 23, 26
data collection: collaborative 5; multi-sited 70

De Fina, A. 20, 167, 195
De Meulder, M. 11, 203
Deumert, A. 3, 24, 27, 36, 109, 129, 180
diaspora 3, 6, 13, 15, 28, 30, 35, 62, 71, 100, 135–9, 141–3, 156, 160–3, 167, 183, 198, 200–2; digital 86, 135, 138, 142–3, 156, 158, 199
Diola *see* Joola
Diop, M. C. 35, 46
Diop, S. 52, 85, 201
Diouf, Makhtar 46–7
Diouf, Mammadou 47
discourse: family 5, 166; interactive written 23, 28–9, 182; metalinguistic 12, 190; public 21, 156, 161, 171; religious 142–3, 150, 152–4, 156, 161

email 27, 39, 100–1, 104, 124
emoji 28–9, 33, 41–5, 55, 80, 111, 115, 120, 122, 127, 129, 134, 142, 145, 152, 159, 194–5, 203
emotion(s) 6, 35, 39, 42, 93, 94, 107, 109, 125, 129, 134, 164, 169, 170, 200
English 1, 23–4, 26, 29, 30–1, 34, 41, 44–5, 47, 49, 55–6, 59, 61, 66–8, 80, 82, 96, 98–9, 102, 112, 115, 127–9, 134, 139, 144–6, 149–50, 156, 158–61, 163, 168, 171, 176, 181–2, 185–93
enregisterment 15, 30, 44–5, 47, 128, 183
ethnography 70, 85, 139; discourse-centred online 70; ethnographic observation 71, 73; linguistic 10, 85; multi-sited 45, 199

Facebook 29, 33, 37, 39, 41, 52, 55, 67–8, 75, 80, 92, 96, 100, 133, 138, 141–2, 146–9, 156–9, 161, 164–6, 185–6, 190; Messenger 1, 55, 65, 75, 80, 82, 92, 96, 98–100, 103–4, 110, 113, 118, 120, 132, 142, 178, 183, 186, 189–90; post 65, 93, 145, 164, 195; profile 100, 113, 142, 147–9, 156, 158, 164; status updates 68
Facetime 104
family: doing 1, 21, 34, 38, 42, 106–7, 134, 199, 204; Language Policy / FLP 8, 16–19, 21–2, 34, 40–2, 166–7, 195, 197, 203; multilingualism 1–5, 8, 16–19, 21, 34, 38, 40–3, 70, 86, 91, 106–8, 160, 167, 198–203; repertoires 6–7, 16, 59, 109, 134, 200; relationships 1, 3, 6, 7, 23, 38–9, 42, 89, 91, 106, 109, 122, 134, 198–9, 201–2; space 21, 75, 200, 204; transnational 2, 5–8, 16, 23, 31, 34–44, 51, 73, 89, 91, 94, 97, 99, 105–6, 117, 133, 135, 139, 141, 160, 183–4, 196, 198–201, 203
Felipe (participant) 55–6, 58–62, 65–8, 89, 98, 100–4, 112, 128, 132, 142, 144–8, 150, 152, 158–9, 163, 170–1
fieldwork 4–5, 54, 57–9, 63, 66–7, 71, 77, 80, 82–3, 85, 96, 147–8, 156–9, 162, 198; *see also* multi-sited
Fishman, J. A. 18, 21, 44
Fogle, L. W., *see* Wright
focus group: data 57, 178; discussion(s) 70, 78, 85, 178; session(s) 77–8, 87–8
framing 6, 32, 39, 86, 93, 156, 199
French 1–2, 4, 14, 16, 24–5, 28, 30, 44–9, 55–61, 64–9, 80, 82, 88–9, 92–3, 96, 98, 101, 106, 112, 116–20, 123–9, 131–2, 134, 139, 141–61, 163, 167–72, 176–7, 181–6, 189–90, 194, 203
Fula/Fulfulde, *see* Peul

García, O. 11, 29
generation 6, 18, 20, 22, 35, 58–9, 67, 77, 97–9, 101, 104, 182–3, 188–9, 195, 201; *see also* intergenerational
Glick-Schiller, N. 34–6
Goodchild, S. 47
Gordon, C. 21, 107–9, 126, 134
Greschke, H. 5, 36, 38–9, 91, 93, 96, 106
group chat(s) 6, 59, 68, 80, 102, 113, 135, 142, 144, 146, 150, 201
Gumperz, J. J. 11, 13, 25

Hanks, W. F. 9
Hannaford, D. 2, 35, 37, 49, 51
He, A. W. 192, 196, 204
Heller, M. 10
heritage language: learning 20, 23–4, 41, 160, 167, 179, 190, 195, 204; maintenance 104, 164, 203; practices 17, 19, 20, 38, 40, 137, 164, 177, 179, 193, 204; repertoire 6, 16, 164, 166, 171–2, 177–8, 180, 183, 196, 199, 202;

Index 233

socialisation 19, 22–3, 86, 180, 203; transmission 203; use 8, 20, 203
Herring, S. C. 23, 129
heteroglossia 4, 6, 10, 14, 29, 31, 51, 110, 140
Hiratsuka, A. 3, 6, 18, 23, 108–9

Ibou (participant) 53, 56–8, 64, 66, 68, 104, 111, 113, 115–6, 181, 183, 186, 188–9
identities 7, 9, 11, 20, 22, 36, 96, 105, 107, 138, 160, 163, 167, 172, 201, 204; diaspora 136, 161; family 21, 42, 107, 199, 202; interactional 200, 202; social 2, 26–7, 136–7, 163
identity 6, 20, 23, 30, 33, 35–6, 46–7, 64, 86, 136, 142, 166–7, 169, 170–5, 177–80, 196, 202; construction 20–1, 23, 26, 35, 105, 135, 163, 166, 180, 202; diasporic 135, 138, 156; marker 67, 169 Norwegian 52; Senegalese 49, 172; social 2, 26–7, 51, 136–7, 163; urban 47; youth 51, 67
ideologies: language 9, 10, 49, 140, 164, 166–7, 169, 171–2, 179, 193; media 42–3, 45; monolingual 11; of language 30, 167
ideology 9, 10, 12, 13, 172, 192; practice and 13, 192; of monolingualism 12
immigration 5, 35, 49–51; see also migration
Instagram 55, 63, 75, 96–7, 170
interaction: digital 2, 3, 4, 19, 34, 50, 57, 62, 64, 77–8, 80, 82, 109, 113, 116–7, 126, 133, 164, 167, 177, 180, 182, 190, 196, 198–9; digitally mediated 1, 7, 17, 32, 43, 59, 61, 85, 180, 189, 202, 204; family 2, 5–6, 8, 18–9, 23, 37, 106, 108–9, 116, 183–4, 190, 203–4; intergenerational 40, 196; mediated 1–2, 6–7, 13, 17, 24, 30–4, 42–3, 59, 61, 78, 85, 107, 110, 141, 156, 163, 180, 189, 196, 198–9, 202, 204; multilingual 24, 106; online 63, 134, 190; peer 186, 190; transnational 2, 40, 66, 94, 103, 110, 133–4, 144, 166, 197; video 38
intergenerational 17, 20, 40, 196; language transmission 166, 202; transmission 18, 170

intertextual: reference 29, 122; repetition 21, 108, 131
intertextuality 6, 21, 86, 109
intimacy 21–2, 35, 38, 107, 109, 122, 124–5, 129–30, 132–3
Issa (participant) 56–7, 60, 66, 73, 115
Italian 42, 49, 53, 55–6, 61, 168

Jacquemet, M. 137–8
Jones, R. H. 9
Joola 1, 2, 4, 24–5, 44, 47–8, 55–8, 60–2, 68, 98, 101–2, 129, 132, 134, 146, 167–8, 170–1, 180, 182, 195, 203
Jørgensen, J. N. 10, 12, 27, 29, 31
Juffermans, K. 58, 141
Juillard, C. 46–8

Kane, O. 35
Kébé, A. B. 48–9
Kędra, J. 19, 40–1, 76
King, K. A. 3, 16–18, 20–2, 70, 106–7, 178, 180
kinship: behaviour 108, 133–4, 189, 201; relationships 130; term(s) 107–8, 122, 132, 134, 164, 195, 201
Kusters, A. 11, 15, 18, 203
Kytölä, S. 35, 106, 109

language: and media practices 1, 12, 42, 199; and superdiversity 13, 71; heritage see heritage language; learning 6, 13, 17, 19–20, 23–4, 41, 43, 49, 65, 89, 160, 164, 167, 178–80, 190, 204; portrait(s) 14, 56, 66, 73, 170, 172, 174, 176; practices see practices; skills 11, 20, 22, 41, 59, 98, 116, 129, 172, 178, 190; socialisation 5, 16–7, 19, 20, 22–3, 38, 86, 126, 129, 166, 169, 179–80, 183, 196, 198, 203–4; transmission see heritage, intergenerational
Lanza, E. 3, 15, 17–19, 21–2, 34, 41–2, 70, 86, 106–7
Leconte F. 48–9, 166
Lee, C. 3–4, 9, 18, 23, 25, 28, 32–4, 73, 180, 200
Lexander, K. V. 4, 9, 14, 19, 27, 30–1, 34, 40–3, 48–9, 62, 68, 73, 125–6, 129, 131–2, 141, 144, 153, 167, 188–9
Li, W. 11, 18, 20, 22, 29–31, 40, 70, 141, 170

Licoppe, C. 2, 37–8
linguistic diversity 13, 24, 26–7, 48, 50–1, 57
linguistic features 10, 15–6, 20, 27–8, 30, 45, 49, 73, 77, 108, 134, 202
literacy 9, 14, 28, 30, 39, 48, 59, 60, 147, 167, 177, 181; digital 4, 8–9, 28, 91, 102, 135, 150, 155; practices 1, 9, 17, 28, 48, 91, 135, 141, 148, 150, 155, 161
Little, S. 17, 19–20, 41, 170–1, 174, 195
Lomeu Gomes, R. 3, 17–18, 21
Lüpke, F. 47–8, 58

Madianou, M. 4, 36–9, 43, 94, 96, 104, 124–5, 139
Mainsah, H. 52, 202
Makoni, S. 11–12
Mamadou (participant) 54, 76
Mandinka 48, 56, 170
Marième (participant) 53–4, 58, 90, 111–2, 122, 174–5, 178
Marino, S. 36, 38, 137–8, 143
Marquez Reiter, R. 136
Martin Rojo, L. 136
Mbodj-Pouye, A. 49, 201
Mc Laughlin, F. 10, 15, 46–48, 137–8, 144
mediagrams 5, 44–5, 70–1, 73, 75–7, 80, 82–6, 89–92, 96–9, 103–4, 167, 180–6, 198–200
media: channel(s) 1–2, 5–6, 39, 42, 44, 70, 73, 80, 83, 85, 92, 96–7, 99–100, 102, 104, 139, 143, 150, 156, 200–1; choice(s) 2, 5, 38–9, 42–3, 45, 71, 73, 77, 80, 82, 85, 91–2, 94, 96, 99–100, 103–4, 139, 143, 183, 196, 199; diaries 70, 77–8, 80, 86; digital 1, 2, 9, 35–42, 44, 70, 103, 133, 135, 138, 145, 148, 156, 160, 163, 180, 196; literacy 39; maps 70–1, 73, 75–8, 80, 82; platform 23, 31, 40, 43, 141–2, 161, 199; repertoire(s) 5, 40, 43–4, 46, 96, 160, 201; social 6, 23, 28–34, 37, 40, 43, 93–4, 113, 135, 138, 141–4, 147, 150, 158, 161–5, 180, 199, 202; *see also* polymedia
Merla, L. 2, 35
messenger applications 33, 92, 138, 143, 161; *see also* Facebook Messenger
metrolingualism 10–11

migration 1–3, 13–14, 22, 34, 36, 42, 49, 51–2, 59, 126, 136–7, 141, 154, 167, 198; trajectories 17, 36, 200
Miller, D. 4, 38–9, 94, 96, 104, 124–5
mobility 2–3, 13–14, 22, 34, 36–7, 46, 48–9, 54–5, 61–2, 135, 168
modality 1, 11, 18, 32, 43–4, 70, 77–8, 80, 82–3, 85, 91, 94, 96–9, 103, 105–6, 129, 133–4, 181, 183, 185, 189, 196, 200, 203; affordances 92; language 44, 73, 77, 97, 130, 180, 182, 196, 201; semiotic 39; *see also* multimodality
mode(s): asynchronous 26–7; communication 4; spoken 92, 150, 186; visual 71; written 27; *see also* modality
Momar (participant) 53–4, 57–9, 64–8, 88, 110, 156, 159, 172, 174, 176–186, 188–90, 204
morality 6, 22, 86, 107–9, 111, 127, 129, 133–4, 201
Mourid(e), Mouridism 47, 55, 59, 66, 153–6
multilingualism 1–5, 8, 10–13, 21–4, 27–8, 49–50, 58, 71, 86, 97, 125, 129, 135, 140–1, 159, 161–2, 165, 167, 200–2; and emotions 125, 129; family 1–5, 8, 16–19, 21, 34, 38, 40–3, 70, 86, 91, 106–8, 160, 167, 198–200, 202–3; networked 24, 27–8, 129; post-migration 138
multimodality 7, 11, 15, 18, 20, 29, 31, 38, 43, 80, 92, 97, 106, 133–4, 137, 150, 152, 155, 158, 161, 198, 203–4

Nabou (participant) 54–5, 59, 63, 127, 129
Nedelcu, M. 2, 5, 35–7, 91, 93, 96, 99, 104, 106, 204
Nemcová, M. 71, 82
networks: diaspora 30, 71; digital 138; personal 29, 31, 52, 71, 76, 87, 198; social 28, 30, 51, 73, 76–7, 91, 99, 138, 149; transnational 99–100, 154
network graphs 70–1, 73, 77
Ngom, F. 47, 59, 154
Norwegian 1, 3, 4, 49–59, 63–68, 80, 82, 88–89, 93, 98, 102, 110–12, 115–17, 125–30, 134, 141, 150, 156–58, 160, 163–65, 168, 171–78, 181, 189, 192–3

Obojska, M. 3, 17
Ochs, E. 6, 17, 20–2, 86, 106–9, 111, 127, 134, 179, 196, 201
orthography 30, 48, 58, 66, 126, 154; *see also* spelling
Otsuji, E. 11, 14–15, 166, 172
Oumou (participant) 51, 53–4, 60, 68, 88, 91–4, 96–9, 101, 104, 106, 111, 116, 118, 125–6, 150, 152, 156–7, 174
Ousmane (participant) 53–4, 65, 67–8, 78, 93–4, 100–4, 110, 117–20, 122–6, 130–1, 133, 144, 147–8, 150, 156–8, 172, 174, 177, 202

Palviainen, Å. 19, 40–41
Pavlenko, A. 125, 129
Pennycook, A. 3, 6, 9–12, 14–15, 18, 23, 108–9, 134, 166, 172
Peul (Pulaar) 4, 16, 24, 45, 47–8, 55–8, 62–4, 68, 96, 101, 129, 134, 149, 164–70, 180, 195, 203
phone calls 1, 37–9, 58, 63, 80, 92–3, 96–7, 100–4, 108, 124, 137, 203
Pietikäinen, S. 139, 141
playfulness 3, 122, 130–1, 133, 183, 195
polycentricity 6, 14, 23, 86, 135, 139, 140–1, 161–2, 172
polylanguaging 10, 28, 31
polymedia 3, 28, 34, 37–40, 42–5, 85, 94, 104, 124–5, 138–9, 154; communication 40; environment(s) 43, 91, 93, 96, 103, 139; practices 43; repertoire 43; research 70, 125, 199; theory 4–5, 38–9, 43, 86, 198
power 21–2, 35–8, 71, 88, 90, 107, 111–12, 116–18, 123–4, 132; and solidarity 21, 37, 107, 109; and connection manoeuvres 6, 21–3, 86, 107, 115, 201
practice(s): communicative 11, 12, 33, 42, 44, 139; digital 4, 7, 19, 102, 142, 156, 160, 200, 203; digital literacy 4, 8–9, 28, 91, 135, 150, 155; family-making 40–1; heritage language 17, 19, 20, 38, 40, 137, 164, 177, 179, 193, 204; language 2–6, 9–10, 13–14, 17–21, 23, 28–9, 34–8, 41–3, 49, 51–2, 58, 71, 78, 88–9, 98, 103, 106, 109, 117, 134, 138, 141, 161, 166–7, 172, 181, 183, 188, 196; language and media 1, 12, 42, 199; literacy 1, 4, 8, 9, 17, 28, 48, 91, 135, 141, 148, 150, 155, 161, 181; media 1, 12, 31, 38, 42–3, 104, 163, 199; morality 6, 86, 109, 111, 134, 201; (-based) approaches 8, 16, 20, 195; social 3, 5, 8–10, 12, 15, 17–8, 44, 204; translingual 11, 18, 29
Purkarthofer, J. 18–19, 21, 71, 203

Rama (participant) 1–4, 25, 32, 43–4, 46, 49, 53–62, 65–8, 97–9, 102–4, 112, 120, 122, 128, 150, 170–1, 182, 190, 202
Rampton, B. 12, 13, 137
register(s): heritage language 6, 8, 13, 15–16, 32, 47, 58–9, 68, 140–1, 153, 167, 183–4, 186, 189, 196, 203; of French 65; of language 10, 30, 140, 144, 189; of mediation 44; of Norwegian 68, 125; of Wolof 47, 59, 155, 189; Senegalese 183; *see also* enregisterment
religion 47, 140, 142–3, 149, 150, 154, 160, 168
repertoire(s) 3–4, 6–8, 11, 13–16, 19–20, 23–4, 43–4, 46, 49, 52–3, 57, 59, 66, 70–1, 88, 109, 134–5, 139, 142, 160, 164, 166–7, 171–2, 175, 177–8, 180, 183, 193, 195–200, 202–3; biographical approach to 16; linguistic 1, 5–6, 8, 11, 13–19, 24–5, 28, 43, 46, 49, 52, 54–7, 60, 64, 66, 70–1, 91, 98, 107, 109, 129, 133, 135–6, 140–2, 160, 163–7, 170–2, 177–8, 198; media 5, 40, 43–4, 46, 96, 160, 201; mediational 1–3, 5, 42–5, 85, 91, 99, 104, 196, 198–9; of mediation 6, 44–5, 97, 135, 139; polymedia 43; semiotic 15, 28, 44, 141, 162
resource(s) 2–6, 11, 15, 17, 19–20, 22–9, 31, 41–6, 56, 85, 97, 102, 106–7, 109–10, 124, 134–5, 142–3, 150, 160, 162, 164, 166–7, 175, 181, 183, 190, 192–3, 195–6, 198–201, 203; linguistic 1, 3–6, 9–16, 18–22, 42–3, 54, 57, 70–1, 86–9, 97, 99, 101–2, 104–5, 124, 134, 143, 160, 164, 166–7, 171–2, 174–5, 180, 188–9, 192–3, 196, 199–203; mobile 14, 16; multimodal 7, 161, 198; orthographic 15; pictorial 29, 143; semiotic 1, 13, 15–16, 18, 20,

27–30, 38, 42–3, 86, 106, 137, 142, 203
Riccio, B. 3, 35, 49, 154
Rosa, J. 136
Røyneland, U. 50–2, 202

Said, F. S. 17, 41, 195
Sall, A. 48
Sall, D. 48
Sara (participant) 54–5, 58, 62–5, 91, 94, 96–7, 99, 102, 112, 126–30, 164–70, 172, 177, 195
Schieffelin, B. 17, 20, 179, 196
script 28–31, 34, 66–7, 161; Arabic 48, 59, 66, 150, 152, 162–3; choice 30; Roman 150
Skype 34, 41–2, 92, 99–100, 103–4, 178
Smith-Christmas, C. 3, 17, 57
Smith, M. 3, 48–9, 52, 167
SMS 44, 68, 75, 80, 82, 92, 100, 103–4, 110, 112, 116, 124–5, 127, 142
Snapchat 1, 73, 82, 97, 99, 104, 185
social media 6, 23, 28–34, 37, 40, 43, 93–4, 113, 135, 138, 141–4, 147, 150, 158, 161–5, 180, 199, 202
solidarity 21–2, 35, 37, 107, 109, 112–17, 120, 126, 131–3, 153–4, 166, 201
Sow, N. 48
space(s): communicative 71, 162; digital 20, 24, 141–2, 144, 177–8, 180, 198, 201, 203; family 16, 21, 23, 75, 200, 204; geographical 21, 34, 154; mediated 135; online 22, 24, 172, 186, 202; social 37, 67, 75, 136, 139, 141; time and 16, 172; translanguaging 11, 18; urban 11, 140
Spanish 55–6, 61, 76, 116, 139, 167–8
spelling 30, 45, 125–6, 128, 154; French 65, 154, 163; non-standard 111; standard 154; unconventional 66; variation 27
Spolsky, B. 17–18
Stæhr, A. 4, 39, 70, 85, 134, 139, 140–1
superdiversity 10, 12–14, 71, 137, 141
Swigart, L. 47
Szecsi, T. 23, 40, 179
Szilagyi, J. 23, 40, 179

Tagg, C. 29, 31–2, 43–4, 77
Tannen, D. 6, 21–2, 86, 106–7, 109, 134, 201
teasing 117, 120, 130–1, 133, 194, 201–2
text message 27, 37, 39, 56, 58–9, 61, 68, 99, 101, 103, 106, 110–11, 115, 117, 122–3, 129, 131, 146, 148, 157, 164, 166, 181–2, 184, 190, 193; see also SMS, texting
texting 29, 31–2, 44, 68, 82, 92, 98, 110, 112, 126, 131, 186, 188, 203
Thiam, N. 47
translanguaging 10–3, 18, 29–31, 45, 56, 149, 153, 177, 186, 192–3, 195, 203; digital 24, 27, 29, 31; as practice and ideology 13
translocality 1, 13, 35–6, 45, 106, 109–13, 116, 118, 125, 133, 135, 141–2, 198, 201
transnational 1–2, 5–8, 11, 13–14, 16, 19, 21–3, 31–2, 34–44, 49, 51, 65–7, 73, 89, 91–4, 97–100, 103–9, 117–18, 132–9, 141–2, 150, 153–7, 160, 162, 179–86, 190, 192, 195–201, 203–4; connectivity 70, 99, 137, 200; interaction 2, 40, 66, 103, 110, 133–4, 144, 166, 197
Trivedi, S. 136

Vertovec, S. 13, 35–6, 137–8
Viber 92, 100, 103–4, 138
video calls 37–40, 58–9, 93–4, 103, 106, 185, 204
visualisation 14, 70–1, 73, 76–7, 83, 87, 199–200
voice message 1, 39, 59–63, 66, 78, 80, 85, 88, 94, 96, 101, 103, 106, 116, 123, 131, 133, 146, 148, 158, 182, 185, 186, 188–9, 193–4

Watson, R. 46, 62, 132
Weidl, M. 46, 58
WhatsApp 34, 42, 44, 55, 62–3, 75, 80, 92, 96, 98–101, 103–6, 116, 132, 138, 142, 146, 148, 154, 161, 185, 188; group chat 59, 102; message(s) 106, 190; voice message(s) 101
Wilding, R. 35–6
Wolof 1, 4, 6, 14, 16, 24–5, 28, 30, 45–9, 52, 54–68, 75, 80, 82, 87–9, 92–3, 98, 101–2, 106, 116–20, 122–6, 129, 131–4, 141, 144–50,

152, 154–61, 163, 167–72, 174–86, 188–96, 202–3
Wright, L. 16–17, 20–1, 37, 108, 180, 201
Wyss, M. 2, 5, 35–7, 91, 93, 96, 99, 104, 106, 204

YouTube 41, 59, 143, 148, 155, 162

Zhao, S. 40–1, 196
Zhu, H. 17–18, 20, 22, 30–1, 40, 70, 170, 203

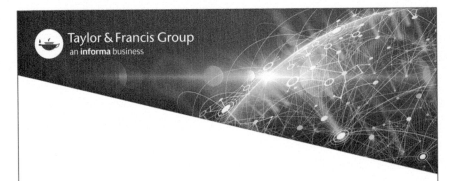